RENTS

HOW MARKETING CAUSES INEQUALITY

GERRIT DE GEEST

Cartoons by Madeline De Geest

Beccaria Books

βB

First paperback edition in September 2018.

For information about special discounts for bulk purchases, please contact sales@beccariabooks.com.

Library of Congress Control Number: 2018908194

De Geest, Gerrit
Rents: how marketing causes inequality / Gerrit De Geest
Includes bibliographical references and index
1. Income distribution—United States. 2. Capitalism—United States
3. Consumer protection—United States
4.Equality—Economic aspects
305.50973—dc23

ISBN 978-1-7325112-0-0 (paperback)
ISBN 978-1-7325112-1-7 (hardback)
ISBN 978-1-7325112-2-4 (ebook-EPUB)
ISBN 978-1-7325112-3-1 (ebook-Kindle)

Book cover and interior design by Leah McDowell
Cartoons by Madeline De Geest

Beccaria Books
www.beccariabooks.com

RENTS

To Christine, Eloise, and Madeline

CONTENTS

INTRODUCTION

I ncome inequality has risen dramatically since the 1970s. But why exactly? Most experts point toward increased productivity differences, globalization, the diminished power of unions, the accumulation of private capital, or the growing success of lobbyists in Washington, DC.[1] In this book, I offer a new explanation: inequality has increased since the 1970s because markets have become less competitive. They have become less competitive because marketing methods that reduce competition and transparency have become more sophisticated. In other words, inequality has increased because of . . . better business schools!

My statement that markets have become less competitive over the past decades may sound surprising. For nearly all products you buy, there are numerous companies on the market, offering numerous items. The internet has also made it easier to acquire information. Moreover, globalization means that American businesses must now compete with companies from all over the world. So, most Americans (and most economists) believe that most markets are highly competitive—and probably even more competitive than ever. Monopolies and oligopolies (markets with only a few competitors) are believed to be exceptions.

This book will show that competitive markets—the ones described in introductory economics courses—have become the exception. Truly competitive pricing has become rare. For most products and services that you buy, you pay a monopoly or oligopoly price. Markets are more distorted than most people realize, and much more than was the case in 1970.

Suppose you need aspirin. Should you buy the "Genuine Aspirin" of Bayer, or the three times cheaper generic version of CVS or Walgreens? Recent research has shown that pharmacists and doctors generally buy the cheaper version for their own use, which suggests that if you paid the brand premium, you were simply misinformed. You mistakenly believed that Bayer Aspirin is better. And you were not alone. One century after its patent has expired, Bayer succeeds at selling its aspirin at premium prices by exploiting those who are misinformed. The market for aspirin is not very competitive because most consumers lack the information needed to make it competitive. As a result, Bayer gains artificial profits.

This book is about artificial profits—called *rents* in economics jargon. (Rents should not be confused with payments of tenants to landlords; in their technical definition, rents are profits that could not have been made in a perfectly competitive market.) The book shows that the Bayer Aspirin is no outlier—rents are a much bigger problem than generally believed. Using a new method, I estimate that these artificial profits now compose at least 35 percent of the economy. This means that for every $100 you spend, $35 on average goes to profits that could not have been made in a perfectly competitive economy.

In 1970, the amount of rents in the economy was only 20 percent. Out of $100, only $20 went to artificial profits. That may still sound like a lot, but it is much less than now. This increased number, by itself, shows how much less competitive markets have become since 1970.

So, what happened? Why did artificial profits go up? How did markets become less competitive? The driving force, as this book will show, is that marketers have become more sophisticated over the past decades. They have become better at turning competitive markets into noncompetitive ones. They have learned how to reduce transparency, separate informed from noninformed consumers, make products less comparable, create lock-in effects, create legal forms of cartels, exploit network externalities, exploit the irrationality of human beings, or make markets fail in numerous other ways.

My view on marketing differs from the rosy view that is taught to business students. According to the rosy view, marketing does not distort markets but improves them by helping consumers find the right products. While I don't deny that marketing sometimes does this, I argue that the true secret behind marketing methods that create "value" for businesses is that they distort the market in some way. Why would marketers do this? In perfect markets, profits tend to be low (as there are, by definition, no rents). Therefore, profits can be increased only by making markets less perfect.

Over the time span 1970–2015, marketing methods have not only become more sophisticated, they have also become more widely applied. Nowadays, it is no longer just Coca-Cola that hires marketing experts. It is small, local businesses too. The impact of this trend has been enormous, not only on the competitiveness of markets but also (and maybe surprisingly) on income differences.

Why does your neighbor make more money than you do? In the standard economic view, it can only be because your neighbor is more productive. Your neighbor works longer hours, works with more energy, is more efficient, has invested more in human capital, or has taken more risks.

This book offers a different view. People with a higher income are not necessarily more productive in a strictly economic sense; they simply receive more rents than you do. They work in a more distorted market than you do, or they exploit market failures better than you do; or, if they work in the same organization, they capture more of the organization's rents than you do. The cynical self-help credo from rent economics is: "If you want a high income, find a market distortion and exploit it. If you can't find a market distortion, then create one."

This is not to say that work ethic plays no role whatsoever. It does, but work ethic can only explain so much. It cannot explain the larger income differences that we observe in market economies. Large income differences are puzzling from an economic view because differences tend to be modest in competitive markets. Even the profits of entrepreneurs, who fill up gaps in the market and therefore may operate in temporary monopoly positions, tend to be modest in a competitive environment. Suppose an entrepreneur comes up with a great idea for a new type of restaurant, "Kentucky's Finest Roadkill." If the restaurant is successful, competitors may soon open competing roadkill restaurants, such as "Under My Wheels" or "Truck Drivers' Catch of the Night." In a perfect market, this will quickly drive down prices and profits.

But markets are far from perfect. In an economy full of rents, getting wealthy becomes less a matter of working hard and more a matter of capturing a share of the rents. After all, 35 percent of the national income goes not to those who do the work but to those who capture the rents. In other words, those who earn a high income typically succeed in capturing an above-average share of the 35 percent rents. They may work hard, but what makes them wealthy is not their hard work.

Because rents tend to end up in the hands of just a few individuals (for reasons I will explain in the book), they make especially the income of the top 1 percent or top 0.1 percent sky-high. My thesis is that these people are not extraordinarily more productive but capture an extraordinarily large share of rents.

The question, still, is why marketing methods designed to make markets fail are tolerated by the legal system. How can deliberately creating a market failure ever be legal if one of the goals of the legal system is to prevent market failures? For each type of market failure, there are many legal rules that try to prevent them. For instance, deliberately creating information failures is forbidden by rules against fraud and deceptive practices. So how can Bayer benefit from misinformed customers if the law's goal is to prevent misinformation?

This brings us to the second component of my new theory about marketing: all marketing techniques that create market failures must, at their core, be based on *subtle* forms of fraud, abuse of trust, monopolization, corruption, duress, cartelization, undue influence, or contract breach—subtle enough to fall through the cracks of the legal system.

So, the story of growing income inequality is the story of a failing legal system. But the true culprit is not what political economists think it is. While lobbying efforts and acts of Congress may have contributed to income inequality at the margins, the true cause is the lack of development in contract law, consumer protection law, tort law, property law, intellectual property law, and competition law.

Why did the legal system fail? The main reason is that, until now, legal scholars and policymakers have underestimated the magnitude of the problem. Law and economics scholars in particular—the experts who try to find the best rules, using economic models—have underestimated the distortionary effect of marketing methods by basing their analyses on Economics 101, not on Marketing 101.

In short, business schools have outsmarted law schools.

This brings me to the final theme of the book. Most economists believe that the best way to reduce inequality is to increase taxes for the wealthy and redistribute the money to the poor. While taxes are harmful to the economy, they are considered less harmful than any other method of reducing inequality.

Yet if most income differences are caused by rents rather than by real productivity differences, the obvious solution is to reduce the amount of rents in the economy. The best way to do this is to let the legal system attack market distortions more aggressively than is now the case.

Indeed, if income inequality is caused by rents, it is in essence caused by distortions. The best way to reduce inequality is to remove those distortions—this is what the legal system can do. Taxes, on the other hand, create new distortions to cancel out some of the income effects of existing distortions. Correcting a distortion through another distortion is rarely the best solution.

A different way to say this is saying that taxes only treat the symptoms of a deeper problem. The legal system can attack the causes of the deeper problem.

This book is divided into three parts. In the first part, I argue that artificial profits ("rents") are the true cause of rising income inequality. In chapter 1, I explain how markets have become less competitive and what role marketing has played in this evolution. In chapter 2, I explain income differences through the lens of rent economics. In chapter 3, I estimate that rents have increased from 20 percent to at least 35 percent of the economy over the time span 1970–2010.

In the second part, I analyze more in detail how marketing distorts markets and why these methods are not attacked by the legal system. (This way, the second part sets the stage for the legal reforms recommended in the third part.) Chapter 4 focuses on legal forms of concealment (including fog making), chapter

5 on legal ways to abuse trust, and chapter 6 on legal ways to monopolize markets. Chapter 7 argues that fraud is a massive problem in current markets, as the legal system underenforces its rules against fraud and even makes some forms of fraud legal.

In the third and final part, I discuss how income inequality can be reduced. Chapter 8 explains why increasing taxes is not the best way to do so. Chapter 9 offers a long to-do list for lawmakers and courts, proposing major changes to antitrust law, contract law, agency law, consumer protection law, intellectual property law, real property law, oil and gas law, and zoning law. The general idea is that the law should target market failures more aggressively than it currently does.

The book is based on three pillars: economics, law, and marketing (though it does not require you to have a background in any of these areas). The book's novelty is that it shows a connection between income inequality, modern marketing techniques, and the law. The book tries to change the way you look at shopping in your daily life and the way you look at income differences around you. And, maybe surprisingly, it tries to show there is a link between what you experience as a consumer and what you experience as an income earner.

Stylistically, the book is written in a more informal, entertaining style than a typical economics book. Yet the more informal style does not mean that this book's goal is merely to popularize existing theories. Its goal is to make a novel contribution to our understanding of income inequality and to outline a new way to reduce it.

PART I
RENTS AND
INEQUALITY

1

HOW MARKETS BECAME
LESS COMPETITIVE

How competitive are modern markets? If you walk through a store, shop on the internet, or even scroll through an old-fashioned telephone guide, the answer seems to be "very competitive." For nearly every good you can think of, there are hundreds of products from dozens of brands. Are you looking for a toothbrush? The choices are endless. Printers? There are too many types to put on display in a single showroom. Cars? So many makes and models that it's hard to squeeze them into a single guide. Water bottles? Every day a new brand enters the market. And the same applies for services, at least if you live in an urban area. Roofers? There may be 500 in your area. Doctors? Too many to count.

So, when you open an introductory book to economics ("Economics 101") and see the three basic market types—perfect competition, oligopoly, and monopoly—you believe that perfect competition best approximates the reality. Not that competition is ever truly perfect (nothing in life is), but modern, globalized markets seem to come close to the ideal of a highly competitive economy.

True monopolies, on the other hand, seem rare. They look more like something from a distant past, when kings granted monopolies to some traders or AT&T was the only telephone company on the market. Maybe your local electricity or water company still has a monopoly, but the government heavily regulates its prices, trying to bring them closer to a competitive outcome. On paper, these companies may have a monopoly position, but you don't pay a monopoly price.

How about oligopolies? These are markets with only a few (two, three, four, or five) competitors. It is easy to name markets with only a few big players, but how many are true oligopolies? Take cell phone companies. You have the big four: Verizon, AT&T, Sprint, and T-Mobile. That's only four. But you also have dozens of smaller companies (like MetroPCS, Cricket, and US Cellular) that compete with cheaper plans. For soft drinks, you have the two giants, Coca-Cola and Pepsi, but they compete with a gazillion smaller companies. In 1987, Red Bull came out of nowhere and hit the market in Europe. The two giants could only watch how two entrepreneurs turned a simple idea into a billion-dollar business.

Other observations seem to confirm that competitive forces in today's markets should be strong. Starting up a business is easier than ever. There are rarely legal barriers to enter a market. Do you want to start your own roofing company, restaurant chain, or energy drink product line? Nothing in the law prevents you from doing so. Best of all, Generation X, Generation Y, and the millennials are creative, out-of-the-box-thinking generations with an entrepreneurial spirit. They have produced tens of thousands of ambitious entrepreneurs ready to fill any gap in the market, like piranhas circling around unwary tourists in the Amazon River, or like a dog waiting beneath the table to snatch up its owner's leftovers.

Imagine someone brings the next hot product to the market: a self-driving bed. It's a four-wheel bed that responds to the beep of your alarm clock by rolling out of your bedroom, down the stairways, out your front door, onto your driveway, onto the highway, and right in front of your office building. From there, it catapults you right into your chair. The demand is enormous—who doesn't want to sleep thirty minutes longer? The profits are high. For a while. Until the market is flooded with competing models—some with a built-in shower, others with a complimentary toaster or coffee maker.

Then, you have the ever-present disrupters. Are taxi companies making good money? That lasts only until Uber disrupts the industry. Is Uber making good money? Don't sleep on it either. That lasts only until a few high school kids write the next billion-dollar transportation app, disrupting the disrupter.

In short, markets are more competitive than ever. Aren't they?

Paying Monopoly Prices in Competitive-Looking Markets

Printer ink is one of the most expensive liquids on earth. A typical HP cartridge may cost $35 for 8.5 ml. This is $4,200 per liter. And that is for an XL size. Regular-sized cartridges may cost over $5,000 per liter. Over the life span of a printer, the toner expenses may be several times the printer's actual price.

It is not that ink is so expensive to make. The reason why ink cartridges are so expensive is that they are "brimming with profits," as marketing consultant Rafi Mohammed wrote in *The 1% Windfall: How Successful Companies Use Price to Profit and Grow.*[2] How is that possible? In the competitive markets of Economics

101, no product can ever be "brimming with profits." And the ink market does seem competitive, if you just walk through a store. There is not just HP but also Canon, Lexmark, and many other brands. Yet in practice, HP does not have to compete with these brands. Your HP printer is designed in such a way that it only works with HP ink cartridges. You have no choice but to buy the ink from HP, at whatever price HP dictates.

What happened is that HP deliberately created a lock-in effect. Once you buy a printer, you are locked in; you can only buy ink cartridges specifically made for that printer. Of course, you could throw away your investment and buy a new printer from a different brand, but that is an expensive alternative. Moreover, once you have bought a different printer, you are again locked in, just to a different brand.

And here we arrive at one of the main paradoxes of modern markets: right in the middle of a competitive-looking market, you may still be paying monopoly prices. Before you bought the printer, the market was competitive. After the sale, you enter a monopoly market and pay monopoly prices for the ink cartridges.[3] The markets for printers may be competitive, but the aftermarket for ink is a monopoly.

Plumbers as Information Monopolists

Suppose that a plumber repairs your bathroom and then charges you for labor and material, including $29 for a bolt. When you ask why such a small, seemingly inexpensive bolt costs so much, he answers that this is a special bolt that is better than the ones available in hardware stores. What he does not say is that the bolt really only costs $1 and that it is not significantly better than regular bolts. But you don't know this, and therefore you pay the $29.

The plumber acquired what is called an *information rent*. "Rent" is a technical name for an artificial profit that could not have been made in a perfect market. In a perfect market, the plumber could not have overcharged for spare parts because in a perfect market, consumers know the market price of every product. An information rent is a rent that is acquired by exploiting superior information. The plumber knew that the price of such a bolt is only $1, but you didn't—after all, you're not a plumber. He also knew that the bolt wasn't any different from the ones you can buy at Home Depot; you thought it must have been a special one. The plumber simply converted his information advantage into an artificial profit. He used his superior knowledge to transfer $28 from your pocket into his. The market for plumbing may look competitive, but you paid an excessive price for that bolt.

Information rents are a relatively new concept in economic theory. The concept first showed up in highly specialized papers and books in the 1990s.[4] The concept has been developed by experts in "industrial organization," who work on "principal-agent theory," a highly theoretical set of models on the behavior of people ("agents") who work for other people ("principals"). The concept of information rents still hasn't made its way into popular economics textbooks. It is possible that you recently majored in economics at college and never heard of information rents.

How high can information rents be? As high as monopoly profits? The short answer is yes. Information rents can be seen as a form of monopoly rents because they are the result of a "monopoly of information," as some economists like to frame it. The plumber has access to some information that you don't have access to. (Of course, literally, you have access to the same information. Nothing prevents you from spending a full week on researching plumber bolts. In practice, you don't have a full week to do this. You buy thousands of products each year and can't afford to spend so much time on every single item.)

The longer answer is that information rents can even be higher than monopoly rents. Suppose I ask my little daughter to make a painting in the style of Picasso. I give her a lot of blue paint. I then try to convince you that it is a real Picasso, worth $100 million. (I add that it is from his Blue Period.) If you eventually buy it for that price, I receive an information rent of $100 million. I know it is not a Picasso, you think it is, and I use my superior information to transfer $100 million from your pocket into mine. (I will also spend some time in jail, if you discover my fraud, because the legal system does not tolerate certain types of information rents, but more on that later.) One hundred million is much higher than a monopolist could ever have charged in a transparent economy. If I had a legal monopoly to sell paintings in the style of Picasso, I could have made a profit of maybe a thousand dollars on some paintings, but never $100 million. No buyer would ever pay that amount if they know it is not a real Picasso.

Thus, information rents are highly problematic. And, as we will later see, in a complex, specialized world, with millions of products, professionals have an abundance of opportunities to acquire such rents.

Why Roofers Are Oligopolists

Suppose the roof of your house is leaking. In your area, there are 500 roofing companies. You call three of them, ask for a bid, and take the lowest bid. At the end of the day, you will pay a fair price for your roof, close to what you would have paid in a perfect market, right? This is what most people think.

Unfortunately, most people are wrong. What you will pay is an oligopoly price—the same as you would have paid if there were only three companies in the market in the whole city. The reason is that only those who make a bid compete. In other words, they are only worried about beating the two competitors selected to submit bids.[5] They know they are not competing with the 497 others. The market for repairing your roof is an oligopoly: only three businesses are competing.

In this example, the fundamental problem is that every roof leak is different. Therefore, there is no such thing as a well-established market price for the repair of your roof. To find out the price, you need to ask for bids from roofers. But asking for bids is a time-consuming process, for the bidders and for yourself. So, you only ask for three bids. Unfortunately, this makes roofers set prices as if there were only three roofing companies on the entire market.

Here is a way to visualize what happens. Imagine that all 500 roofers are standing on a football field. Unfortunately, there is a very dense fog, so you can only see the three standing closest to you. These three form the entire market for your roof's repair. The other 497 have no effect on the price you pay. Some of them may have significantly lower prices, but you can't see that. Thus, the degree of competition is not determined by how many competitors there are on the foggy football field but by how many the consumers can see. "Seeing" in this context means more than just knowing that they exist (it is easy to look in the phonebook and see the list of 500 roofers, but this in itself does not tell you anything about each roofer's quality or price). "Seeing" means that consumers know the price and know whether the suppliers offer sufficient quality.

But wait—isn't there at least an implicit threat in the existence of the other 497 roofers in that when the price of the three bids is too high, nothing prevents the consumer from soliciting more bids? That is correct if the consumer knows that the three are charging too much. Yet this is exactly the problem. To know whether the three are charging too much, you must know how much the others are charging. Unfortunately, there is so much fog on the football field that you can't see the others.

Still, you may ask yourself, does it really matter whether three or 500 roofers are competing? Even if there are only three roofers, they better give their best price if they want to get the job. In other words, isn't it enough to have a few competing businesses to get highly competitive markets?

This question comes down to whether prices are the same in an oligopoly as they are in a perfectly competitive market. The short answer is no—oligopoly prices are much higher than competitive prices. How much higher? That depends on the model used to predict them. Take the most popular model—the Cournot model.[6] (The Cournot model is built on a number of assumptions, which I explain in an endnote, but don't worry, you don't need to understand the technicalities of the model to be able to grasp the main point I am making here.) For instance, in a simple version of this model, when the monopoly price is $150 and the perfectly competitive price is $100, the price under an oligopoly with two is $133 and under an oligopoly with three is $125.[7] The longer answer is a little more complicated. Prices in an oligopoly have an unpredictable variable: they depend on how the players play the game. For instance, if businesses fight a price war, the price may equal the perfect market price. This is the outcome of the Bertrand model.[8] But if they are very nice toward each other, and nobody ever starts lowering the price, they may charge the same price as a monopolist. You could consider this an *implicit cartel*, which is an unspoken agreement between competitors to fix the price in an industry without openly agreeing to do so. Cartels are illegal when they are explicit, that is, when competitors *do* meet and openly agree to fix prices; but when they never exchange a word, the practice of just "being nice to each other" and never undercutting the other's price is legal.

The more players there are on the market, the more likely it is that one of them will start a price war. On the other hand, the more fog there is on the market, the less likely it becomes that businesses will compete on price. That also applies to fog related to quality. How good is a roofer? That's hard to know. This makes it an interesting strategy for bidding roofers to set their prices high, just in case the customer doesn't trust the other roofers quality-wise.

Here is the bottom line. Those who believe that competitive bidding will result in a perfectly competitive market price as long as there is some competition implicitly apply the Bertrand model. The argument basically assumes that as long as there is some competition, the outcome will be the same as in a perfect market. Again, this is not theoretically impossible, but it is based on the Bertrand model, which draws the rosiest picture of oligopoly markets. A more realistic prediction is that the fewer competitors there are, the higher the price will be.

So, if consumers have time for only two or three bids, competition is seriously undermined.

Enter the Marketers: The Razor-Blade Model

These were just a few examples where consumers pay monopoly or oligopoly prices in competitive-looking markets. In the pages that follow, I will show they are not outliers. Over the past decades, more and more markets have become distorted. The driving force is a generation of business school graduates whose full-time job it is . . . to distort markets.

In the ink cartridges example, the HP marketers applied a method known in the marketing literature as the "razor-blade model." In 1903, Gillette offered the first razors with disposable blades. Depending on the patent situation and the competition it faced, Gillette sometimes made the razor expensive and the blades cheap, or the razor cheap and the blades expensive. By coincidence, it was discovered that the latter combination (cheap razors and expensive blades) generated higher profits. This was a surprise because economic models predicted that it would not matter: in theory, rational consumers should take the total costs over the life span of the product into account. In practice, consumers turned out to be less rational. Maybe they didn't do the math. Or maybe they lacked the information to do the math.

Business schools now teach the razor-blade model to all students. It is praised as a great technique to "create value" for businesses. And yes, marketing books point to the fact that profits are higher in HP's printer division than in any other division. "Seventy percent of Hewlett-Packard's operating profits are from its imaging and printing division, most of which comes from printer supplies such as toner refills," Rafi Mohammed writes. His colleagues Nagle, Hogan, and Zale add that the profit ratio of HP's inkjet division is twice that of the company in general.[9] What they don't write is that the "value" that is created for businesses is, at its core, an artificial profit generated by monopolizing an aftermarket.

How Your Local Store Acquires Information Rents

Remember the plumber example, which showed how artificial profits (information rents) can be obtained by exploiting superior information? Marketers now apply this insight at a massive scale when they set prices in stores. A few decades ago, stores determined prices by looking at the wholesale price and adding a fixed percentage to cover their costs. But now, pricing is entirely based on exploiting asymmetric information.

Here is how it works. Each store has thousands of products.

Do you know how much each product costs in competing stores? Maybe you know this for a few items, such as tomatoes. Yet for the vast majority of products, you have no clue what they cost elsewhere. A can opener costs $14.99 in your local store, but what is the market price for the same can opener elsewhere? You don't know—after all, a can opener is not something that you buy weekly. So, pricing consultants recommend stores to set low, competitive prices for products like tomatoes and add high markups on products like can openers. Because the store doesn't charge much for tomatoes, consumers may think that profits are low on all products. The store knows that this is not true, but they won't tell you that. They have superior knowledge on the true costs of products and exploit that to obtain information rents. If you ever wondered how the Waltons (the owners of Walmart) became one of the wealthiest families in the world, the short answer is: information rents.

One obstacle marketers had to overcome is that there are always a few well-informed consumers. In the past, stores tended to lower prices for everyone in order not to lose these informed customers. Modern marketers no longer make this mistake: they have learned how to split the informed and noninformed consumers. One way to do so is to give the informed customers coupons (which are found only by those who do their homework). Those who don't have coupons are typically those who are less informed about market prices as they spend less time searching.

Another way is to offer a best-price guarantee: when the better-informed customers discover that the product costs less elsewhere, the store offers to "match the price." At first glance, this looks like a great way to make clear that a store is committed to offering the best possible prices. They tell their customers that they are working day and night to make sure they always have the lowest prices. Because of those efforts, customers can have "peace of mind." Indeed, there seems to be no reason for customers to worry about being overcharged. There is also no motive for them to search elsewhere; the store has built in a mechanism that guarantees that customers will not be overcharged. It looks nearly impossible that prices are lower elsewhere because if they were, it would probably already have been discovered by other customers, and prices would have been adjusted.

But here is the catch: when a customer discovers that it is cheaper elsewhere, the price is not lowered for all customers. Instead, it is lowered only for the one who discovered it. The store drives a wedge between those who are informed and those who are not informed. Uninformed customers think they can free ride on the efforts of informed customers, but they cannot. The main effect of "peace of mind" pricing is that consumers search less, and this, in turn, allows prices to be set higher.

The Art of Making Fog

The roofer example illustrates another insight: any competitive market can be transformed into an oligopolistic market by creating "fog." Marketers apply this insight by making it costly to know the real price. Sometimes, the technique is as simple as refusing to publish prices on the internet or giving prices only upon request, after a visit to the store or a personal meeting at the end of a sales pitch. At other times, marketers create fog by designing highly complex price plans. Cell phone companies are good at this.

Fog can also be created by "shrouded pricing." You initially see only a part of the price and learn the total price at a much later stage. I once booked a rental car for $29.95 a day. Well, that turned out to be $86.22 after I paid "Rental Car Protection" ($12), "Tax recovery charges and fees" ($15.27), "RSP" (I forgot what this stands for, but it cost me $4.99), "CDW/LDW" (same remark, cost me $22.99), and the "Concession Recoup Fee" ($1.02). And that's without counting overpriced refueling and sales taxes. Instead of receiving a midsize sedan for a modest price, I was treated to a surprise fee feast!

Sometimes the fog is not related to the price but to the quality of products. I mentioned already that pharmacists and doctors don't buy Bayer's "Genuine Aspirin" but buy the three times cheaper generic versions instead. Who buys Bayer's "Genuine" version at the premium price? Those who are misinformed and believe that Bayer Aspirin is better.

How exactly are buyers misinformed? In essence by putting two products on a shelf without giving much comparative quality information. If one of these products is three times more expensive, then some consumers will think that this product must be better. The marketing method is, at its core, a way to mislead people. But the misleading is achieved in such a subtle way that it does not fall under the legal definition of fraud.

The manufacturer may also help your store stop price comparison in subtler ways. Breathe Right Nasal Strips ("Extra") are sold per 44 in Costco and per 26 in Walmart. A quick search on the internet reveals that Breathe Right sells its products in packages of 10, 12, 26, 28, 30, 44, and 50. So by the time you are in that other shop, you have probably forgotten how many items were in the other packages. Since it is too hard to compare prices, you may occasionally buy it where it is most expensive.

Another way to stop price competition is to make products incomparable. If products are different, comparing them becomes like comparing apples and oranges. One way to do this is to sell a product under different brand names. Is your local store worried that its shoppers will discover that its dog food is overpriced? No problem. The manufacturer will make sure that the dog food in your local store looks slightly different and has different brand names than the ones in the store next door.[10] When products are different, prices are harder to compare.

A more sophisticated way to make products incomparable is to bundle commercial goods with charity contributions. Alternative food giant Whole Foods has become a master at this. Consumers who buy at Whole Foods pay more for products than those who shop at Walmart, but they also help save the environment, for instance by purchasing products from local farmers (which reduces transport-related pollution) or by shopping in a store that is built from sustainable materials. Also, Whole Foods proudly supports local initiatives. (Of course, Whole Foods is not the only company that does this. "If you buy goods from us, you help us give back to local communities" is a slogan that you may have heard in many stores.)

This bundling of goods, environmental benefits, and charity may have benefits for the environment and for local communities, but it definitely creates commercial benefits for Whole Foods. How? Because bundling substantially reduces price transparency. Suppose I pay $100 for a product in Whole Foods and only $90 in Walmart. Is the $10 difference justified by the environmental and community benefits that Whole Foods offers? Suppose Whole Foods is five miles further from my home than Walmart. Do the environmental advantages of buying vegetables from local farmers outweigh the extra gas that I need to drive to the Whole Foods? Suppose I want to give to local communities. Does it make sense to give through buying products at slightly higher prices at Whole Foods, or would local communities benefit even more if I just gave that money to them directly? I've never been able to find the answer, and I would guess that you haven't either. But that is great news, at least from a marketing perspective. The bundling makes the prices at Whole Foods incomparable to those at other stores. And this reduces price competition.

Two Views on Marketing

What is the role of marketing in the economy?* Does it improve the economic system, or does it make it worse?

According to the standard, rosy view taught to business students, marketing improves the economy by reducing market failures. Suppose a business has developed a superior product, but uninformed consumers keep buying older, inferior products. This is a market failure. Now, enter the marketers. They identify potential consumers and truthfully inform them about the superiority of the new product. At the same time, they set prices in such a way that the innovator captures enough of the value it has created. At the end of the day, the market failure has been removed. Consumers have found the best product and innovators have been paid for their work. Marketing has made the world a better place.

Here is my own, competing theory: marketing harms the economy by making markets fail.

Why would marketers want to make markets fail? Well, their

---

* Marketing, I should clarify, has a broader definition than some people think. It includes not only advertising but also sales pitching, product choice, and product pricing. Marketing refers to decisions businesses make about what product versions to bring to the market, what prices to charge, what channels to use for distribution, and what information to add to the market.

ultimate goal is to increase the profits of their clients—the businesses. But profits are low in a perfect market because there are no rents. Receiving rents is possible only if markets fail in some way. Therefore, marketers will do whatever they legally can to create market imperfections.

More specifically, marketers do two things under this alternative theory. First, if businesses operate in a failing market, marketers help them to *better exploit the market failure.*[11] Second, if businesses operate in a competitive market, marketers will try to *make the market fail.* The goal of marketing, in short, is to exploit a market failure, and if there is none, to create one.

A major constraint for marketers, however, is that marketing methods must be legal. Satisfying this constraint is less obvious than it sounds. After all, one of the goals of the legal system is to prevent market failures. The legal system forbids plain forms of fraud, monopolization, abuse of trust, corruption, duress, cartelization, exploitation of irrational parties, and contract breach. All these examples are archetypes of ways to distort markets. Fraud, for instance, distorts markets by spreading false information. Rules against fraud (and related rules such as rules against deceptive practice) are therefore serious obstacles for those who want to acquire information rents. Thus, successful marketing techniques must be based on *subtle* forms of fraud, monopolization, abuse of trust, corruption, duress, cartelization, undue influence, or contract breach—subtle enough to fall through the cracks of the legal system.

At the outset, I want to clarify that I believe that the first, rosy view of marketing captures a part of the empirical reality as well. Sometimes marketers do help innovators bring their superior products to consumers. Sometimes marketers *do* make consumers better informed. They definitely give consumers *some* information, and a limited amount of biased information is usually better than no information at all. Sometimes, the pricing strategies help innovators recoup their investments. But sometimes is not always. Marketing can be good for the economy, but it can also be bad.

In the rest of this book, I will focus on the second view on marketing because of its implications for income inequality. When marketers create subtle market failures, they create rents. *When marketers get better at this over time, they increase the total amount of rents in the economy, and therefore income inequality.*

The Growing Impact of Marketing

Over the time span between 1970 and 2015, marketing methods have not only become more sophisticated; they have also become more widely applied. In the old days, only giants like Coca-Cola hired marketing experts. In the current era, small, local businesses hire them too.[12] A few years ago, the air-conditioning system in the house of a friend of mine broke down. He called a small, local repair company. The technician discovered after ten minutes that the system had lost R-22 ("Freon") cooling gas, and he fixed the problem by adding four pounds of this gas into the system. The entire service only took about 30 minutes, but he was charged $405 in total—$105 for the service call and $300 for four pounds of R-22 gas. When he asked why the price for R-22 gas had increased so much (two years earlier he paid only $35 per pound and now he paid $75 per pound), the technician explained: "The government is making it more expensive because it harms the ozone layer. It's gone up three different times now, and we have no other choice than to pass it on to customers."

My friend checked the story on the internet and found that the price of R-22 had indeed increased because of government policy. But then he looked further and discovered that the wholesale price was still less than $11 per pound! The real price had increased from $5 to $11, but the price he was billed had increased from $35 to $75. He paid $300 for four pounds of gas that had cost the repair company only about $43.

Before continuing, let me say that this story illustrates another theme: that those who try to acquire information rents usually come up with a story to prevent their rents from being discovered. These stories are a part of marketing too. To be credible, the stories must contain some true facts. In this case, it was true that the government had tried to phase out a harmful gas, and that its price had recently been increased on three different occasions. But two half-truths do not make the whole story true.

Here's the rest of the story. My friend called the owner of the company and asked why the price had increased so much more than the wholesale price. The owner explained that it was not him who had determined those prices. He had hired business consultants and they had recommended him to double the price of R-22.

What these business consultants did was perfectly in line with what marketing books prescribe. When customers are locked in (which they are, after paying a $105 visit fee) and uninformed about prices (which they are, because most don't know how much R-22 costs elsewhere), the demand is "inelastic" and the price should be increased. ("Inelastic" is a technical economic term meaning that most people will still buy the product if the price goes up.) In other words, in those situations, there is an opportunity to acquire an information rent on top of a lock-in rent. Thus, the consultants were simply acting in accordance with marketing theory to drive profits up.

While these marketing techniques are not purely American inventions (it was Simon-Kucher & Partners, in fact, the

German consultancy firm, that started the professionalization of pricing in Bonn in 1985),[13] the new marketing insights have been applied on a larger scale in the United States. This helps to explain why income inequality has grown faster in the US.

A friend of mine experienced this when he went skiing for the first time in the United States. In Austria, where he used to go skiing, ski pass prices are transparent: they are announced long before the beginning of the season, they do not change during the year (prices are higher during peak periods, as is openly announced beforehand), and it does not matter where or when you buy the tickets—the price is always the same.

When he played with the idea of skiing in Colorado, he checked the ski pass prices in Winter Park on the internet. Since they looked reasonable, he booked a hotel. But when he arrived and went to buy the ski passes, he was shocked to learn that the price would be more than twice of what he had seen on the internet.

It turned out that there were many types of passes. Some you could no longer buy in March. Others you could buy, but only if you bought them before you drove to Winter Park. The price of day passes also varied. Those that you could buy in Winter Park were very expensive. He could get cheaper passes, but only if he called a certain number. There he was told that he could get a lower price, but only if he booked the day before. He could get a better price if he found a coupon. There were coupons all over the place, but they would not tell him where he could find them—they were hidden like Easter eggs. He ended up not skiing the first morning; he went on an Easter egg hunt instead—the only way to avoid being overcharged.

Here is what happened. In Austria, prices are still calculated like in the good old days: the real average costs are estimated, a markup is added, and a simple, transparent, and fair-looking price list is published. In Colorado, prices are set by pricing consultants who have been trained at modern business schools. They know that they can increase profits by making prices less transparent. They also know that tourists who book a hotel without first buying lift tickets bring the ski lift owner into a temporary monopoly position: the tourists can no longer move to another ski region and must pay whatever prices are asked if they want to ski at all. Pricing consultants design schemes that maximally exploit these information failures and lock-in effects. And I must say they did a great job. Even after the egg hunt, my friend ended up spending more on ski passes than ever before in his life.

But these new marketing insights are coming to the rest of the world as well. The Coupon Disease has now reached Europe too. The Law of One Price (the prediction that in a competitive economy everybody pays the same price for the same good) is becoming something like a cougar or a tiger: at school, you learn that they exist, but you never see one in the real world.

Market Structure Analysis:
Most Markets Are Oligopolistic

It is easy to give examples of where you pay a monopoly or oligopoly price. But how often does that happen? For all the goods and services you bought last year, how often did you pay an oligopoly or monopoly price? What evidence do we have that truly competitive pricing has become rare?

Ideally, we would look at data about the degree of competition in the entire economy. Unfortunately, such data have not been collected yet. Therefore, we have to look at proxies. We have to develop tests that give rough indications of competitiveness.

The first such test is a variant of what antitrust lawyers have been using for decades—a *structural analysis* of a market. Traditionally, such a structural analysis simply counts the number of competitors within a market. Take the market for aspirins. If there is only one manufacturer, the price you observe must be a monopoly price; if there are a few manufacturers, the price you see is an oligopoly price; and if there are many, the price you see should roughly correspond to the price in a perfect market. If you apply this traditional structural test (i.e., if you count the number of competitors), you conclude that 90 percent of all markets are highly competitive. Indeed, for nearly every product you can think of, there are numerous competitors on the market.

The main shortcoming of the traditional structural test is that it assumes either that there are no search costs or that they have no effect on pricing. (This shortcoming should be no surprise, since search costs were neglected in economic scholarship until 1970.) In reality, prices are not determined by how many competitors there are on the foggy football field, but by *how many competitors the consumers can see* at the time they make a decision. Seeing means that consumers know the price and know whether the suppliers offer enough quality to at least meet some minimum standards.

So here is what an *improved structural test* should look like: Count the number of companies where the average consumer is sufficiently informed about the company's products at the time of making a decision. Being sufficiently informed means knowing the final prices and knowing enough about the quality. Exclude from the number those products the consumer does not trust enough quality-wise and therefore does not really consider. In the roofer example, if the average consumer asks for three bids but disqualifies one, the real market structure is a duopoly. If for cars, the average consumer considers cars from eight different brands and disqualifies none of these (because nearly all cars are quite reliable nowadays), the real market is a weaker oligopoly with eight competing brands. In markets where consumers do not ask for a second bid, such as in the repair market, we may assume monopoly pricing, even if there are 500 firms in the market. The same applies to upsale markets or markets with lock-in effects (such as the market for ink cartridges).[14]

If we make such an improved structural analysis (that takes search costs into account), we quickly see that in most cases, consumers compare only a few companies. For roofing work, consumers typically compare two or three bids. For legal services, they typically consider only one bid. For plastic surgery (which is not reimbursed by health insurance), they consider one or two bids. For goods that can be bought on the internet, they rarely compare the prices of more than a few websites (though for some products they may be assisted in their comparisons by websites such as Google Shopping, eBay, or Amazon).

The outcome gets even worse when we also consider how little information consumers know about the quality of the products. If the average consumer is poorly informed, you can expect oligopoly pricing (because it is easy to trick a consumer into believing that an expensive product is better than a cheaper alternative). As a rule of thumb, one can assume that whenever a consumer buys a brand-name product, an oligopoly price is paid.

More Value-Based Pricing Suggests
Less Competitive Markets

Additional evidence that competitive pricing has become the exception can be found in marketing books.[15] Those books, and the literature on which they are based, are written by experts who know how markets work in practice as opposed to theory. They tell us that a remarkable evolution has taken place over the last couple of decades.

Many years ago, the most popular pricing method was "cost-plus" pricing. Under this approach, you would calculate your costs and then add an extra value to the price called a linear markup. For instance, if you set your markup at 30 percent of the true cost, then a product that cost you $100 would be priced at $130 and a product that cost you $1,000 will be priced at $1,300. (Whether this markup is a rent or just an amount to cover overhead costs is irrelevant in this context.)

Modern marketing books consider cost-plus pricing an old, lazy method of pricing that leaves too much money on the table. The new trend is to use "value-based" pricing.[16] Under this method, you do not ask how much it costs to produce the good, but how much the consumer values it. You set prices in such a way that you capture as much as possible from this "value." The costs are irrelevant, except for determining the price floor: if the true cost of a product is $100, the price must be at least $100 in order not to make a loss. Yet whether the price should be $130, $200, or $5,000 has nothing to do with true costs—only with how much consumers are willing to pay for the product.

In practice, of course, it is not possible to capture 100 percent of the value of every product. One reason is that you do not perfectly know how individual consumers value the product, especially because each consumer has a different valuation. By using the right techniques, however, the consumer surplus can be minimized and the producer's profit maximized.

The value-based pricing method looks logical, and even fair. If your product creates value, why shouldn't you earn a fair share of that value? But as logical and fair as it sounds to the ears of many people, it sounds equally as startling to the ears of an economist.

Value-based pricing is startling because it runs squarely against one of the fundamental features of competitive markets: value is in principle irrelevant to the price of a product. Clean water is cheaper than wine, not because it is less valuable but because it is cheaper to produce. A car is cheaper than a helicopter, not because it is less valuable (I'd rather have a car than a helicopter, if I had to choose only one), but because a car is cheaper to make. Laptops have become cheaper over time, not because they have become less useful but because production costs have decreased.

The only markets in which value is decisive for pricing are those that are insufficiently competitive. Monopolists and oligopolists can capture a part of the "value" of the products they sell, but these are supposed to be the exceptions, not the rule, if we read Economics 101 books. In sufficiently competitive markets, the price is determined by the costs, so that the good old "cost-plus markup" method makes sense.

So, we might expect marketing books to write: "Apply cost-based pricing, unless you are dealing with the exceptional situation in which your firm is a monopolist or oligopolist; in those few markets apply value-based pricing; but realize that there are few markets in which firms have oligopoly or monopoly power." This would be consistent with what most economists (and commentators) believe.

But this is not what marketing books say. They say that in principle you should apply value-based pricing, and in a few exceptions, apply the good old cost-based pricing. This is another indication that oligopolistic markets have become the norm and strongly competitive markets the exception.

The Death of Commodities: The Austrian Propane Market

Another way to measure the degree of competition in an economy is counting the number of *commodities* on the market. Commodities (as defined by economists) are goods that many competitors are able to make. The term in essence refers to goods that are sold with zero rents. Goods that are not commodities are either goods that have not been reverse engineered yet (so that nobody else is able to make them) or goods that are still patent protected (so that nobody else is allowed to make them).

Economics 101 suggests that, at any given moment, the vast majority of all products should be commodities. Indeed, patents expire after twenty years, and most goods are not that hard to reverse engineer (moreover, there are strong incentives to reverse engineer, because the first to do so temporarily receives the rents associated with a duopoly).

But how many of the products that you buy are true commodities? And even if they are commodities, how often do you realize that? Generic aspirin may be the same as Bayer Aspirin and yet you may have paid Bayer's premium price because you didn't realize it was a commodity.

One of the greatest "success stories" of marketers is that they have been able to turn commodities into differentiated products. Sometimes they do this by making consumers believe their products are different, or sometimes by slightly changing the products and making consumers believe that the differences are enormous. Some other times, they do it in even more ingenious ways, as the story of the Austrian propane market illustrates.

In Austria, a country with beautiful mountains, the demand for propane is larger than in many other countries because the mountains make it expensive to build natural gas pipelines.[17] Propane gas (also called butane gas or LPG) is a waste product of petroleum oil; in contrast to natural gas, it can easily be compressed and transported in large cylinders.

A few decades ago, Austrian sellers of propane faced what they considered to be a serious problem: low profit margins. Margins were low because competition was intense, and competition was intense because propane is a "commodity." Indeed, all sellers offer the same product, and many companies are able to produce it; therefore, price competition tends to be intense, eliminating rents on the market. From a welfare economics perspective, this is a great situation. From the perspective of the propane sellers, however, this was a bad situation. So, marketers had to find a way to reduce price competition. But how?

Using propane requires building a huge tank in the customer's backyard. Initially, customers owned their tanks and were free to buy gas from any dealer. Then, dealers stopped selling propane tanks and offered long-term leases instead. At first sight, this offer looked attractive to customers: upfront costs were lower and total lease payments were often lower than the normal purchase price. Sure, the contract stipulated that the company "owned" the installation and therefore was the only one that could service it or deliver propane gas, but at that time, their prices were not higher than elsewhere in the industry. Once many customers were locked into long-term leases, however, the company started to increase its prices. Competing companies imitated the business model, locked in their customers, and increased prices too. This further helped spiral up prices.

The marketing strategy in the Austrian propane industry is an ingenious application of the razor-blade model. Before marketers went to work, there was a highly competitive commodity market. After they went to work, the market became monopolistic because of the lock-in effect. While there were still many companies on the market, each individual customer had no choice but to buy propane from only one supplier—the company that owned the installation in the backyard. Similarly, each customer could buy services from only one company—the same one. The long-term contract had locked the customer in. Gone was the price competition.

Was this legal? A higher Austrian court decided it was. Indeed, contracts are binding, there was no plain fraud or duress, and apparently no antitrust violation—just two free parties agreeing on a long-term contract.

Pricing experts Steinmetz and Brooks give a remarkable piece of advice: don't ever let your products be treated like commodities! In their book *How to Sell at Margins Higher Than Your Competitors: Winning Every Sale at Full Price, Rate, or Fee*, they write: "When prospects say *commodity*, they're trying to denigrate. . . . They are trying to put down your product or service. In doing so, they are both denigrating what it is that you sell and are simultaneously trying to scare, frighten, and intimidate you into believing that what you sell is of no more value than your competitors."[18]

There is something startling about this statement: in perfect markets, products are commodities. In essence, Steinmetz and Brooks say: if your products are treated as if they are in a perfect market, you should feel disrespected. But in a sense, they are right: with so many marketing techniques to transform competitive markets into noncompetitive ones, you are simply not trying hard if you settle for a perfect market.

Does product differentiation lead to higher profits? For

pricing experts, there is no doubt that differentiation is a way to increase profits. Steinmetz and Brooks consider it the essence of selling: "A salesperson must differentiate his or her company's product or services from the competitor's somehow, some way. That is what selling is about." Their colleagues Holden and Burton give a simple piece of advice: "When products are regarded as commodities, add services to differentiate products and prop up prices."[19]

Either way, look around and you will see that the number of pure commodities on the market has become astonishingly small. A bar of chocolate or a can of soda? They are differentiated goods, not commodities. A simple loaf of bread or a bag of chips? Same remark. Even salt and drinking water have become branded, differentiated goods! This is another indicator that truly competitive markets have become rare.

Price Discrimination as a Sign of Market Power

A related piece of evidence for declining competitiveness is the increased use of price discrimination. Price discrimination means that different consumers pay different prices for the same products. There is a strong form and a weak form of this phenomenon. In the strongest form, consumers pay different prices for exactly the same good. A traditional example is a movie theater, where children pay less to watch a movie although they receive the exact same experience as adults. In the weaker form, consumers who pay more officially get a better product, but in reality the higher production costs do not outweigh the higher price. A clear example can be found in some airplanes, where business class passengers get the same type of seat as coach passengers but receive an extra drink.

Price discrimination comes in many forms. One form lowers

the price for those who have found coupons for the products. A different form (identified by economist Hal Varian) varies the prices of a good over time: one month the product is expensive, the next month it is cheap.[20] Price-shoppers know this and only buy the product when it is priced cheaply; less informed consumers pay the higher price, except when they are lucky enough to go shopping on a low-price day. Another form of price discrimination consists of allowing price negotiations; those who are well informed, or who are just skilled at negotiating, pay less.

Price discrimination is a puzzling feature of modern markets. It is puzzling because your Economics 101 book probably treated this subject under the chapter "Monopoly Power." Indeed, monopolists traditionally try to apply price discrimination in order not to lose the so-called "inframarginal" customers. These are the customers who are no longer interested in the good when it is offered at the inflated monopoly price, but who still are willing to pay more than the true costs. When the monopolist can sell the product at lower prices to this group while still selling it at the higher prices to other buyers, the rents can be even larger, and the so-called "deadweight loss" (the social loss due to underconsumption of the good) gets reduced.

Price discrimination may also be applied by oligopolists, to the extent that they are able to set the price above the true costs. But it is impossible in a perfect market. In such a market, all buyers and sellers are "price takers," not "price makers." All buyers pay the same price for the same good; this is the so-called Law of One Price. Price discrimination is the opposite: different buyers pay a different price.

A popular justification for the increased presence of price discrimination is fixed costs. Fixed costs are costs that remain constant, irrespective of the number of goods that are produced or services that are delivered. Take a movie theater as an example. The costs of building the theater, heating or cooling the theater, making the movie, and playing the movie are the same, irrespective of whether one person or two hundred people watch the movie. The cost of letting one individual use an empty seat is nearly zero. Nonetheless, the admission price will need to be higher than zero, because otherwise the fixed costs cannot be paid back. In addition, not all visitors need to pay the same price—children and seniors may pay less, because they tend to have a lower budget and may therefore not be willing to pay as much.

But this type of price discrimination requires transparent prices: students have to know they pay less or they may not come. Search-cost-based price discrimination—the one that has become dominant in recent years—is very different in nature. It consists of charging more to consumers who are insufficiently familiar with the market prices.

In sum, the increased use of price discrimination cannot be explained solely on the basis of fixed costs. It is also an indication of less competition or less transparency.

Another Sign of Market Power: Loyalty Cards

Here is a surprising piece of evidence of the decline of competition: the increased use of loyalty programs. In modern markets, it has become a challenge for consumers to get all their loyalty cards into a single wallet. Moreover, loyalty programs are now being offered in many versions. Consumers first may become silver members, then gold members, then platinum members, then platinum elite members, then premium platinum elite members, and finally premium platinum gold elite five-star reward members—the highest rank in the mini-society of locked-in consumers.

At first glance, loyalty cards look like harmless business practices that only result in winners. Indeed, loyalty cards must be good for the businesses, because otherwise they would not offer them. They also look good for the consumers who get all the rewards. And they seem not to harm the consumers who decide not to participate in loyalty card programs, because they just continue paying the normal price that they would otherwise pay.

Recent economic scholarship, however, has drawn a more negative picture of loyalty cards.[21] First, loyalty cards create subtle lock-in effects. Suppose you belong to a frequent flier program with American Airlines. What happens when you find a United Airlines flight that is slightly cheaper than a comparable American Airlines flight? If you choose the United flight you may save money in the short term, but you may not have enough American miles to pay for that family trip to Florida for which you've been saving up miles.

Second, loyalty cards may reduce competition by creating barriers to entry in the market. Indeed, if all customers become loyal to the incumbent firms, entry becomes much harder for firms hoping to join the market. And third, loyalty cards may reduce search efforts—customers who stay loyal no longer search for the best price in the market.

That loyalty programs are designed to reduce competition should not come as a surprise. Loyalty programs, as the name suggests, reward loyal consumers. Why do sellers do that? Obviously to make consumers either loyal in the first place or even more loyal than before. Paradoxically, the fact that the seller does *not* always offer the best value in the market is the very reason why loyalty programs are used. If the seller always offered the best value for its products, consumers would automatically stay loyal to the company and wouldn't need to be courted by special loyalty programs.

What is even more worrisome is that recent scholarship has shown that loyalty programs are in themselves an indication of market power. Indeed, in perfect markets, loyalty cards would not exist. If the perfect market price is $100, a seller who wants to give the eleventh purchase for free must increase the price of the first ten purchases to $110, but there is simply no motive for consumers to participate in such a program. This may explain why internet sellers who face tough price competition seldom offer loyalty cards. Outside this competitive island, however, loyalty programs are widespread, and this in itself is an indication of the declining competitiveness of most markets.

2

EXPLAINING INCOME DIFFERENCES

Why do some of your neighbors or friends make more money than you do? This is, of course, a complicated issue. Many factors determine the income associated with a certain profession; for instance, jobs that many people would love to do (like working in the arts sector) tend to pay less than jobs that are considered unpleasant (like plumbing). Yet it is good to realize that the dominant economic viewpoint on inequality ties income to productivity. The underlying idea is that in a market economy, income reflects productivity. This would mean, by implication, that if your neighbors make more money than you do, your neighbors must be more productive. Maybe they work longer hours, work with more energy, are more efficient, have invested more in human capital, or have taken more risks.

In this chapter, I will develop a different view. I will show that people with a high income are not necessarily more productive in a strictly economic sense—they simply receive more artificial profits caused by market imperfections. I'll show that rent economics better explains the extreme income differences that we observe today.

And they are extreme. A fast-food cook makes about $19,000 per year.[22] A CEO of a large corporation easily makes $11 million per year—or nearly 600 times more than a fast-food cook.[23] An anesthesiologist makes nearly thirteen times as much as a fast-food cook.[24] A partner of a large law firm makes seventy-five times more than a fast-food cook.[25] The owner of a small roofing company may easily make five times more than those who work for that company. Even school teachers (who aren't really overpaid if you realize that their income is still below average) make three times as much as fast-food cooks.[26] Although these income differences are mind-boggling, they are often "explained" on economic grounds. Let's take a closer look at these economic grounds.

Productivity Differences?

The common explanation for income differences is that well-paid people are simply more productive. There are two variants of this view. One is that well-paid people are more productive than others who have the same job. The other is that well-paid people have jobs that are intrinsically more productive.

The underlying view of both variants is that markets are brutally honest. Markets, so goes the argument, are like nature: the best hunters get the largest meal. If caveman Og catches a deer while caveman Ug catches only a fly, caveman Og will be well fed, and caveman Ug will be hungry. Markets inevitably create income inequality because they make it painfully clear that not all human beings are equally productive.

But what is "productivity"? The popularity of the standard view is partly caused by confusion surrounding that term. In business economics, productivity means "generating money for yourself." When Warren Buffet makes $1 billion in a year, his "productivity" in that year was $1 billion, because that is the money he made for himself. If a fast-food cook makes only $19,000 that given year, this worker was about 52,000 times less productive than Warren Buffet because he made about 52,000 times less. So, yes, in the business economics definition of productivity, income differences and productivity differences go hand in hand. But in this definition, it is misleading to say that income differences are caused by productivity differences. They aren't caused by them; they are the same.

In welfare economics, "productivity" is defined in a more meaningful way. It refers to how many goods or services someone adds to the economy. Productivity differences within the same job, however, are usually modest because unproductive workers tend to quit. If plumber Gerrit is ten times slower than plumber

Joe, plumbing may not be his true calling. Once Gerrit comes to this realization, he may try out something else—like writing a book on plumbers. Second, professionals tend to learn from each other. Why is Joe twice as fast as Bob? Maybe he uses better tools. But Bob may soon find that out.

Working more hours cannot fully explain the large income differences that we observe either. You can work 80 hours when your neighbor works 40 hours, and in that case your income may be twice that of your neighbor. But even if you never sleep, there are only 168 hours in a week. That is only about four times as much as your neighbor works. So, working more hours can never explain why you make ten times or one hundred times more than your full-time working neighbor.

Earning back investments also explains less than often believed. People who go four years to college have a 10 percent shorter career than those who start working at the age of eighteen. This, in itself, explains an income difference of only 11 percent in the remaining years. Study loans may amount to the postcollege income of another couple of years. This explains a wage difference of another 5–15 percent. For doctors, you may multiply this all by three. After college, they must spend another four years in medical school, where tuition tends to be even higher. (After medical school, doctors also must take a "poorly paid" fellowship, but "poorly paid" is compared to what they will later earn, not compared to what fast-food workers earn.)

Plug all those factors into the equation, add some others (like the fact that interest must be paid on study loans and that doctors may work longer hours), and you may explain why doctors make three to four times more than fast-food cooks. But ten to twenty times more? This is hard to explain from a strictly economic viewpoint.

Could it be that performing a surgery is intrinsically more

productive than grilling a hamburger? No. *There is no such thing as intrinsically more productive professions.* Leading a meeting or performing a surgery is not, by its very nature, a more productive act than flipping a hamburger or cleaning a restroom. Writing a legal memo is not intrinsically more productive than cooking a meal. Making an X-ray of a French bulldog's broken paw is not intrinsically more productive than making a satin sofa on which he can sit to watch TV.*

Could it be that some of these services create more "value" than others? *This explanation, however, violates a fundamental principle of economics—that in a perfectly competitive economy, prices (and wages) are not determined by "value" but by cost.* Nothing is more valuable than clean water, and still, it is one of the cheapest products on earth. If wine is more expensive than water, that is not because wine is more valuable but because making wine is more work than purifying water. So, if some professionals capture a part of the "value" they create, this proves that they operate in markets that are not perfectly competitive.

A related explanation for income differences is differences in responsibility. Responsibility, however, is a vague concept, and so it all depends on how the term is defined. If responsibility is defined as the ability to physically endanger others, then bus drivers should be paid more than law professors. If responsibility is defined in a moral way, then CEOs may claim that their work affects the well-being of all workers; but social workers may challenge that and argue that they affect happiness in a more direct way. To avoid endless discussion, we need to go back to our

---

* For another way to see why, ask yourself: Do we need people to cook meals, make sofas, make X-rays, write legal memos? The answer is yes. Then ask yourself: Could cooks and sofa makers be more productive in their job? Maybe they could work 10 percent faster, but that probably holds for radiologists and attorneys too. Therefore, we cannot conclude that cooks and sofa makers are intrinsically less productive in their job. This does not mean that all people would be paid the same in a perfect market, because some work longer hours, spend time at college, or took more risks. But the cause of income inequality is not that some jobs, by their very nature, are less productive than others.

goal—to try to come up with an *economic* explanation for income differences. In economic terms, *responsibility means that if you fail, you pay money out of your own pocket* (or spend some time in jail or remain unemployed for a while). Responsibility then largely coincides with financial risk. So how much can risk explain?

The risk explanation has the same shortcoming as the other explanations for income differences: risk may explain some things, but less than you would think. It is true that a CEO has a risky job, but what risks does a CEO actually face and how large are they? The legal liability risks are quite low. First, CEOs rarely face personal liability—if they make a mistake, their employer is usually the one who pays. Second, many of the more serious legal risks (such as jail time) presuppose bad faith (think Enron), which is a personal choice and not a risk. (Indeed, there is an easy way to eliminate this risk: don't commit fraud.) Statistically, the chance that a CEO acting in good faith will end up paying a legal bill is extremely small.

Of course, if we are talking about the risk of getting fired, the risk becomes real. CEOs get fired sometimes. But lower ranked workers face similar risks. True, there may be a difference with respect to finding a similarly paid job after dismissal. This risk is virtually nonexistent for unskilled workers—if you lose a minimum-wage job, your next job cannot possibly pay less. CEOs do face a risk of having to take a lower paid job. But this risk argument is circular—the CEO needs to be overpaid because he risks losing his overpaid job.

How about the risk for business owners? Here, it is true that there is a serious risk. Not all businesses are successful, and if your business fails, your losses can be significant. Still, many businesses require very little initial capital (think Microsoft, Google, or Facebook). If things go bad, the owner may need to reduce the workforce or give up some projects. But this risk does not consist of losing something, but of failing to obtain a higher income. True, some businesses require a significant amount of capital (think of a high-end restaurant). If such businesses fail, the owners may end up in poverty. There is a simple way to check whether business risk can explain income inequality. Suppose a business owner makes ten times what she would otherwise have made as a worker, and suppose that this higher income is solely a compensation for her risk-taking. A simplistic back-of-the-envelope calculation suggests that the success chance here was only 10 percent.[27] That means that for every successful business owner with an income of ten times the average income, there should be nine failed business owners who live in complete poverty. But can you really find such large numbers of impoverished entrepreneurs? *If you go to the poorest neighborhoods of your city, you will find minimum-wage workers, not failed entrepreneurs.*

Ricardo's Discovery

If income differences are so much larger than can be explained on simple economic grounds, something else must be going on. And that "something" was discovered in 1817 by an English economist named David Ricardo.[28]

Ricardo was not a professor—unlike Adam Smith, Thomas Malthus, John Mill, and other great classical economists. He didn't even go to school very long; when he was fourteen years old, he started working for his father. But his father had a very uncommon job—he was a stockbroker in London (the Wall Street of that time, so to speak). While the young Ricardo never learned economics from the books, he learned it in action. And learn it he did! By his midtwenties, he had made a fortune.

Ricardo began reading economics books only at a later age. And to his surprise, he noticed that the economy depicted in these books was very different from the economy he had experienced in real life. For instance, in the view of Adam Smith (the founding father of modern economics), getting wealthy was a matter of becoming productive. If workers could make more pins by working in a pin factory, wealth would go up. If farmers could produce more on the same land, they would become wealthier.

But Adam Smith was an unworldly, absentminded professor— the type that is depicted in slapstick comedies. One day, Adam Smith was visiting a tanning factory. He was so focused on explaining his theories that he fell in a large pool of goop.[29]

Ricardo had a different personality. And as a stockbroker, he had experienced that becoming wealthy was not so much a matter of working hard or being productive in a technological sense. Nobody worked as hard in the early nineteenth century as the members of the working class, and they made just enough to stay alive. The workers in pin factories (Adam Smith's favorite example) were much more productive than pin makers before the Industrial Revolution, but their income had largely remained the same. In Ricardo's experience, becoming wealthy was a matter of predicting where extraordinary profits would arise, and finding ways to capture these profits.

Who received most of these extraordinary profits in England around that time? In Ricardo's view, it was the landlords. The reason is that good agricultural land is scarce in the strictest sense of the word. You can't make more land—it is produced by nature. Of course, you could develop less fertile, rocky land. That is what you need to do as population grows and demand for food increases. But this makes good land even more valuable.

So, landlords are in the best possible position. They don't have to work and still get wealthy. All they need to do is collect huge sums of cash from the farmers who use their land. And the farmers have no choice but to pay these sums, as they compete to get the best land.

Ricardo needed a name for the artificial profits he had identified and used the term "rents"—the plain-English term for what farmers pay to landlords. That made sense because, at that time, agricultural land was the single biggest source of artificial profits. But in the meantime, the economic definition of the term has become much broader.*

Rents versus Quasi Rents

What exactly is a rent? As we have seen, a rent is a *profit that could not have been made in a perfect market.*[30] Suppose that the price of a product is $100 in a perfect market. But now suppose that the king gives a seller a monopoly to sell this product. Because there is no longer competition on the market, the price for the product goes up to $150. In this case, the seller receives a rent of $50 (the difference between the real price, which is $150, and the hypothetical price in a perfect market, which is $100).†

It is important to repeat that a rent is not the same as a profit. A rent is an artificial profit, a "superprofit." In perfect markets, businesses need to make some profits to stay alive. They need to give investors a reasonable compensation for letting them use their capital and give entrepreneurs a reasonable compensation

---

* Ricardo did more than just coining the term. He also discovered two fundamental principles of rent economics: the rents associated with good land go to the landlord (not to the farmer who works on the land), and the magnitude of the rents depends on the legal system. He argued that the English import restrictions on cheap Polish corn (the so-called "Corn Laws") artificially increased domestic food prices and thus artificially increased the rents for English landlords. As an economist, he argued against these Corn Laws. But as an investor, he was pessimistic enough about the political system to predict that the Corn Laws would not be repealed. So he bought land, and became a landlord himself!

† How do we know that the price would have been $100 in a perfect market? Rents are easy to define but hard to measure in practice. How much of a doctor's or CEO's income comes from rents? This is hard to say because measuring rents requires knowing what lawyers call a "counterfactual," that is, the reality that would have existed had the facts been different. The measurement difficulties explain why rents are understudied by economists, and why tax authorities have given up the idea to have a special tax on rents. Yet, the fact that rents are hard to measure does not mean they do not exist.

for all the time spent setting up and running the business. Rents are profits that go beyond that.

The modern definition of rents is broader than what Ricardo had in mind. For instance, the idea that monopoly profits are rents comes from John Stuart Mill (1848), not from Ricardo.[31] The idea that a better-informed party may acquire such a thing as an "information rent" (like a plumber who overcharges for spare parts) is only a few decades old. Modern economics makes a direct link between rents and market failures. Monopolies and asymmetric information are all market failures. Whenever there is a market failure, there is an opportunity for artificial profits. The more competitive the market, the lower the rents. In a perfect market, there are no rents.

As it turns out, Ricardo's land rents are atypical. These rents are caused by the absolute scarcity of land. Are they caused by a market failure? In a philosophical sense, yes. In an ideal world, the market would produce more land as soon as there was a shortage of land. The market for land would be like the market for laptops: if there is a shortage of laptops, the market quickly increases supply. But in the real world, it is technologically impossible to increase the supply of land. The same applies to oil, gold, and other natural resources. The rents associated with all these goods are now called *Ricardian rents*. They are atypical because they are not caused by market failures but by the absolute scarcity of natural resources.

Rents should not be confused with quasi rents. Quasi rents, as the name suggests, look like rents, because they look like overpayments at first glance. But upon closer inspection, what appears to be an overpayment is just the compensation for costs made at an earlier stage. People who went to college have a higher average income than people who didn't. But to the extent that the higher income is just compensation for the tuition paid and the shorter career, the income difference is a quasi rent, so it's not a rent at all.

A special case of quasi rents are the gains of a lottery winner.

Suppose you buy a $10 lottery ticket that gives you one chance in a million to win $10 million. If you win the $10 million, this looks like a rent, but upon closer inspection, you paid what economists call an "actuarially fair price" for the chance to win this amount.[32] Even in a perfect lottery market, there would be lottery winners. So, it is incorrect to see this as a rent—it is a quasi rent.

Now it becomes trickier. An indirect way to buy a lottery ticket is to participate in a winner-take-all-market. Consider movie stars in Hollywood. For every star who makes $20 million per year, there may be 1,000 unknown actors who hardly make any money. If one actor out of 1,000 receives $20 million, the average income for actors is $20,000. Therefore, what appears to be a rent ($20 million per year) may, in reality, be a quasi rent. From this perspective, the famous actors who live in mansions in Beverly Hills are just lottery winners.*

Is it possible to have truly wealthy people in a perfect market? At first sight no, because there are no rents. (You can make more money than your neighbor by working longer hours over the course of your life, working with more energy, or doing the same task more efficiently, but that will only take you so far.) But since there are still quasi rents in perfect markets, and there is still risk, lucky gamblers can end up wealthy. These include both the winners of explicit lotteries, and the winners of implicit lotteries such as winner-take-all markets. So, the only ones who live in mansions are lottery winners, actors who won the Hollywood lottery, and successful entrepreneurs who won the Silicon Valley lottery. But technically, these wealthy individuals received quasi rents, not rents.

---

* Suppose an entrepreneur studies the restaurant business for years, comes up with a great idea for a new restaurant chain, "Kentucky's Finest Roadkill," and eventually sells her business for $10 million. Is this a rent or a quasi rent? If it cost her $100,000 to develop the idea, and the chance of success was only 1 percent, the $10 million is a quasi rent. It looks like an artificial profit, but statistically, it is just the compensation for entrepreneurial costs. This doesn't mean that all excessive-looking incomes are quasi rents, though. In the following chapters, I will try to convince you that there are more rents and fewer quasi rents than people believe.

Rents Tend to Go to the Owners
(of the Business or Property)

Now, let's move to the question that matters most for income inequality: If there are rents somewhere in the economy, who gets the rents?

David Ricardo, the founder of rent analysis, asked the same question for the rents associated with good farmland. Do they go to the farmer who works on it, or to the landlord who owns it? At first sight, you might think it is the farmer who is the lucky one. He will have to work less hard than a farmer with bad land to obtain the same harvest. If both farmers work equally hard, the one with the best land will have the larger harvest.

Ricardo, however, concluded that this was a fallacy. The reason is that farmers compete with each other to get the best land. If good land generates $100,000 more harvest, farmers are willing to pay up to $100,000 more to acquire the farming rights. In equilibrium, the higher payment to the landlord completely offsets the higher harvest. Farmers with the best land aren't any better off than those with the worst land—the entire surplus goes to the landlord.

Although Ricardo had landowners in mind, economists later realized that the principle is more general. The principle that "rents go to the owners" applies to all types of owners, including business owners.

Who receives the rents associated with HP's expensive ink cartridges? The owners of HP (that is, the shareholders), not the employees. Who receives the rents of overpriced roofing services? The owner of the roofing company, not the roofers who do the hard labor. Who receives the rents in a $2 million fee that a law firm receives for settling a class action (more on that later)? The partners of the law firm (they are the owners), not the administrative assistants or associate attorneys who may have done most of the work.[33]

What will happen with the plumber who discovers he can overcharge for spare parts? He may start a business that hires ten plumbers. These plumbers, who do the work, receive no more than the market wage (for instance, $30,000 per year). The owner of the business makes $200,000. All the artificial profits acquired by overcharging for spare parts (say, $20,000 per plumber) get concentrated into the hands of one person, the business owner.

Ricardo's finding has another surprising implication. Should you invest your money in "equity" (that is, become shareholder of a company), or should you invest it in bonds (that is, lend your money for a fixed interest rate)? Over the past two centuries, shareholders (the holders of "equity") received consistently higher returns on their investment than bondholders. The difference (called the "equity premium") is estimated to be between 4 and 8 percent interest per year.[34] To be clear, the data does not say that shareholders receive a higher return than bondholders because shareholders have a higher risk to lose their investment in a bankruptcy. Instead, it shows the difference *after* you have taken those losses into account. This suggests that you are better off buying shares, as you will receive 4 to 8 percent more interest per year in the long run than when you buy government bonds.

What exactly explains the equity premium? Economists have come up with many explanations, but none of them are considered convincing. This is why the topic is known in the literature as the *equity premium puzzle*. But the puzzle is not so hard to solve if you apply rent economics: shareholders receive more money because they capture more rents. They capture more of the rents received by businesses because they are the owners. Remember, rents tend to go to the owners of businesses, and yes, shareholders—and not bondholders—are legally the owners.*

Ricardo's finding that rents go to owners is firmly supported by modern economic theory. It can be seen as an application of a more general theorem of principal-agent theory. This theorem holds that in principle, *the principal will not leave rents with the agent.* Let me briefly explain what this means. Principal-agent theory analyzes at the most abstract level the economic relationship between two parties. The "principal" is the party for whom the work is done; the "agent" is the party who does the work. In an employment contract, the employer is the principal and the employee is the agent. It is easy to understand intuitively why the principal will usually not pay rents to the agent. If you know that an administrative assistant with a certain skill set costs $30,000, why would you pay a salary of $100,000?

Of course, there are cases where employers overpay some of their workers. But these are special cases, in which the agent has superior information on the cost structure (more on that later). When the principal has access to the same information, she will not pay more than is strictly needed. Principals don't leave rents with agents.

First-Generation Owners Tend to Get All Future Rents

A second fundamental law of rent economics was discovered by the American economist Gordon Tullock in the 1970s.[35] This law holds that, in principle, all future rents will go to the first

---

* Why do private-sector bondholders receive slightly more than government bondholders? Because occasionally, some of the rents of private companies leak to the bondholders. Although the owners of private companies try hard to avoid leakage, they can't fully eliminate it because there may be only a few investors on the market with sufficient information on the company's true risk profile. In other words, competition among bondholders is not always perfect. Government bonds, in contrast, are the one investment for which no single investor can exploit an informational advantage—after all, information on the government is public. Therefore, they are the one investment on which no rents are paid.

generation of rent receivers. Tullock was a political economist (one of the founders of Public Choice Theory), so he focused on rents acquired through political lobbying. Yet the principle is more general.

Suppose that taxi drivers successfully lobby for a regulation that restricts access to the taxi market to those who hold a "taxi license." Only incumbent taxi drivers receive a license; from then on, new entrants have to buy the license from an existing license holder. Because the demand for taxi services is growing over time, there is soon a shortage of taxis, which increases prices, so that the first generation of license holders acquires a rent.

Yet, when this first generation sell their licenses to the next generation, they acquire a second rent. Indeed, there is a competitive bidding process for these taxi licenses, much like the bidding process among farmers to get the best land. Suppose that a taxi license is expected to generate $300,000 rents over the next thirty years. In that case, new entrants are willing to pay $300,000 for a license. As a matter of fact, new entrants are willing to pay even more. Indeed, they know that when they will retire, they will be able to sell their license for a high price. If the competition for licenses is perfect, the market price will equal the sum of all future rents ("discounted to present value," as economists will add).

This mechanism, again, *concentrates rents into the hands of a few*. If rents are expected to be available in the sector throughout five generations, the first generation runs away with all the rents that would belong to the next four generations. For those subsequent generations, what looks like a high income is just a normal income after they have paid back the entry price. For them, a rent has been transformed into a quasi rent.

Tullock's first-generation law applies to everyone who owns property rights that generate rents. Who receives the rents HP receives by selling overpriced cartridges? The current owner, that is, the current shareholders? According to Tullock's law, it is the first generation of owners, i.e., the founders of the company. The reason is that, when the next generation of shareholders bought their stock, they paid a competitive price that took the expected future rents into account.

Here is the paradox: rents go to shareholders, but becoming a shareholder does not help you get rents because the market price you pay for the shares will in principle equal the expected value of all future rents.

In practice, however, there is a lot of leakage to later generations. We have already discussed the equity premium puzzle, which tells us that people who buy shares have a 4–8 percent higher return on their investment than people who buy bonds. If you *buy* shares, you are never the first-generation owner; nonetheless, you still capture some rents. Or imagine you lease an apartment in Manhattan. The price is high as it includes a (Ricardian) rent. Will this economic rent go to the current owner? Probably not fully, because the current owner paid a high price to the previous owner, who in turn paid a high price to the previous owner. If we take Tullock's law to its extreme, all rents went to the Lenape people who sold the land to Dutch colonists in the seventeenth century. But that is clearly not the case, and not just because the original sellers lacked negotiation experience.[36] Then what explains leakage of rents to later generations? Maybe we simply incorrectly defined what the first generation is. As we will see in the next chapter, rent sources can be analogized to oil wells that pop up and later disappear. Who is the first generation in the case of an oil well? It is those who owned the land when the oil was discovered, not those who developed the land many centuries before. Therefore, the rents may not go to what is literally the first generation. Neither the Lenape people nor the Dutch colonists knew that the land would later become a great source of rents. That is why the rents did not go to their generation.

Occasionally, Rents Leak to Employees

In principle, rents go to owners, not to employees. Occasionally, however, rents may get leaked to employees who are better informed than their bosses.[37] CEOs, for instance, may know better than shareholders (who are the owners) how qualified an individual CFO is compared to other candidates. They may use their informational superiority to convince the shareholders that the current CFO needs to be paid at least $3 million, on the argument that he is so much better than most of his peers (which may or may not be true—the fact is that it is very costly for shareholders to check such statements). If the CFO gets $3 million, that makes it only logical to give the CEO $5 million ("more responsibility"). This $5 million then includes an information rent, though a very subtle one.[38]

Still, leakage is not the sole privilege of CEOs, CFOs, and other people whose position starts with a C. Consider Goldman Sachs. In the aftermath of the 2008 bailout, there was public outcry when newspapers reported that numerous employees kept receiving huge bonuses. To be fair, a bonus is not the same as a rent, but since the base wage of Goldman Sachs employees was already high, these bonuses are probably a good proxy for leaked rents.

Before continuing, let me remark that the public outcry missed the point. What is problematic for society is not so much that some of Goldman Sachs' rents leak to its employees. *The problem is that Goldman Sachs obtains rents.* Whether the shareholders or the employees get those rents is of secondary importance. (It is also not clear which of the two is worse from an income inequality perspective without knowing the identity of the shareholders.)

How can Goldman Sachs acquire rents? Some may say that Goldman Sachs works in an oligopolistic sector, but a more obvious explanation is information rents. As Greg Smith, the author of *Why I Left Goldman Sachs*, put it, "How does Wall Street make so much money anyway?... Two words: asymmetrical information. . . . Because Wall Street facilitates business for the smartest hedge funds, mutual funds, pension funds, sovereign wealth funds and corporations in the world, it knows who is on every side of a trade. It can effectively see everyone's cards. Therefore, it can bet smarter with its own money. . . . With opaque unregulated derivatives, there are no cameras. In this smoke-filled room, there is maximum temptation to try to exploit unsophisticated investors and conflicts of interest."[39]

Back to the rent leakage issue. Why don't the owners of Goldman Sachs succeed in keeping the rents for themselves? The answer is simple: the employees are better informed. For instance, how high should bonuses be to attract good employees and make them work hard? The manager of a department may know this, but for outsiders such as the owners, it may be difficult to find that out. Managers also have an incentive to propose overly generous bonuses for those below them—after all, this justifies that they get even higher bonuses.

The fact that the leaked rents are information rents nonetheless explains why higher-end employees have a higher chance of getting overpaid. Employees that are higher up in the organization typically have more information. Therefore, rent economics predicts that CEOs are the ones who capture the most leaked rents.

CEOs are also more likely to receive another source of rents—*search cost rents*. Suppose a CEO, who is paid $10 million per year, does a great job leading the company. Out of the seven billion people on this planet, are there any others who could do an equally great job for only $1 million per year? Definitely. The only problem is that it is hard to find out who they are. Of course, we could look at people's CVs, but how great someone is in a particular job becomes clear only once someone does the job. Suppose the new CEO turns out to be slightly less great. This could cost the company $100 million. Therefore, companies may choose to overpay someone who is known to be good. It is too risky to experiment with cheaper alternatives.

Occasionally, even low-skilled workers may be able to extract rents because of search costs. I know busy professionals who pay $25 per hour for cleaning services by someone who would only make $9 per hour in the normal labor market for relatively low-skilled work. This is puzzling because there may be thousands of other low-skilled workers out there who are willing to do the same job for much less. But how can customers know which are the ones who are equally good? The search costs are high, and therefore customers may prefer to overpay someone they know is good. In a sense, they pay a "brand-loyalty" premium.

That said, search cost rents are more likely to be acquired by highly specialized workers. Also, rents for low-skilled jobs are more likely to be captured by "rent entrepreneurs." These are home-service businesses that identify the good workers, pay them $9 per hour, and bill the customers $25 per hour. The search cost rents no longer go to the low-skilled workers, but to the business owners.

Cherry-Picking Rents

A specific form of rents that employees may receive when they are better informed than the owners are *cherry-picking rents*. These are the rents acquired by cherry-picking the overpaid parts of a job and skipping the underpaid parts.

Suppose you have an orchard of cherry trees and you want to hire workers to pick the cherries. But you have a problem: you live 1,000 miles away and can't watch them while they are working. You even have no clue how many cherries are on the trees this year. Even then, you have no way to know whether the workers picked all the cherries.

So, how should you pay the workers? If you pay them per hour, they may slow down—or even falsely report the hours they worked. If you pay them a fixed amount for the whole orchard, you have two other problems. First, you don't know how much work there is this year, and second, you have no way to check whether they really picked them all.

Thus, you decide to pay them per bucket. But how much should you pay? You vaguely know from previous years that filling a bucket requires on average $10 work. You know it costs less for the low-hanging cherries and more for the high-hanging cherries, but on average, $10 is a correct price. So, you make an arrangement with a local store and tell the workers you will pay $10 for each bucket they bring to this store.

What happens? Only the low-hanging cherries are picked. Nobody is willing to pick the cherries at the top of the tree.

Why? Implicitly, you have made the mistake of paying the same price for jobs that require different effort levels. Picking low-hanging cherries is easier than picking high-hanging cherries. You have essentially offered to always pay the price that corresponds to the average effort cost—say, the effort cost of picking cherries halfway up the tree. This means you are overpaying for the easy jobs and underpaying for the hard jobs. The workers decide to do only the overpaid jobs and leave the underpaid jobs to others (or to the birds!).

By choosing this payment form, you have created two problems. The first is that the high-hanging cherries are not picked. The second is that you have overpaid for the low-hanging cherries. As a result, the workers receive rents.

Here is another way to look at it. Suppose for simplicity that picking costs vary from $1 to $20 per bucket. If the workers pick the easiest cherries, it requires an effort cost of $1 per bucket, but they get paid $10 and so receive a rent of $9. If they pick cherries that require an effort cost of $4, they get paid $10 as well and receive a rent of $6. If the effort cost is $10, they are still willing to pick the cherries, and only in that marginal case, they are correctly paid. They are not willing to pick cherries that require an effort of more than $10—in that case, they prefer to move on to the next job.

If you look at the problem at a more fundamental level, you will see that the source of the rent is the asymmetric information between you and your workers. You know only on average how much it costs to fill a bucket of cherries, but you do not know for each individual bucket where they were picked and how much effort they required. The workers, by contrast, know for each bucket how much effort it takes (and can easily predict how much effort the next bucket will take). The workers, in other words, have superior information on the effort costs and get a rent by exploiting this information.

If you could find a way to make them honestly reveal the effort cost for each bucket, you could easily remove their rent. Indeed, if they told you (honestly) that the effort cost of a specific bucket was only $1, you would only pay $1, and if it was $7 you would only pay $7. But obviously, the workers have no incentive to reveal that information—they prefer to exploit it to obtain a rent. Because the rent is caused by superior information, *cherry-picking rents* are just a special form of *information rents*.

It is easy to solve the rent problem by paying less. But this will only exacerbate the other problem—that the higher-hanging cherries remain unpicked. Indeed, if you pay $5 per bucket, you will overpay less for the buckets that require a $1 effort, but now the cherries will remain unpicked as soon as the effort costs are higher than $5. Conversely, it is easy to solve the underpicking problem by worsening the rent problem. You can indeed make the workers pick the high-hanging cherries by paying them $20 per bucket. But in this case, you overpay even more.

This paradox—that you can improve the first problem only by worsening the second problem—is known in the economic literature as the *efficiency versus information rents trade-off*. Efficiency (just another word for economic optimality) requires that all cherries be picked. But to reach full efficiency, you need to pay high information rents. Very often, the optimal trade-off consists in compromising somewhat on both inefficiency and rent reduction. You pay some rents and leave some cherries unpicked because any other combination of these two "evils" would be even worse for you.

But can't you solve the problem simply by paying workers per hour and making sure you are in the orchard when they pick the cherries? That is true—this would solve the problem. If you are watching, the cherry pickers will no longer shirk or falsely report the number of hours they worked. But it only solves the problem because you would have more information. Acquiring this extra information, however, may not be free. Traveling a thousand miles may be quite costly. And then the *efficiency versus information rents trade-off* reappears.

Salespeople may receive cherry-picking rents too. Suppose you are a car dealer and have hired many salespeople. How would you pay them? Paying them a fixed wage may not be a good idea, since it is hard to define what exactly they need to do to get a successful deal. So, you decide to give them a percentage of the sales and let them decide how much effort they will put into each sales opportunity. But what percentage should you pay? At first sight this looks simple. Find out the market wage for this type of job (say, $30,000) and set the percentage just high enough to get a $30,000 yearly income on average. Suppose, for instance, that this percentage is 10 percent of the markup.

This 10 percent, however, does not give perfect incentives. After all, the salesperson bears 100 percent of the effort cost and receives only 10 percent of the extra money that is being made because of more effort. You can improve incentives by paying more, but then you will also pay rents. In short, you are faced with the *efficiency versus information rents paradox*. You will look for the optimal compromise, where the marginal overpayment equals the marginal increased profit. At the end of the day, this optimal percentage may give the salesperson $50,000 per year—a $20,000 rent.

To see why the rents of salespeople are cherry-picking rents, keep in mind that their contract does not tell them what to do, but offers them a menu of choices. They pick out the sales opportunities that are overpaid but decide not to chase the sales opportunities that are underpaid. The crux of the problem is their superior information. How much effort will a specific sale cost? Is it worth going after that customer? The employer does not know, but the salesperson does; and she exploits that information to obtain an information rent.

Why the Pharmaceutical Industry Is So Profitable and Bill Gates So Wealthy

Cherry-picking rents are a type of rents that can be acquired by employees. Yet technically they can be acquired by any other "agent," that is, someone who works for someone else. Therefore, they can also be acquired by employers, to the extent that these employers are "agents" in another relationship. Pharmaceutical companies, for instance, can be seen as "agents" who work for the government (or society), developing new drugs. Why is the pharmaceutical industry more profitable than the average industry?[40] Because they receive cherry-picking rents.

Before I explain why, you should understand that

pharmaceutical companies are paid in a somewhat special way. They do not just receive an amount of dollars for each successful drug discovery. Instead, they receive a patent. A patent is a monopoly right; only the patent holder is allowed to sell the drug. Like all monopolists, patent holders tend to make high profits. The longer the patent lasts, the higher the total profits. So, if we ask how much pharmaceutical companies should be paid for discovering new drugs, the question is not how much money they should be paid by the government, but how many years of monopoly they should receive.

So, how long should a patent last? Twenty years? Three years? Seventy years? Economic theory says that should depend on the research costs (including the costs of what later turn out to be unsuccessful research programs), and on the demand for the product. For some medical discoveries (the low-hanging cherries, so to speak), one year would be enough. For others, it may be three years, eight years, nineteen years, or thirty-three years. For some (drugs for rare medical conditions, for instance), a monopoly of forty years may be needed to fully recoup the investment.

A perfect legal system would give just enough patent protection to recoup the research costs. After all, the goal is not to give inventors a rent, but to give them a quasi rent (a profit that may look high but that is just compensation for earlier costs). This means that for some inventions, patent protection would be three years; for another, fourteen years and five months; for some other, thirty-three years. In reality, calculating the optimal patent duration is difficult, and therefore the legal system works with a general protection of twenty years for all inventions, irrespective of their research costs.

It is not difficult to see that this fixed twenty-year protection leads to cherry-picking rents. Suppose the development costs of a certain drug can be earned back after a single year. The profits for the following nineteen years then are pure rents. As a general rule, rents are earned whenever a protection of less than twenty years would have been sufficient.

Moreover, the fixed twenty-year protection leads to underresearching, because only the drugs that can be earned back within twenty years or less of protection will be developed. A drug for a relatively rare disease that can only be earned back with a protection of, say, thirty-four years, will not be developed.

Now, you may say that the numerical examples I have given underestimate the challenges of pharmaceutical companies in several ways. For instance, you may argue that getting a drug approved is not only a very costly process but also a long one, so that the effective monopoly position in reality lasts less than twenty years. That may very well be true, but this criticism misses the real point: whenever the legal system offers a *fixed* duration of patent protection, you will get both cherry-picking rents and some cases of underresearching.

As always, the rent problem and the underresearching problem are in conflict with each other. You can improve the underresearching problem by extending general patent protection to, for instance, fifty years (as has been proposed by some). But then you overpay even more for the drugs that would have been developed under the current regime.

The fact that cherry-picking rents are a form of information rents can be illustrated with this example as well. The deeper reason why pharmaceutical companies gain rents is that they know better than the government how much the expected development costs will be and how profitable the drug will be. (Okay, they may not perfectly know these numbers before they start doing research, but they have some idea of the likely costs and profits.) Because of this information, they avoid developing drugs that are not profitable under the current twenty-year scheme. If the government did possess the same information, it could adjust the patent duration for each individual drug. But the government has great difficulties in acquiring this information, and the pharmaceutical companies have no incentive to spontaneously reveal it. In a sense, they outsmart the government, just like the cherry pickers outsmarted the orchard owner.

Here is another real-life example of cherry-picking rents, though it is a little harder to recognize: the legal protection of MS-DOS and Microsoft Windows. How long should the legal protection last? Just long enough to let the developer recoup the investment costs. (After that, it should become legal to copy software—at least, that is what Economics 101 prescribes.)

But the duration should not only depend on the investment costs but also on how fast money can be made. And here there is something very special about operating software: it is a good that tends to have so-called *network externalities*. Network externalities are positive externalities for other users of the good.[41] Imagine that nobody else on this planet had a telephone; would you buy one? Probably not. But the more people that have a telephone, the more useful it becomes to buy one too— everyone who buys a telephone creates a positive effect on other potential users of the "network."

No doubt, operating software has such characteristics. Why did most people use MS-DOS, and now Windows? Because of its superiority to Apple's operating software or Linux? No, because most other people had MS-DOS or Windows as well. And why did those people have this software? Because most others had it.

Network externalities are not innocent from an economic point of view. They naturally distort competition. They lead to *natural monopoly.** The term natural "monopoly," however, should not always be taken literally. Microsoft never had a 100 percent monopoly in the operating software market (though it depends, of course, on how you define the market; if you define it as "the market for IBM-compatible operating software," they had a monopoly until Linux showed up). But the pricing power they had was akin to that of a monopolist. Because of that, enormous profits could be generated. Therefore, patent protection should have been very short—maybe as short as a few months for each version.[42]

The current legal system, however, did not adjust the duration for MS-DOS and Windows. It gave the same (in practice lifelong) protection to all software, irrespective of whether there were network externalities involved. The difference between the profits that Microsoft made and the profits that were strictly needed to recoup the investment are rents. Good news for Bill Gates, who acquired billions of dollars because of . . . an imperfection in the legal system.

Radiation Rents: Those Who Can Threaten to Get Rents Elsewhere Get Rents!

Professors at American medical schools are better paid than professors in history departments. Why? At first sight, both labor markets seem equally competitive. In both markets, there are many schools and many candidates. In both markets,

---

* The textbook example of a natural monopoly is utilities infrastructure: it would be wasteful to have twenty competing water mains on your street. The cheapest solution is to have only one, sufficiently large pipeline. Imagine water provision were left to an unregulated market. What would happen? Maybe there would be wasteful investments in the short run—five companies sending bulldozers to your street to build their own water main. In the long run, however, markets tend to move to the technically optimal solution, which is a monopoly in this case. Network externalities lead to similar equilibria. Surprisingly, the legal system treats them differently.

schools have plenty of information about the candidates (they can read the candidates' publications and teaching evaluations) and candidates have plenty of information about the schools. In short, there seem to be no reasons to expect rents in any of these markets.

Why, then, are medical professors paid more? Because they have different outside options. Medical professors can threaten to become full-time doctors, while history professors can only threaten to become full-time high school teachers. So, here is the puzzling fact: if doctors receive rents, then medical professors need to be paid rents as well to keep them away from this rent-earning market. Therefore, the rents in the doctors' market radiate to the medical professors' market. It is as if an infection in one place spreads to another.

Radiation rents are rents that have radiated from distorted markets to competitive markets. They are paid in highly competitive markets in which rents can, in principle, not exist. They are paid to prevent talented workers from moving their talent to other markets in which there are rents.

The conditions under which radiation rents may occur have not been fully theorized yet in the literature. As a matter of fact, there isn't even a technical term for this phenomenon—and so I herewith introduce the term "radiation rent." While the term may be new, the principle itself is a straightforward application of a fundamental principle of labor economics—that wages are determined by the employees' outside options. If their outside options include rents, that must affect wages.[43]

To how many sectors of the economy do rents in one sector radiate? Theoretically, that is unclear. You could easily make an extreme model, in which the rents in a single, small sector radiate to the rest of the economy (as I'll explain in an endnote).[44] So, rents may radiate to sectors where you don't expect it. It may be possible for elementary school teachers to receive radiation rents, if they can threaten either to become car salespeople, start their own plumbing companies, or move to another sector where information rents are acquired. The fact that teachers make three times as much as unskilled workers is puzzling from an economic viewpoint—even though teachers are not "overpaid" in the broader scheme of the economy.

In theory, it is even possible that radiation rents in turn cause more radiation rents! If teachers receive radiation rents, then everyone who can threaten to become a teacher should in principle receive the same amount of rents.

What percentage of the GDP consists of radiation rents? This is extremely difficult to estimate. Measuring radiation rents in one sector requires not only measuring the rents in other sectors, but also measuring the switching costs to those other sectors. But it is not because something is hard to measure that it does not exist.

This brings us to another fundamental problem of rents: they make it harder to measure economic data, such as true productivity. Rents distort prices, and in a market economy each price may in turn affect other prices. So, when some prices get distorted, some other prices get distorted as well, and in the end, it becomes very difficult to determine which prices are indirectly distorted, and what the prices would have been had the initial distortion not occurred. And that, in itself, is quite problematic. After all, the efficiency of a market economy depends on whether the market prices truly reflect the costs.

Land or Natural Resources Rents Don't Cause Income Inequality If Competition to Acquire Them Is Perfect

If you own land in Manhattan, you may receive a lot of money because land is very scarce in Manhattan. If you own an oil well in Texas, your income may be high as well because there is less oil on this planet than there is demand for oil.

These rents are called "Ricardian rents." We have seen that these rents are atypical. They are not caused by market failures but by the absolute scarcity of natural resources—we wish Mother Nature had given us more of these goodies. Unlike other sources of rents, it is not desirable to bring the price closer to the true costs. If the government would artificially lower the price of land, it may no longer end up in the hands of those who value it most. Similarly, if the price of oil is artificially lowered, oil may get wasted.

If it is not even desirable to eliminate Ricardian rents, don't they inevitably create income inequality? After all, there will always be someone who owns the land, the oil field, or the gold mine, won't there?

It is true that the scarcity of natural resources inevitably leads to rents. But here is the amazing thing: these rents do not necessarily lead to income inequality. Indeed, *Ricardian rents only lead to income inequality if there is imperfect competition to acquire these resources!*[45] If landlords or oil magnates get wealthy, it must be because they paid less to acquire the land or the oil than they would have paid in a perfectly competitive setting. An extreme case of imperfect competition happens when the government simply gives these resources away for free.

Unfortunately, property law often gives away rents on a

massive scale. This is the case, for instance, when mining rights are given to those who happen to live above a mine.*

Consider the Kidd Creek Mine case that is discussed in some Contracts classes in law school.[46] The Texas Gulf Sulphur mining company had developed new technology that allowed them to predict where sulfide deposits could be found. This new technology (which involved analyzing aerial pictures) led them to discover the Kidd Creek sulphur mine in Ontario, Canada— one of the largest sulfide mines in the world. The property law of Ontario, however, stated that the ownership of a mine belonged to whoever owned the land above it. This created a serious problem for the mining company: if they would approach the landowner and reveal what they knew, the landowner could essentially free ride on their entrepreneurial efforts, using this information to sell the mine to competitors at the full market price. So, they used the following "trick" to obtain information rents. The company offered to check the subsurface of the land at their own expense, pretending they knew less than they actually did. They paid the owner $500 for the right to check the land, and the contract further stipulated that if minerals were discovered, 10 percent of the value would go to the owner. The owner signed, and of course, Texas Gulf Sulphur did "discover"

---

* Another scarce resource is a radio frequency. In 2003, a small company named Mediasales received a Dutch radio license, possibly worth 23 million euros, for only 8,000 euros. How did they do that? Well, the Dutch government chose a type of auction that economists called a "beauty contest." In a beauty contest, the winner is not the one who offers the most money, but the one who presents the most impressive project. In this case, participants had to present a project for a new radio station that would focus on Dutch productions (participants also had to tell how much they would pay for the license, but that played only a secondary role). Radio giant RTL Nederland, generally considered the unbeatable favorite, offered to play Dutch music 35 percent of the time and pay 23 million euros. Mediasales offered 70 percent Dutch music and 8,000 euros. A court eventually decided that Mediasales had to be awarded the license. See http://en. wikipedia.org/wiki/100%25_NL. Unintentionally, the Dutch government had given away millions of euros of rents to a few people. See also Paul Klemperer, *Auctions: Theory and Practice* (Princeton: Princeton University Press, 2004), 171 ("A beauty contest, by contrast, can give away valuable assets at a fraction of what they are worth"). Note that beauty contests can be rational in rare circumstances—for instance, for architectural designs, when the competition is on quality *given a predetermined price* that is expected to reflect the market price (taking risk into consideration).

a mine. When the owner later found out he had been tricked, he sued the mining company. The case was settled: the owner accepted 10 percent of the mine's value (as stipulated in the contract), probably because he realized that this, in itself, would make him the richest man in Canada.

When this case is discussed in Contracts classes, the debate usually revolves around who should get the rents: the landowner or the mining company? Some students feel that it is the landowner who should get the whole $1 billion because after all, it is *his* land. Others feel that the billion dollars should go to the mining company because it was its entrepreneurship that led to the discovery of the mine. That is indeed the question under contract law. But the more important legal question must be answered under property law: Should the legal system give away Ricardian rents for free? Sure, the mining company needs to be compensated for its investment, but why should it be overcompensated with the mine's full value? If it costs $1,000 to discover that you have a certain medical condition, why would you pay the doctor $100,000?

Now for the most generous spiller of Ricardian rents: zoning regulation. Building land near a city is naturally scarce, but zoning regulations typically make it even scarcer by restricting the places where houses can be built (and sometimes rightly so, because open space such as a park increases the value of the surrounding land). If you own agricultural land and suddenly it is declared building land, you win the lottery.

In one of the suburbs of Ghent (Belgium) where I used to live, there was one house in a beautiful subdivision that was larger than the surrounding houses. How did the owner succeed in becoming one of the wealthiest individuals of the suburb? Well, it turns out that he just happened to own agricultural land. The day the city transformed it into building land, he became a millionaire.

If governments give away land rents for free, societies may become more similar to a medieval society than most people realize. In medieval times, a few lords lived in castles, and most others had to work hard in the fields to sustain the local lord's standard of living. In our society, many people must work long hours to be able to pay off the loans they needed to acquire a small lot of building land. Many young couples in my old Belgian suburb lived the following routine: At 7 a.m. they had to drop their baby off at daycare and head to their office in the capital, where they worked long hours. At 7 p.m., they would return and pick up their baby. Why did they work so much more than they would have wished? Because they wanted to have a backyard for their child, and to afford one, they needed to pay a lot of money to the local lord—I mean, to the one who won the zoning lottery.

Will All Rents Turn into Quasi Rents through Rent-Seeking Costs?

Before discussing the overall impact of rents on income inequality, we need to answer a preliminary question: Do rents really exist? Can they ever occur at a large scale in a market economy? The question may sound absurd, but economists often argue that rents disappear like snow under the sun whenever there is competition for rents. I will call this viewpoint the "There Can Be No Rents in Markets Fallacy." At the outset, I should make it clear that there is some truth in a weaker version of this reasoning—that *in some cases* rents will be transformed into quasi rents. But the viewpoint that rents *must* be low in market economies is both theoretically and empirically incorrect.

The argument used to deny the existence of rents goes as follows. Imagine that plumbers can acquire information rents by overpricing components. In that case, plumbers make more money than those with comparable jobs. The higher income, however, will work like a magnet, attracting new entrants to the plumbing market. From then on, plumbers will have to compete to get a share of the market. They may have to spend money on expensive advertising campaigns or professional-looking trucks. In equilibrium, these costs (which are technically "rent-seeking costs") may equal the rents. In that case, plumbers make no more money than those with comparable jobs, so goes the argument. They don't receive rents, but quasi rents.

This argument could be used to deny that HP gets rents from overpriced ink cartridges. If on average $500 rents can be earned on cartridges during the printer's life span, firms will compete to get the opportunity to sell overpriced cartridges, and this competition will bring the price of printers down to $500 below the true costs. In other words, even if there is a lack of competition in the secondary market (the cartridge market), the competition in the primary market (the printer market) will make the rents dissipate. At the end of the day, the consumer pays a correct price for the total package. She may pay $500 too much for cartridges but also $500 too little for the printer.

The hypothesis that rent-seeking costs may equal rents was first made in a political context by public choice economists.[47] Their reasoning went as follows. Suppose a king announces that he will approve only one new medieval guild. This guild will have the right to restrict competition, which would generate $100 million rents for its members. The king also announces that the guild will go to the profession that offers him the most money. How much will the winning profession pay (assuming that all professions overcome the collective action problems associated with the fact that many self-interested individuals have to act as a group)? All participating groups know that if they offer only, for instance, $90 million to get the $100 million of rents, they will likely be outbid by another group that offers even more. So, to win the auction, groups have to offer close to $100 million. If you take this reasoning to its mathematical extremes, you find that the winning offer will equal $100 million. In other words, the rent-seeking costs will equal the rents.

The argument that rents may not even exist in monopolized markets is implicit in the work of the Austrian economist Joseph Schumpeter.[48] Schumpeter is famous for being the intellectual father of the economic study of entrepreneurship. Yet he was also the first in the history of economics to say something positive about monopolies. Indeed, since Adam Smith, monopolies have been considered the worst possible market structure. Schumpeter, however, pointed out that innovation often happens through firms that hold a temporary monopoly. In Schumpeter's view, monopolists do face competition, but that competition takes place at an earlier stage, when many firms are still fighting for the market. The winner of the competition-for-the-market may be generously rewarded, but this reward may no longer be excessive if you consider the costs incurred to obtain the market (including the costs incurred by those who lost the race).

Schumpeter did not formally argue that the total costs to obtain a market will always equal the rents that can be obtained on that market. But he did suggest that, if competition for markets is sufficiently intense, the rents in the second market will dissipate. If we reason like Schumpeter, we may conclude that Bill Gates did not earn any rents. All he did was win a highly competitive winner-take-all-lottery, so, what looks like rents are in reality quasi rents. Bill Gates's wealth, in that case, did not come out of the pocket of the users of MS-DOS. It came (at least virtually) out of the pockets of the other entrepreneurs who spent billions trying to create the industry standard but who lost the battle. All these entrepreneurs plus Bill Gates bought a lottery ticket at an actuarially fair price. Bill Gates won, the others lost—at least in Schumpeter's framework.

If rents are dissipated through rent-seeking costs, they are still problematic, because rent-seeking costs are intrinsically wasteful. But rents can then no longer explain income inequality: everyone who received a rent paid for it in some form. What appears to be a rent is, in reality, a quasi rent.

Time to look at empirical data, starting with political rents! As it turns out, rent-seeking costs tend to be much lower than rents. Regulation in Washington, DC, can be bought for a few cents on the dollar. For instance, the prescription drug industry paid only $116 million to lobbyists to prevent Medicare from reducing drug prices—a windfall of $90 billion annually. Similarly, companies that lobbied on the 2004 American Jobs Creation Act got $220 in benefits for every $1 spent on lobbying.[49] But also in the private sector, marketing and other rent-seeking costs do not completely erase the profitability of the market. The HP printer division (with its overpriced ink cartridges) is much more profitable than its other divisions.[50]

Let's now analyze the rent dissipation argument on a theoretical level. Under what conditions will the expenses to acquire a rent equal the value of the rent? The total rent-seeking expenses are the product of the number of candidates who try to acquire the rent, and the average costs they incur in the hope of acquiring it. This implies that there are two general conditions: first, there must be a sufficient number of candidates, and second, they must be able to spend enough.

Imagine the US government places a $10,000 golden egg in one of the million streets in the country, without giving any hints about the region or state where it's located. The government announces that the finder of the egg can keep it. Will you jump out of your chair and start searching? No. Statistically, the chance of finding the golden egg is so small that the search costs would clearly outweigh the benefits of searching. Only those who happen to be in the right place at the right time and happen to see the egg should put forth the effort to get the egg. Now, suppose there are three individuals who walk in the right street at the right time. When they see the golden egg, they start running toward it as fast as they can. The winner receives the golden egg in return for running hard for ten seconds. The two others, who arrived a split second later, have lost a running cost investment of ten seconds. The total "rent-seeking costs" of those three are thirty seconds of running—very small compared to the value of the rent.

Why didn't rent-seeking costs equal rents in this case? First, there were too few individuals who could compete. Second, their spending was limited to a physical effort of ten seconds, whereas the egg was worth far more. Now, suppose the golden egg was visible to 10,000 people at the same time, and that all of them were about a two-minute run away from the egg. In that case, the sheer number of participants could make it possible that the rent-seeking costs would equal the rent. But even then, it is possible that 9,990 of the runners would stop running after ten seconds, when they see that the others are far better runners.

In practice, there can be several reasons why competitors may not be able to spend enough to fully dissipate the rent. First, negative prices cannot exist. Suppose that the real cost of a printer is $200, and that the ex post rent acquired by selling overpriced cartridges is $500. To fully dissipate the rents, printers would have to be sold at a price of negative $300, that is, consumers would have to receive $300 for being willing to take home the printer. But paying consumers to simply take a good may not be possible, for instance, because it creates "moral hazard" problems—consumers may throw away the printer after cashing the $300.[51]

A second reason is that a price reduction in the primary market can be erroneously interpreted by the consumers as a signal of low quality. Suppose that when consumers see a $50 printer, they believe it must be low quality. In this case, the price of the printer may have to be kept at the true cost level.

A third reason is that entry fees may be illegal. This is the case for dentists and doctors, who may not be charged a fee to enter the profession (though they can be made to pay in subtler ways, for instance, by having to do night work at below-market fees during their training).

Fourth, there can be practical reasons why too few candidates compete for the rents. Very often, exploiting a rent opportunity requires some expertise, and too few people happen to have this expertise at the time the rent opportunity becomes visible. When IBM put the biggest golden egg ever for grabs (the opportunity to write the operating software for their newly invented PCs), Bill Gates was one of the very few people on the planet who knew about this opportunity and had the opportunity to compete (which required not only software expertise but also the right social networks). And when rents became available in the growing Swiss tourism industry in the 1950s, only the Swiss farmers who happened to own land near what turned out to be tourism centers had the opportunity to turn their farms into bed-and-breakfasts, later into cheap hotels, and still later into luxury hotels.

Here is the paradox. To fully transform rents into rent-seeking costs, the market-to-acquire-rents must be perfectly transparent and competitive. However, the market in which there are rents is by definition *not* perfectly transparent and competitive. In other words, if rents are caused by market imperfections, why would the market-to-acquire-rents be perfect?

Why Rents Lead to Income Inequality

Okay, rents exist. But do they always increase income inequality? Suppose that rents go to an individual plumber, whose income would otherwise have been below average. Thanks to the rents, he has an average income. Don't those rents reduce inequality by bringing someone's income closer to the average?

In some cases, this may happen. But in practice, this rarely happens. Based on the fundamental laws of rent economics, rents will *nearly always* increase income inequality.

For starters, keep in mind that rents are overpayments. Rents are artificial profits that could not have been made in a perfectly competitive market. So, by their very nature, rents nearly always increase inequality. After all, those who receive them are overpaid. If you are overpaid, you typically end up with an above-average income.

Rents only reduce income inequality if they go to people with below-average incomes *and* if they are relatively small. The latter condition is important: if rents are large, they may "overshoot" and create a problem at the other side. If someone who was in the bottom 30 percent ends up in the top 10 percent, that is further away from the average. In this case, rents increase income inequality, even though they go to someone who was initially relatively poor.

In reality, rents tend to get concentrated in the hands of a few, so that those who receive them get large doses of them. In addition, rents tend to go to people with an above-average income to start with. Just look again at the fundamental laws of rent economics.

The first law of rent economics is that rents tend to go to the owners. This has a concentration effect. Do plumbers receive rents by overcharging for spare parts? Soon, there will be businesses who hire plumbers as wage workers. From then on, the plumbers (who do the work) receive only the market wage; all the rents go to the business owners. If a typical business has ten plumbers, rents get concentrated by a factor of ten. In other industries, the factor is much larger. Sometimes, the concentration factor is so large that those who receive the rents become billionaires.

A second law of rent economics is that rents tend to go to the first generation of rent receivers. This has a concentration effect as well.

A third law is that the rents a business receives may get leaked to employees who have an informational advantage. Since information is spread unequally over all employees, the leaked rents are spread unequally as well. Typically, those at the top receive a disproportionally large share of the leaked rents. After all, they are the ones with a disproportionally large informational advantage.

A fourth law is that the "talented" or "smart" tend to get the rents. Rents are like golden Easter eggs: the first to pick them up get them. In practice, this often requires outsmarting someone else. So, those who would have received an above-average income anyway tend to be the ones who receive the rents. Also, grabbing a rent requires seeing a rent opportunity, and this information is spread unequally as well. Seeing a rent opportunity may require some luck as well, and luck is, once again, distributed unequally.

Finally, ownership of land and natural resources tends to be unequally distributed as well. When these resources are given away or sold by the government below the perfectly competitive market price, the rents tend to go to a small percentage of the population.

"Talented" People Tend to Get the Rents

When we discussed the "economic" explanations given for income inequality, I argued that productivity differences cannot explain much. But how about "talent," defined as some form of intelligence that is useful in the modern economy?[52] If you look at people who become wealthy, they seem to have some form of "talent" that few other people have. Bill Gates may simply be "smarter" than most of us. Surgeons may be "smarter" than the fishermen who catch all those salmon they eat. (Fishermen may have talents most surgeons don't have, but unfortunately, that is not the type of talent the economic system needs most, so goes the argument.)

Here is my view: *talent may explain who gets the rents but not why there are rents in the first place.* Talent may explain who gets the best-paid positions in our society, but it doesn't explain why these positions are so well paid. Bill Gates is a talented man. His talent may explain why he was the one who acquired the rents associated with operating software for PCs, but it does not explain why these rents were up for grabs in the first place. (As we have seen, the fundamental cause was an imperfection of the legal system.)

Let me illustrate this with an old fairy tale (that I have just made up). Once upon a time, there was a king who built a dozen castles each year (financed with tax money, but that is a detail omitted in fairy tales). Because he could live in only one castle, he decided to give all the others away to the winners of local poker tournaments. Winning such a poker tournament was the only way to become wealthy in this kingdom. Therefore, kids started taking poker classes at the age of three. At the age of eighteen, the most talented were admitted to a poker college, where they played poker twelve hours per day. Even then, only the very best of them would ever win a castle.

No doubt, those who ended up living in a castle were smart. From their perspective, the castle was the well-deserved, "normal" compensation for their talent. So, who got the most overpaid positions in this society? The most talented poker players. But that doesn't explain why poker players were so overpaid in the first place.

To be fair, it is theoretically possible that there is such a thing as *talent scarcity* for some *much-needed jobs.* Not everyone can compose songs like Paul McCartney or discover scientific theories like Albert Einstein. Their talent is scarce; we wish that more people were born with such talents.

But for how many professions is talent really the limiting force? Is there really a talent scarcity for doctors? Of course, not everyone is talented enough to become a doctor. But that is not the question. Not everyone is talented enough to become a fisherman either. What matters for talent scarcity is not how many people have the talent but how many have the talent relative to how often the talent is demanded. What matters for the doctors' market is not whether everyone could become a doctor, but whether there are enough talented people available on this planet to fill up the number of doctor positions needed.

Modern psychology suggests that intelligence is very fluid, at least at a young age. There are few professions that require a very specific talent. Look around, and you will surely find many people who aren't doctors but could have been good doctors. This suggests that, even if there were a shortage of doctors, this shortage would be short-lived, since the high earnings associated with shortages tend to attract new talent. Maybe the legal system creates entry barriers, but then those entry barriers explain the high earnings, not the talent scarcity.

Why the Best-Paid Profession in the World Is Selling, Not Inventing

So, what is the best-paid profession in the world? Maybe you expect the answer to be inventors, artists, manufacturers, or contract law professors. In their book *How to Sell at Margins Higher Than Your Competitors*, pricing specialists Steinmetz and Brooks argue that the best-paid profession in the world is selling![53] As puzzling as it sounds, they are probably right.

The best-paid profession is not necessarily the one that adds the most to the progress of mankind. The best-paid profession is the one that generates the highest artificial profits—rents. We have seen that the holy grail of rents is the information rent. Who is in a better position to acquire information rents than sellers, broadly defined, who have a natural informational advantage over their customers?*

Rent economics also explains why inventing is not the best-paid profession. Innovation is the future! That is what we tell our kids. We tell them they should work hard in math and science class because our country needs more engineers and scientists— they are the ones who will make us wealthier. What we don't tell our kids is that engineers and researchers are not the best-paid professionals. Sure, there are a few who started their own business, obtained a few patents, and eventually became wealthy. But if you look at the top 1 percent of the best-paid people, you will find few engineers or researchers. Occasionally, you may find a few CEOs who used to be engineers early in their careers. Yet they typically started making big money when they stopped working as engineers.

The fact that so few engineers and researchers find themselves in the top 1 percent of income earners is easy to explain. The best-paid jobs are those that receive the most rents. Therefore, the best-paid professionals are those who are best at rent extracting, not those who are best at engineering.

---

* Selling is of course more than just trying to capture an information rent. Selling is first and foremost bringing the produced goods to the users who value them most. In this sense, sellers offer valuable services to end users.

Moreover, sellers typically acquire expertise on the good they are selling. This expertise allows them to advise customers—another valuable service. But the same expertise allows them to exploit customers in subtle ways. As a result, selling can be one of the best-paid professions.

The tragedy of rents, then, is that the most talented people move toward the jobs that create rents, not toward the jobs that create long-term growth. Do you know a math major who obtained a PhD in physics? I bet she is no longer working in a lab but doing math for a hedge fund on Wall Street. This pays better. Rents reduce innovation in many indirect ways (more about this later). Attracting talent to the wrong professions is one of them.

3

RENTS ARE AT LEAST
35 PERCENT OF THE ECONOMY

I t is easy to give examples of distorted markets. Yet anecdotes alone do not prove a claim. And this book makes quite a few bold claims: (1) the degree of market distortion is high in the economy; (2) market distortions are the best explanation for income differences; (3) markets have become more distorted in recent decades; and (4) this is the main reason why income inequality has increased.

How do I prove this scientifically? How do I show that this is more than a wild hypothesis, or more than an "it is so just because I tell you so" story?

To do that, I need to make my reasoning analytically precise, and therefore I utilize a technical concept called rents. "Rents," as we have seen, are artificial profits that could not have been made in a perfect market. Rents are anything that goes beyond competitive profits—they are "superprofits."

Why do we need the concept of rents? Because it allows

us to make a bridge between market distortions and income inequality. *Rents are, in essence, the distributional side effects of market distortions.* They are the extra income that some people receive because of market distortions. They make some people wealthier (those who receive them) and others poorer (those who overpay for goods and services). The more distorted markets are, the more distributional side effects they generate, and the more income inequality is created.

The concept of rents has a second analytical benefit: it allows us to put a number on the degree of competitiveness. Expressing the competitiveness of markets in numbers is hard; this is the very reason why there is no data available on degrees of competitiveness in the entire economy.

That said, rents are also notoriously hard to measure. How much of a plumber's income would not have been made in a perfect market? That is hard to tell. This is one of the reasons why there are no "rent taxes" (the government prefers to tax things that are easy to measure) and why direct data on rents is not available. The main contribution of this chapter is to develop a new method to estimate rents. Indirectly, these estimates will also measure the degree of market distortion in the overall economy. The estimates are based on a reinterpretation of indirect data, that is, data that measure something else (like national income, the capital share, the labor share, the total amount of capital in the economy, the total value of building land, the market interest rates, certain types of transaction costs), but indirectly say something about the magnitude of rents.[55]

To reinterpret all these empirical materials, we need some theory. And as it turns out, theory changes quite a bit once we apply insights from rent economics. Let's start with a simple question: What is capital?

The Breathing Permit Fairy Tale:
Some Capital Is Just Expected Rents

How much capital is needed to run the US economy? At first glance, there seems to be an easy measure: domestic private capital. It adds up all marketable capital related to private assets in the US: land, buildings, US corporations, private-sector bonds (not government bonds), and all other private investments. In 2010, the US domestic private capital was $55 trillion, or 435 percent of the national income.[56] (Note that I take "national income" [NI] and not "gross domestic product" [GDP] as a measure for the size of the economy. The NI is a more accurate measure; the GDP overestimates the size of the economy. The reason why is technical. I'll explain it in an endnote.)[57]

But here is the problem: a part of this $55 trillion is not real wealth but just air—it is no more than the expectation to receive rents in the future. If HP has a high capitalized value, it is not because it has so many machines, buildings, or cash. It is because investors expect that HP will continue to be able to make artificial profits on overpriced ink cartridges. "Capital" can therefore mean two different things. It can mean saved labor (for instance, in the form of machines, buildings, inventories) but also future rents. If a company is worth $1 billion, that sometimes just means that people expect it to capture $1 billion of rents in the future.

Let me illustrate this with the Fairy Tale of the Breathing Permits. Once upon a time, there was a kingdom in which breathing air was free. One day, however, the king told the citizens that they had to buy breathing permits if they wanted to continue breathing. Those who needed more air needed more expensive permits. Those who wanted to have a baby had to buy breathing rights for the baby. Breathing rights were granted for one year and needed to be renewed every year. The king set the total number of breathing rights at 5 percent below the normally used volume so that there was a slight shortage. Moreover, he gave all future breathing rights for the next fifteen years to a single individual—the one who won the National Breathing Rights Lottery.

Given the artificial scarcity, families had to spend large portions of their budgets on breathing rights. Employers who demanded physical activity from their employees had to do the same. In total, the breathing rights business generated $1 trillion per year. The lottery winner's newly founded company was estimated to be worth $15 trillion—the value of a fifteen-year long breathing rights monopoly.

Here was the upside of introducing breathing rights: on paper, the kingdom had become $15 trillion wealthier overnight. Indeed, the sum of the private capital owned by all citizens had increased by $15 trillion. Now the downside: in reality, the country had become poorer. Before the rights existed, citizens could do any physical activity they wanted. After the rights had been created, they had to restrict such activities. They hiked less, biked less, played less with their kids, and skied less.

In a neighboring kingdom, a fairy found a stick that granted her magical powers for one night. During that night, she could do as much work as the rest of the population in a whole year. In a single night, she built millions of homes and thousands of factories—something that would normally have cost $15 trillion. The fairy put all this property into a corporation and gave it away to a little girl. (I vaguely recall the fairy did this because the girl had just lost a tooth. I always forget the nonfinancial details of fairy tales.) The girl's corporation immediately obtained a $15 trillion market value. Overnight, the private capital in this country increased by $15 trillion as well. But unlike the case of the breathing rights, the country had truly become $15 trillion wealthier. It had more buildings and more machines.

The point of the fairy tale is that there are two types of capital. First, there is what I will call *real capital*, which reflects true investments in valuable goods (houses, machines, etc.). Second, there is what I will call *rent capital*. This is the capitalization of expected rents. Rent capital is not real but *illusory capital*.

Why is it illusory capital? Because for every $1 rent someone expects to receive in the future, there is $1 rent someone else will have to pay. So, the expectation to receive $15 trillion rents must be accompanied by other people's expectations to pay $15 trillion rents. The company that issued the breathing rights was worth $15 trillion because that is how much the citizens had to pay in the future. (In accounting terms, when one firm counts a future payment as an asset, another firm will have to count it as a liability. If you owe me $100, I can write in my ledger that I am at +$100, but you must write in your ledger that you are at -$100.)

In this sense, $15 trillion rent capital is analogous to $15 trillion in government bonds. These bonds are not added to the official national wealth statistics because they correspond to a $15 trillion government debt. Indeed, it would be illusionary to say that a country is wealthy because its citizens have financed government debt.

What other forms of capital are illusory? As it turns out, *land capital* is also largely illusory. (The only part that is not illusory is the part that represents real investments in the land, such as roads or sewerage.) This may sound surprising—isn't land truly useful, because you need it to produce certain things? That is true, but so is air. You should also keep in mind that if total land values are high in a region, that does not reflect that the region has a lot of land—to the contrary, it reflects that there is not enough land. So, a country with high land prices like the Netherlands is not a country with a lot of land but a country with a shortage of land. Seen from another angle, land capital simply expresses the expectation that future users of the land can be charged more than the true costs (of developing the land) because there is not enough land. In other words, the land value is the sum of the future Ricardian rents that need to be paid by those who want to use the land. This means that for every $1 trillion of land "wealth," there is an implicit $1 trillion debt to pay these Ricardian rents.

For an individual, though, it does not matter whether an investment represents true capital or illusory capital. Both generate *real* income for the owner. Both can be sold on the market for *real* money. For a country, however, it makes a big difference. The country that received $15 trillion worth of buildings and factories from the fairy had received something of real value. The country with the $15 trillion breathing license company had also a $15 trillion breathing license debt. Overall, the country gained nothing. Its $15 trillion capital was illusory.

As a matter of fact, the country with the breathing permits had even less than nothing. Indeed, the breathing rights requirement made people hike less, bike less, ski less. Paradoxically, a country with more rent capital is, in reality, a poorer country.

Rent Sources as Oil Wells: Why the Dow Jones Going Up Is Bad News

Imagine you have an oil well in your backyard, giving you a yearly rent of $1 million. How much could you sell it for? That depends on how long the well will last. If it produces oil for another ten years, it is worth $10 million on Day 1.[58] Halfway through the life cycle, it is worth only $5 million. Let's translate this into a simple formula for those of you who like math. The capitalized value of a rent source (C), is the average yearly rent (R) times the remaining duration (d) of the rents. So, $C = Rd$.

This simple formula applies to other forms of capitalized rents as well. Suppose the local government artificially restricts the number of taxis and gives you a ten-year license. Each of these ten years, you expect a $100,000 rent. *If* you could sell the license on Day 1, it would be worth $1 million.[59]

The word *if* in the last sentence is crucial. If you are not allowed to sell it, you can no longer capitalize the rent, and it will no longer show up in national wealth statistics (which are based on *marketable* assets, that is, things you can sell). This does not mean the license would have no value for you—it still generates $1 million over those years. But it has become similar to a medical license—highly valuable, but not sellable and therefore not in the statistics.

So, rent capitalization requires two conditions. First, the rent source must have been appropriated by someone. (There may be many future rent sources we can think of, but as long as nobody has laid their hands on them, they don't increase national wealth.) Second, the rent source must be legally transferable. It is only through the ability to bring something to the market that it receives market valuation.

It is important to realize that capitalized value of a rent source depends on its *duration*. Rent sources are like oil wells. They never last forever. The longer they last, the more valuable they are.

Wait—isn't land a rent source that lasts forever? No, it isn't. While land may always generate *some* rent, the magnitude of its rent evolves for several reasons. First, the type of land that generates most rents varies over time. In 1770, agricultural land was highly valuable; its capitalized value equaled 166 percent of the national income. Now it is worth only 12 percent.[60] Two centuries ago, land next to a beach was pretty worthless (who was interested in sandy land?). Now it is highly valuable.

Second, building land prices are constantly evolving too. In the late nineteenth century, the "hot spots" (that were most in demand) were right in the center of the city. Then they moved up a mile. Then they moved up again. Eventually, they moved even farther away from the center as cars and highways reduced travel times. But recently, some urban neighborhoods have become trendy again.

Third, the success of cities changes over time. Detroit used to be expensive but is now in decline. Los Angeles and Miami used to be cheap but are now expensive. It's an endless show of Ricardian wells popping up and disappearing again.

What holds for land also holds for commercial rent sources— at an even faster pace. Ink cartridges are brimming with rents since marketers discovered how to apply the razor-blade model. How long will this party continue? Maybe a few more years, maybe a few more decades. But one day, the party may be over, for instance, because technology evolves, or because the legal system wakes up.

How can we explain that land tends to give a lower "return on capital" than many other investments? If you buy land, the yearly income is often said to be around 3–4 percent on the investment.[61] If you buy a business, the income can easily be twice that number. The explanation is amazingly simple once you understand rent economics: the duration of the rent source is longer in the case of land. Locations may remain hot spots for sixty or more years. For businesses that acquire rents, the party may not last that long.

To see why the longer duration leads to the lower "return," go back to the oil well in your backyard. The first year, when there were still ten years remaining and the capitalized value was $10 million, the yearly rents were 10 percent of the rent capital. Five years later (halfway its life cycle), when the capitalized value had dropped to $5 million, the yearly rents of $1 million corresponded to 20 percent of the capital. This may give the false impression that the "interest" was 10 percent in the beginning, and 20 percent halfway the oil well's life cycle.

So, if the yearly income of land appears to be 3 percent of the land value, that may just mean that the place is expected to remain a source of rents for another thirty-three years. If all hot spots are on average halfway through their life cycle, this suggests that the average life cycle of a real estate rent source is sixty-six years.[62]

The problem is that these percentages can easily be misinterpreted as the true return on capital, especially when we look at numbers for the entire economy. In 2010, the total domestic private capital was 435 percent of the national income, and the capital share was 29 percent. May we conclude that the "market interest" on capital was 6–7 percent (that is, 29 "return" on 435 percent "investment")? That would be correct in an economy without rents. In such an economy, all capital is real capital and all capital income is a competitive market interest. (Moreover, the fact that machines and buildings wear out over time is already accounted for in the 29 percent because that's the number after capital depreciation.) In an economy full of rents, however, the number of 6–7 percent says more about the expected duration of rents sources than about the market interest on capital.

Time for an application. France has more private capital wealth per national income (575 percent) than the US (410 percent). Does this mean that the French save more? That's the standard explanation (and also Piketty's). This would be true if all the differences were related to real capital. But why would the French economy need more capital to operate than the American? Both are highly developed countries using the same technology.

What is more likely to differ is the amount of rent capital. And indeed, upon closer inspection the whole difference comes down to the difference in real estate capital (371 percent of the national income in France versus 182 percent in the US). Real estate consists of land and buildings, but since there is no reason to believe that the French have better buildings, the difference must be related to land rents. How could these be higher in France? First, yearly land rents could be higher because French zoning regulation is stricter or because all French want to live in the same places, like Paris or the Cote d'Azur. Second, the expected duration of the rent sources could be longer if hot spots and hot cities change at a slower pace. This could very well be the case: Paris has been the economic center for ages and will remain so in the foreseeable future, while American economic centers seem to come and go (think Detroit and Pittsburgh).

So, the French don't necessarily save more. They only have more illusory capital.

Here is another application. If the Dow Jones index goes up on a given day, is that good news? Business analysts usually see it that way. They see it as a sign that the economy is doing well, that pension funds are increasing in value, that there is confidence in the future, and that the true value of the listed corporations has increased. The higher the Dow Jones, the wealthier the country, so it seems.

This view would be correct if the capitalized value of a company represented only true capital. Unfortunately, the value largely represents illusory rent capital. Rent capital, as we have seen, is no more than the expectation that rents will be gained in the future. The market value of HP says more about the expectation of investors that ink cartridges will remain expensive than about the number of buildings or machines that HP owns.

To be fair, the Dow Jones index also picks up some psychological phenomena. If consumers and investors become pessimistic about the future, the economy can get trapped in a vicious cycle, and *real* investments can go to waste. Still, this possible waste of true capital plays a minor role in the overall picture. The Dow Jones index, by its very nature, says more about expected rents than about true economic performance.

The Dow Jones going up means that the expectation of rents in the economy is going up, or that the expected duration of rent sources is going up. In the latter case, that means that the competition on the market-for-the-market is expected to be less fierce. In this respect, the Dow Jones index measures the *lack* of competition—both on the product markets (where the rents occur) and on the market-for-the market.

The Dow Jones going up may be good news for some investors, but it is usually bad news for the rest of the economy.

The Capital Share Would Be 3 Percent in an Economy without Rents

Let's now move to a central step in the new method to estimate rents: estimating how large the capital share would be in an economy without rents.

The capital share is the part of the national income that goes to capital owners (such as business owners, shareholders, bondholders, or landowners) and not to workers (who receive the "labor share"). The capital share is close to 30 percent. The other 70 percent represents the labor share—the part of the national income that goes to those who supply labor, such as employees or self-employed workers. To understand what this means, consider that the American economy consists of a working population of roughly 150 million people and that the national income is about $15 trillion, or approximately $100,000 per worker. Of this amount, only $70,000 goes to workers; the remaining $30,000 goes to investors.

More precisely, the capital share in the US is estimated to be about 29 percent (in 2010). This is probably an underestimation because the statistics are based on tax data. A conservative estimate is that the true capital share is *at least* 2 percent higher.[63] Still, let's continue on the assumption that 29 percent is the correct figure.

Why is the capital share so high? The standard explanation is that it is the culmination of two factors. First, operating a modern economy requires enormous amounts of capital—about four to five times the national income (435 percent in 2010). Second, the owners of this capital receive interest, at a rate determined by the market, and this turns out to be 6–7 percent (controlling for inflation). Multiply both numbers, and you find that capital owners need to receive about 30 percent of the national income. This may be large, but it is the inevitable outcome in an economy that needs so much capital and where the interest rate is determined by the market, or so goes the argument. Bad luck for the workers! If they produce a good worth $100, they can only divide $70 among themselves.

Now here is my bold estimate: *in an economy without rents, the capital share would have been around 3 percent over the last decade.* In other words, 90 percent of the capital share is rents. How do I get to this astonishing number? To start, the private capital needed to run the economy was not 435 percent (in 2010) but between 200 percent and 300 percent. In addition, the pure market interest rate on capital was not 6–7 percent but 1 percent over the past decade. Multiply these numbers and you get at most 3 percent, not 29 percent.

To see why, let's first estimate how much capital the economy really needs. In other words, let's estimate how much of the 435 percent is illusory capital, that is, how much is no more than the expectation to receive rents in the future. I have already explained that land is illusory capital. The total agricultural land value is 12 percent of the national income (NI).[64] Building land was worth 56 percent of the NI in 2010.[65] If you add these two numbers, you already find that 68 percent of the 435 percent is illusory capital.

Now the more difficult question: in 2010, the stock market capitalization of US companies was 128 percent of the NI.[66] How much of this corporate capital is illusory and how much represents real capital (buildings, machines, trucks, inventory, cash, etc.)?

There is a strong theoretical reason to believe that most corporate capital is illusory. Modern companies try to finance most capital goods (such as buildings, machines, trucks, and inventory) with bonds (which are essentially just loans). The reason is that bondholders do not receive a share of the rents (remember, rents go to the owners, and bondholders are not the owners of the company); so, the fewer shareholders there are, the more rents they will each receive. If companies do this to the extreme, then companies no longer own any "tangible assets." Their buildings, cars, and machines are leased, and the products that are waiting to be shipped are financed by banks. If a company no longer owns any tangible assets (because they are all financed by bondholders), 100 percent of the stock market value represents expected rents. In practice, companies may not be able to reach that ideal. For instance, they may stockpile some cash while thinking about the next acquisition. To be on the safe side, let's make the conservative estimate that only half of the stock market capitalization represents rent expectations. In that case, the illusory part of corporate capital corresponds to 64 percent of the NI.

Adding the value of agricultural land, building land, and the illusory part of the stock market capitalization (12 percent + 56 percent + 64 percent), we obtain 132 percent illusory capital. This means that of the 435 percent domestic private capital, only *303 percent was real capital.*

This estimate of 303 percent may still be generous. To see why the US economy may need even less real capital, consider the 2010 data for the German economy, which uses similar technology and may therefore require about the same amount of capital.

The domestic private capital in Germany was 373 percent; the larger part of this number represents housing and land (235 percent).[67] If we assume that German buildings have the same value as US buildings (126 percent), the land itself represents 109 percent. Now, let's make the *extreme* assumption that the illusory part of German corporate capital is 0 percent (which would mean that German corporations receive no rents at all!). Then, we find that *the German economy requires only 264 percent real capital to operate.* If we make the more realistic assumption that the illusory part of the German corporate capital represents as much as we assumed in the US (64 percent of the NI), the German economy requires *only 195 percent real capital* to operate.

Taken together, the private capital needed to operate the US economy is somewhere between 200 percent and 300 percent of the US national income. That is the number we get when we delete all forms of illusory capital in the American economy.

Next, let's estimate the pure market interest on capital. Earlier, we mentioned that the average return on capital seems to be around 6.6 percent. This number, however, is not the pure "market interest rate"; it also includes all the rents picked up by the owners of businesses. (Remember that rent economics predicts that most rents will go to owners.) Therefore, the 6.6 percent is the sum of the *market interest plus rents.* How much is the true market interest?

The best measure of the pure market interest rate are long-term government bonds. Government bonds may be the one investment that does not pick up any rents. After all, the interests are determined in highly transparent, competitive markets. The interest rates are not set by the government—they reflect what the market demands in return for the use of capital. Therefore, they are most likely to reflect the pure market interest rate for riskless capital.

But what about the risk? Shouldn't the return on stocks be higher because they contain more risk? And since many investments in a modern economy are risky, isn't it possible that we end up with an average interest of 6–7 percent?

The term "risk," however, includes different components. The first is the statistical cost of losses due to failed projects or bankruptcies. The 6–7 percent number, however, already accounts for these losses as it is calculated after the deduction of all failed projects and bankruptcies. The second component is the compensation for the willingness to live with risk—the pure risk aversion premium. This premium may have been significant in older times, when people still laid all their eggs in one basket. With modern financial diversification techniques, however, the risk aversion premium can be made insignificant. Of course, collecting a portfolio of investments (with risks that cancel each other out) requires work. But the compensation of the financial experts who do this work are costs that typically show up in the labor share, not in the capital share.

To be fair, shareholders bear a long-term upside risk—it is unknown how many rents corporations will capture in the future. It is incorrect, however, to say that because of this upside risk, shareholders should receive higher return rates. The causation works in the opposite direction—it is because there are unknown rents that there is upside risk. Risk aversion among rent receivers can't explain why rents are so high.[68] If stock is risky in some ways, so are government bonds (even aside from political risks). First, the market interest on government bonds fluctuates over time; this means there is a significant long-term interest fluctuation risk. (Some people don't realize this, but if you buy government bonds, and then interest rates go up, your government bonds are suddenly worth less on the market.) Second, they are nominal instruments and therefore subject to inflation risk—contrary to stock. (If you invest $100 in government bonds and the next year there is a 10 percent inflation, your bonds are suddenly worth 10 percent less; if you invest the same money in a machine, the machine will keep its true value.) So, it is not clear that buying stock is truly riskier than buying government bonds—the risks are just of a different nature.

How much is the current pure market interest? Some have suggested it may be as low as 0 percent or even be negative.* I estimate that *the pure market interest rate on capital over the last decade was around 1 percent* (or perhaps slightly above 1 percent). This is indeed the average rate for government bonds over the past decade, controlling for inflation. The calculations themselves are technical, so I explain them in an endnote.[69]

Let's summarize: The US economy needs between 200 percent and 300 percent capital to operate, and the competitive market interest over the last decade was around 1 percent. Multiply these numbers (200 to 300 percent and 1 percent), and you find that in an economy without rents, the capital share would have been 2 to 3 percent of the national income. This means that the other 26–27 percent must be rents.

The fact that most of the capital share (26 out of 29 percent) consists of rents may sound surprising, but it follows directly from a fundamental principle of rent theory—that rents tend to go to owners. Moreover, principals (the business owners) try to avoid rent leakage to their agents (the employees). Therefore, we should expect to find more rents in the capital share than in the labor share.

How high were these rents in 1970? Using the same data and methodology, I find that the real domestic capital was 237 percent of the NI (while the illusory part was only 90 percent) and that the inflation-adjusted pure market interest on capital was about 1.75 percent around 1970.[70] Therefore, the capital

---

* Note that a negative interest on capital is not a logical impossibility. Think of your own savings account the past few years: the interest was lower than the inflation. A negative interest essentially means that capital owners are willing to subsidize the economy in order to keep their capital alive.

share would have been 4–5 percent in 1970 in the absence of rents. Let's assume it was 5 percent. Since the capital share was 21 percent, this means that *in 1970, 16 percent of the NI were rents captured by capital owners.* So, the rents received by capital owners went from 16 percent in 1970 to 26 percent in 2010.

At Least One-Sixth of the Labor Share Is Rents

While most rents can be expected to show up in the capital share, some rents should show up in the labor share as well. As a matter of fact, wage inequality—in other words, inequality within the labor share—has increased significantly in the US. The 10 percent best-paid employees now receive nearly 35 percent of the total wage mass; that number was less than 26 percent in 1970.[71] This suggests that the rents picked up by workers have increased too.

But by how much? Before taking a closer look at the data, let's take a look at theory. Rent theory suggests that employees can have four sources of rents.

A first source of rents for workers are rents that "leak" from their firms (which obtained those rents on the product market). In other words, some of the rents that would normally go to the capital share now end up in the labor share. Capital owners will of course try to prevent that, but employees, especially those at the top, may exploit informational advantages to camouflage the leakage.

Leaked rents must have increased since 1970 because the amount of rents received by capital owners has increased—so that there is more to leak from. (Remember, rents in the capital share increased from about 16 percent in 1970 to 26 percent in 2010.) In addition, businesses have also become larger (with fewer that are still family-owned), so there may be a larger loss of control than before. Moreover, the economy has become more complex and specialized, which may have further increased the informational advantage of employees over owners.

A second source of rents for workers are the cherry-picking rents employers have to pay to give them the right incentives (remember the *efficiency versus information rent trade-off*?). These information rents have likely increased as well because of the very same informational changes.

A third source of rents for workers are radiation rents. In an economy with plenty of rents, talented people have many opportunities to acquire rents. Very often, the only way to keep them away from these overpaid jobs is to overpay them. While estimating radiation rents is even harder than estimating other forms of rents, labor economics suggests they can be significant, as wages are determined by outside options. Radiation rents have likely increased too, since the options to obtain rents have increased.

Finally, employees may form unions and receive cartel rents by threatening to strike. (Some of those rents may technically be leaked rents as more profitable sectors tend to pay higher wages to unionized workers. But some may be more than just leakage, especially in countries with stronger unions.) Labor union rents have likely decreased.

Where will these rents show up in the wage distribution? The first three are more likely to show up at the top. Only the fourth (union rents) are likely to be spread out more equally over the workforce (that is, the highest paid workers do not get disproportionally more union rents than the lowest paid). In other words, labor union rents typically increase the labor share but do not alter the distribution within the labor share itself. Still, indirectly they may flatten out the distribution by softening the inequality effects of the other rent sources.

Back to the data—starting with the increase of the top decile from 26 percent to 35 percent.[72] As explained earlier in this book, it is hard to come up with a "productivity" explanation for this increase. Moreover, this same number has not increased in France (where it stayed around 27 percent), and it is hard to see how technologically similar countries would suddenly require so much more "productivity" at the top. In addition, most of this increase happened in the top 1 percent of wages. This all suggests that the 9 percent increase can easily be interpreted as a rent increase.[73] Note that 9 percent of the labor share corresponds to about 6 percent of the national income.

If rents in the labor share have increased by 6 percent (of the national income) between 1970 and 2010, how much were they in 1970? They can't have been zero, because shareholders and business owners did not have *perfect* information to prevent leakage and information rents. Moreover, labor unions were still stronger, so some of the rents must have leaked for other causes than informational ones.

Here is my best guess, based on the theoretical arguments we just discussed: in 1970, rents in the labor share were at least 6 percent, and now they are 6 percent higher, so at least 12 percent (of the national income). To be fair, this is no more than an "educated guess." To add plausibility to the 12 percent number, I make some other back-of-the-envelope calculations in an endnote.[74]

By adding the estimates for the rents in the capital share (16 percent in 1970, 26 percent in 2010) and in the labor share (6 percent in 1970, 12 percent in 2010), we find that total rents in the economy increased from 22 percent to 38 percent of the national income. To make these estimates more conservative, we could conclude that rents have increased from at least 20 percent to at least 35 percent over the time span 1970–2010.

Ricardian Rents Are 8 Percent
of the National Income

If rents have increased from (probably) 22 percent in 1970
to 38 percent in 2010, how much can be attributed to higher
oil prices, higher land prices, and higher natural resource
prices? The rents on these goods are called "Ricardian rents."
They are atypical rents because they are not caused by a
market failure in a strict sense but by the absolute scarcity
of certain goods. Knowing how much they changed in the
time span 1970–2010 is important if we want to know the
net effect of marketing.

There is plenty of anecdotal evidence that Ricardian rents are
significant. Look at the wealthiest individuals in the world and
you will see that many are active in oil, mining, or real estate. It is
also no coincidence that some of the most profitable companies
(such as Exxon) operate in the oil or mining industry.

Ricardian rents can derive from natural resources (which
include oil, natural gas, coal, minerals, and forest resources) and
land. Let us first estimate the rents related to natural resources.
Here, we are lucky because the World Bank has a dataset that
estimates the worldwide rents in each of these five categories.[75]
According to this dataset, 4.92 percent of the world GDP went
to natural resource rents in 2005–2014; that was only 1.18
percent in 1970.[76]

These are the averages for the entire world. How much of
these rents were paid by US residents? Unfortunately, the World
Bank doesn't collect data on national consumption (only on
national production). To estimate how much oil, gas, and coal
was consumed in the US compared to the rest of the world,
we can use data of the US Energy Information Administration
(EIA) and make some assumptions.[77] Overall, I find that in

1970, 1.11 percent of the US national income went to natural resources rents, versus 4.97 percent in the period 2005–2014. In short, *Ricardian rents on natural resources have increased from about 1 percent to about 5 percent of the national income* over the last few decades.

Next, let's estimate land rents. As we have seen, the scarcity of land (especially in metropolitan areas) drives up land prices; this creates rents as the price for using the land exceeds the true cost of developing it (which may be zero, as that forest may have been cut down centuries ago). You pay for these rents in two ways. In a direct way, they increase the rental payment for your house or the monthly payment for your mortgage. In an indirect way, they increase prices for products and services because businesses have to pass on their land rent expenditures to their customers. If you buy an expensive cup of coffee in New York, a part of the price is for the use of the expensive real estate.

To make matters more complicated, there is a third way in which land rents increase your expenditures—through their *local inflation effect*. Indeed, if a cup of coffee is more expensive in New York, that is not only because the coffee shop has to pay more to rent the building but also because wages are higher in New York than in most other places. Why are wages higher? Because life is more expensive in New York, as apartments, coffee, and services are more expensive. So, it all starts with expensive land and ends with expensive goods and services. (Land is expensive, which drives up prices, which drives up wages, which in turn drives up prices, which again drives up wages, and so forth.) In theory, this local inflation effect may spiral up until it is many times higher than the original land rent. In an endnote, I estimate the land rents plus their local inflation effect to be around 15 percent of the national income, but I also explain why most of it is likely just local inflation.[78]

How could we measure the pure land rents? Could we start

from the total land value in the US (which was about 68 percent of the national income in 2010) and impute a "reasonable" rate of return on this capital, for instance, 4 percent? Unfortunately, this violates a fundamental principle of rent economics—that capitalized rents (such as land values) are not only a function of the yearly rent but also of the expected duration of the rent source. There is no way to know the "reasonable rate of return" without knowing the expected duration.

Here is a better way to measure land rents. First, look at how much families spend on housing. (This doesn't measure how much families indirectly spend on commercial land rents in the form of higher prices for goods and services, but we'll estimate that later.) In 2010, this was about $1.6 trillion, or 12.76 percent of the national income. (In 1970, it was 9.76 percent of the NI.)[79] These numbers, however, are based on what landlords would ask for a similar home, and landlords have to cover some other costs (such as property taxes, financing costs, and transaction costs).[80]

When all these costs are deducted, we find that 6.92 percent of the national income was spent on residential housing itself (5.29 percent in 1970).[81] How much of this went to the land and how much to the building? In 2010, land rents represented about 31 percent of the total real estate value (compared to 21 percent in 1970).[82] This gives us 2.14 percent for 2010 (1.11 percent for 1970). If we add land rents associated with commercial real estate and agriculture, we find that *total land rents were 2.68 percent of the national income in 2010 (1.64 percent in 1970).*[83]

If we put rents from natural resources (oil, natural gas, coal, minerals, and forest products) and land together, we get about 8 percent (5 percent + nearly 3 percent). So, our overall estimate is that *8 percent of the national income was spent on Ricardian rents in 2010 (versus 3 percent in 1970).*

This means that non-Ricardian rents (caused by market

distortions in a strict sense) have increased from 19 percent in 1970 to 30 percent in 2010. In other words, *most of the increased income inequality can be linked to increasingly distorted markets.*

What Do Rent-Seeking Costs Tell Us About the Magnitude of Rents?

Let's do another robustness check. Let's estimate rent-seeking costs and see whether we can reconcile the results with our estimates of rents.

Rents lead to rent-seeking costs. If you see a golden egg worth $10,000 at the other side of the river, you will spend up to $10,000 to cross the river to get the egg. In the economic literature on rent seeking, the term "rent seeking" originally referred to lobbying costs, but the idea that rents lead to rent-seeking costs can be applied more broadly.

In the context of private businesses, rent-seeking costs are all the types of wasteful spending that businesses do to acquire a rent. Rent-seeking costs can consist, for instance, of advertising costs made to attract rent-paying customers. They also make up a large part of a salesperson's time. Car dealers usually do not publish final prices on the internet, but require you to meet with a salesperson, who will first talk with you for half an hour to find out what type of consumer you are and how much you may be willing to pay. All the energy that goes into this pricing game represents rent-seeking costs.

Rent-seeking costs make sense for those who make them, but from the perspective of society, they are 100 percent wasteful. They don't add anything to the output of the economy. If rent-seeking costs had been spent to produce more goods or services, society would have been richer.

In a sense, those who work in the rent-seeking business

are as productive as those who stand still in a traffic jam. All economists agree that traffic jams are extremely wasteful: if all those wasted hours in traffic had been used more productively, the country would have been richer. But the same could be said about all those hours spent to get a rent. (And then we are not even talking about rent-avoiding costs at the consumers' side, such as spending half a day talking with car dealers about prices, or clipping coupons.)

Now, here is the interesting thing about rent-seeking costs estimations: *indirectly, they give an indication on how large rents are.* Indeed, rents may partly get dissipated in the form of rent-seeking costs and therefore the magnitude of the dissipated part may give us an indication about the magnitude of the nondissipated part.

The more difficult question is how much of the national income goes up in rent-seeking flames. A starting point can be McCloskey and Klamer's estimation that in 1994 about 26 percent of the economy was spent on what they call "persuasion."[84]

McCloskey and Klamer noticed an upward trend of about

3 percent since the previous decade. Using similar data, I estimate that persuasion costs rose from about 22 percent in 1970 to about 30 percent in 2010.[85]

Persuasion refers to "sweet talk"—the judgmental part of transaction costs that goes beyond a mechanical transmission of information. McCloskey and Klamer's definition of persuasion, though, does not fully overlap with our definition of "rent seeking." For instance, when an employee tries to persuade her boss that there is a cheaper way to produce a good, or when a defense attorney tries to persuade a jury that his client is innocent, this falls under "persuasion" but not under rent seeking. Still, the efforts of the car salesperson to make you accept a higher price than average, or the time spent by other salespeople to give biased information definitely fall under rent-seeking costs. If we assume that half of the "persuasion costs" of McCloskey and Klamer fall under our "rent-seeking costs" (I know, that is an arbitrary assumption, but in the absence of data, all we can do is to make the best possible guess), then this type of rent-seeking costs rose from 11 percent in 1970 to 15 percent of the NI in 2010.

What other rent-seeking costs should we add to this number?[86] Rent-seeking costs may also consist of, for instance, the costs of flooding the market with different-looking products to create fog, the costs of duplicative research in patent races, the costs of impressive bank buildings or fancy law firm offices, the costs of setting up exclusive distribution channels to make product comparison harder, and even the costs of education (OK, you learn a lot at medical school, but you first need to spend four years in college, so a part of those eight years is not needed to become a doctor but just a wasteful expenditure to limit access to the profession). So, if we assume that all these other costs add another one-half, we estimate that *rent-seeking costs increased from about 16 percent in 1970 to 23 percent of the NI in 2010.*[87]

Keep in mind, though, that our goal was not to make a precise
estimate of rent-seeking costs (that would be a project in its own)
but to check whether our general rent estimates (which were
based on national accounts data, if you remember) are plausible.
The total rents we estimated based on national accounts are 38
percent of the NI, the Ricardian rents are 8 percent, and the
non-Ricardian rents are 30 percent. I'll explain in an endnote
why our estimates of rent-seeking costs, speculative as they are
in themselves, add plausibility to this number of 30 percent.[88]

Can Marketing Really Cause That Much Income Inequality?

Non-Ricardian rents have increased in four decades from about
19 percent to 30 percent. Can marketing methods really have
had such a major impact on income inequality?

It is probably not hard to see that market failures may have a
major impact on income inequality. It is also not hard to see that
marketing may prevent the market from being transparent and
competitive. Yet some people may have a hard time believing that
marketing truly affects inequality because they see marketing
as something subtle, something innocent looking. Can subtle
distortions really have such a major impact on income inequality?

Well, let us reframe the question as follows. Market-distorting
marketing methods are, at their core, *subtle forms* of theft, fraud,
coercion, contract breach, or cartelization (more on that in the
following chapters). Let us first discuss the income inequality
effects of *less subtle forms* of fraud and theft.

Imagine that once upon a time (here comes another fairy
tale) there was a kingdom in which fraud and theft were allowed.
In this kingdom, the overwhelming majority of farmers were
poor. These farmers worked hard, but their harvests were often

stolen by thieves. There were also a few families that lived in castles, each having an hourly income of 2,000 times an average farmer's hourly income. What was their secret for making so much money per hour? Stealing crops from farmers. A farmer needed 2,000 hours to produce the harvest, but a thief needed only an hour to steal that harvest. Therefore, robbing was 2,000 times more "productive" than farming—of course not in the true economic sense, because thieves do not produce wealth but merely redistribute it from their victims to themselves. Still, robbing was more "productive" when productivity is defined as creating "value" for oneself. (I know, this is an odd definition, but believe it or not, this is the standard definition at all business schools!) In this fairy tale, the robbers worked as many hours per year as the farmers. But at the end of the year they made 2,000 times more than those farmers who were not the victims of theft, and even more than the farmers whose harvests had been stolen.

The fairy tale was about physical theft, but the "higher productivity" lesson applies to subtle forms of fraud or theft as well. Consider again the plumber who worked forty hours per week but had double the income of other plumbers who worked the same number of hours. The plumber in our example did this by overcharging for spare parts. His income consisted of two equal parts. One part of this income came from working forty hours per week, and the other part from overcharging for spare parts. The first part required hard work and many hours. The second part, in contrast, required hardly any work. All the plumber had to do was change a price of $1 to $29 on an invoice. It costs less than one second to change the number 1 into the number 29 on a form. At most, the plumber had to come up with a story for why the bolt was so expensive, but that was only necessary in the rare cases in which the consumer became suspicious, and even then, it cost him only a few minutes to tell this story.

Let me make it clear, though, that it is not my position that acquiring a rent is a form of theft. But the opposite is nearly always true: theft is the acquisition of a rent. Indeed, robbers receive "compensation" for their robbery activities that they would not receive in a normal market. (If you do not point a gun at a bank employee, you do not get a transaction that makes the bank worse off.) Moreover, this "compensation" must outweigh the compensation that thieves can acquire in a legal way, at least if the thieves are rational—because if theft was not better paid than working, the thieves would just work. So, because theft is the acquisition of a rent, the income inequality effects of allowing theft may tell us something about the income inequality effects of allowing information rents.

The bottom line is that *those who are in the rent business can make much more money per hour than those who are in the productivity business.* This implies that, as soon as there are information rents up for grabs in the economy, income inequality will increase. And this insight holds for other types of rents as well. Rents are, by definition, payments received on top of costs. In their most extreme form, rents do not require any effort—all they require is being in the right place at the right time and in the right position to take advantage of them. In practice, some efforts may be required to get into that position, but there is no reason why these efforts would equal the value of the rents. Because rents are not compensation for the effort expended in acquiring them, the effort required per rent is usually small compared to the payment received.

Can business schools really have such an impact on income inequality? Well, to understand what role great schools can play, just imagine a society in which stealing is perfectly legal. The only thing that prevents thieves from stealing even more is their own lack of sophistication, and the sophistication of some potential victims. Then, imagine that business schools start to offer master's degrees in theft. Some of the brightest people in the country take the courses from some of the brightest professors in the country on how to steal more efficiently. Armed with the newest theft techniques, those brilliant young people start to work as "theft consultants," advising gangs how to operate more efficiently. Would you be surprised if theft increased significantly?

This is of course not what happened. Business schools teach you to maximize income under constraints, and one of the constraints is the law. So, business schools will never teach you something illegal. Still, what happened is that business professors figured out that the law is full of cracks. They also figured out that markets are not as transparent as their colleagues in law school tend to assume, and that markets can be made less transparent with a few simple tricks. Moreover, they figured out that the newest psychological insights could not only be used to make people more rational, but also to make them *less* rational. Within a couple of decades, most highly competitive markets were transformed into oligopolistic or monopolistic ones. Are you surprised that income inequality increased?[89]

PART II
A NEW THEORY
OF MARKETING

4

THICKEN THE FOG!
LEGAL FORMS OF CONCEALMENT

O ver the next four chapters, we analyze how marketing methods create distortions. We examine what types of market failure they create and why they fall through the cracks of the legal system. The basic insight is that, at their core, all these marketing methods are based on legal forms of fraud, concealment, abuse of trust, duress, price cartelization, monopolization, undue influence, or corruption.

The single most effective way to distort markets is to create fog. This is what we will focus on in this chapter. Fog works in two ways. First, fog transforms competitive markets into oligopolistic ones. Remember the analogy with the foggy football field in which you could see only the three roofers standing closest to you out of 500? The fewer alternatives buyers see, the less competitive the market is. Second, fog makes it easier for businesses to acquire information rents. Such rents can be acquired only if the seller knows more than the buyer (as shown in the plumber example). So, the harder it is for the buyer to get information, the easier it is for the seller to exploit asymmetric information.

In an ideal world, marketing would be the antidote of fog. Whenever markets were foggy, marketers would come in, provide accurate information, and help consumers find the best products and the best prices. But that's the rosy view on marketing. In practice, marketing may do the opposite: *deliberately* create the fog.

As we will see, some methods are straightforward (don't publish prices on the internet, offer complex price plans), while others are more refined—so refined that most people no longer recognize their fog-creation effect.

Total-View Search versus Sequential Search

Do you know any lawyers, doctors, accountants, sprinkler service companies, car repair shops, appliance repairers, roofers, or plumbers who publish their prices on the internet? I don't. This, in itself, is a perplexing observation. The internet is an incredibly efficient forum for spreading information. Consumers are incredibly interested in prices, and yet they can't find prices on the internet.

From the service suppliers' perspective, this is a smart tactic. Imagine that all the air conditioner repairers in an area published all their prices. This could initiate fierce price competition that could remove most of the current information rents from the market. But if prices can be known only after a personal appointment with an air conditioner repairman, price competition becomes difficult.

To better understand how fog affects price competition, it is important to understand how searching works in practice, and how a total-view search process differs from a sequential search process.

In a total-view search process, you immediately see all products on the market. Suppose that you are shopping for knee surgery (and assume for simplicity that you are not covered by your insurance). Under a total-view search, you immediately see all the surgeons in your area who perform such procedures. You also see the total price of the procedure (not only the fee for the surgeon but also the fee for the anesthesiologist, the hospital, etc.), the next available date of the surgery, and objective quality information, such as success rates and the surgeon's experience. Where exactly do you see this? Well, it could be on your computer, or in an old-fashioned printed catalogue—it doesn't matter as long as you have immediate access to all information.

Now contrast this with a sequential search process. Here, you schedule an appointment with one surgeon, and receive information on price, next available date, and quality. Then you may choose this surgeon or continue your search by scheduling an appointment with a second surgeon, in which case you will again receive the same information. After your meeting with the second surgeon, you may choose one of the first two surgeons or meet with a third one. This process continues until you decide to stop searching.

Sequential searching comes in many variants. Asking for bids from roofers is one variant (after each bid, you may select one of the bids or request another bid). But even an internet search can be sequential. Suppose you need insulation material for your basement. Unfortunately, you find no single website that lists all products on the market with exact prices and objective quality information. So, you go to one company's website, study their products, then consult another company's website, study their products, and so on, until you make your choice.

It is obvious that total-view searching is intrinsically superior to sequential searching. Total-view searching is the most efficient search process because all pieces of information have already been collected in one place. Sequential search, in contrast, requires every single buyer to do this collection job again—it's like *forcing them to reinvent the wheel*. So, sequential search is, by its very nature, more costly. Therefore, buyers end up less informed when searching is made sequential.

Sequential search, imperfect as it is, may be the best search process when collecting total-view databases is too costly. That was usually the case before the internet era. Printing thick books that listed all products, prices, and quality information was costly; continually updating them was even more costly. So, before the internet was invented, sequential searching was the imperfect process we had to live with.[90]

Surprisingly, even in this IT age, the sequential search process is still the most common search process. It is the search process for knee surgery, plumbing services, car repair services—you name it. Even for mass-produced consumer goods, a true total-view search process is rarely possible. Sure, when you want to buy a vacuum cleaner, you can look on Google Shopping or Amazon, but there is no place where you get a complete overview of all products on the market with all their final prices (including rebates and coupons), and with carefully organized, accurate information on dimensions, features, noise levels, suction power on hard floors, suction power on carpet floors, durability, energy costs, and the expected cost of repair and filter bags. Of course, you can read users' reviews on Amazon, but reading them for each vacuum cleaner is a time-consuming, sequential search process.

Why is total-view searching so rare in practice? One reason is that it requires standardization (more on this in chapter 9). But another is that it requires cooperation from businesses. And this brings us back to the role of marketers. Because total-view searching destroys rents, marketers will try to turn it into sequential searching. For instance, marketers will recommend businesses to not publish prices on the internet. In addition, they will try to make sequential searches even costlier through tactics such as revealing prices only after a personal sales pitch rather than over the phone.

Why the Internet Did Not Wipe Out Information Rents

In the internet's early years, economists were hopeful about its possible effect on the competitiveness of markets. The idea was that the internet would increase competition by increasing the number of sellers on the market. In the past, you could only buy goods at a few local stores, but using the internet, you can buy goods from hundreds of stores all over the country. At the same time, economists believed that the internet would make it harder to overprice goods since consumers could easily figure out the market price of any good on the internet. Moreover, search engines would help consumers find the best product for the best price. There is no hiding on the internet; if Google can find it, everyone can find it. Overall, the expectation was that the internet would lead to lower prices, lower product margins, and above all, the return of the good old Law of One Price: everybody would pay the same price for the same product.

After more than two decades of the internet's existence, it is time to lower these expectations. Have you ever tried to find the lowest price on the internet for simple things like hotel rooms or airplane seats? If you really want the lowest price, it can take you a full evening. As it turns out, there is no booking site that always finds the lowest price for either of these items. It is even worse for consumer goods (sure, there is Google Shopping, but if you click on the sites with the lowest reported price, the full price often turns out to be different than what you saw at Google

Shopping). And for services, from sprinkler repair services to medical services—forget the internet. Services providers do not publish their prices on the internet.

Why aren't search engines and booking sites more effective? It is not because they hire lousy programmers but because they need businesses to cooperate. Unfortunately, businesses have no incentive to fully cooperate.[91] A single hotel may offer as many as 500 possible room rates.[92] If you own a hotel, why would you make your prices fully transparent by cooperating with all booking sites? It is much smarter to use these booking sites to segment the market. Sites that are good at reaching "high-value customers" can be used to extract higher prices from these customers. Booking sites that are good at identifying low-value customers should get the low-price products.

McKinsey consultants Baker, Marn, and Zawada were exactly correct in their 2001 *Harvard Business Review* article when they wrote: "The fundamental value of the internet lies not in lowering prices or making them consistent but in optimizing them. After all, if it's easy for customers to compare prices on the internet, it's also easy for companies to track customers' behavior and adjust prices accordingly."[93] (Note that the term "value" is used here in the business sense, not in the social optimality sense; the internet has "value" when it allows businesses to acquire rents; rents are obviously not good for society. It is a strange use of the English word "value," but it is the standard definition in business economics.)

Baker, Marn, and Zawada continue: "A visitor entering a store is a statistical mystery. Sales staff have no idea what that customer has bought in the past, what combination of price and benefits would trigger a purchase, whether that person generally buys items at full price or only on sale, or if he needs an incentive to go beyond browsing. The mystery is cleared up on the internet." One real-life example they mention is a site that sells electronic components using the buying histories of its customers to determine whether they are regular or occasional customers. The latter, who probably buy only when the site's competitors do not have products in stock, are charged as much as 20 percent more than regular customers. And, as Baker, Marn, and Zawada add, the occasional customers "gladly pay that premium for the assured supply in emergency situations."[94] (Note again that the English term "gladly" is used in a somewhat strange sense, but maybe marketing specialists have a somewhat strange sense of humor.)

Companies can use the internet in many ways to increase prices. One way is to experiment with price increases during very short periods of time and observe how customers react. Another is to use clickstream data or the customer's buying histories tracked by cookies on their own computers to find out the customer's "type." If a company finds out that you tend to accept the first offer you see, they can safely increase the price. If they find out that you are an active searcher, they know they have to lower the price for you. This is just another way to acquire information rents by charging more to those who do not know the market prices.

Making It Costly to Know the Real Price

"Dynamic pricing"—a new buzzword in marketing—allows businesses to "optimize" prices by changing them from day to day, from moment to moment, or from customer to customer. In the marketers' wildest dreams, prices in a store change every time a different customer looks at them. Two marketing professors from the Wharton Business School wrote, "The day may soon come when a customer walks down a supermarket aisle and prices on the electronic monitors positioned next to the goods in the aisle start to change, in recognition of the purchase history of the customer, inventory levels of the goods at the time, the number of customers in the store, or even the weather outside."[95]

Dynamic pricing is lauded as a fancy way to "create value" for businesses. Yet what it does, upon closer inspection, is to increase fog by making it nearly impossible to compare prices with competitors. How can you compare prices if they change every minute? (As a rule of thumb, the more often prices are updated, the costlier it becomes to stay informed. So, if prices are updated ten times more often than in the past, price information costs have increased ten times as well. No wonder that prices that are "optimized" every split second are the marketer's dream.)

Marketers argue that in a constantly changing world, constantly updated prices may better reflect the true costs of a product. If oil prices on the world market change every hour, gas prices at the pump should also change every hour. In addition, they argue, it's a form of price discrimination. In practice, however, dynamic pricing has little to do with reflecting true costs. That it is a form of price discrimination is true. Unfortunately, it is a form that is based on exploiting uninformed buyers. Take one of the simplest variants (the one described by an economist named Varian), in which businesses constantly vary the price of a product, so that it is expensive in one period, cheap in the next period, and so forth.[96] The official justification is that those who value the product the most are least likely to wait until the product is cheap. But if its goal was to make customers who can't wait pay more, the future prices would be clearly announced. That is usually not the case; even employees of the shop may not know how expensive the good will be next month. Moreover, asking a premium price for instant delivery would obtain the same result.

A different marketing method that makes it tougher to know prices is to make the real prices paid different from the "list prices." In some markets, such as the market for new cars, rebates have become so common that nearly nobody pays the full list price. In that case, what is the point of setting the list price so high? If the list price for a car is $20,000, but in reality most customers pay $18,000, why isn't the list price just set at $18,000? Well, the point is that there are still a few naive customers who pay the full list price. Even if that is only 5 percent of all customers, that means there is still a rent in 5 percent of the transactions.

Sure, mathematically it would be easier to work with a list price of $18,000 and making those few naive customers pay a "naivety penalty" of $2,000. But if it were framed that way, naive customers would be alarmed. So, it is better to keep the official price at $20,000 and give a rebate only to those who demand it.

Another marketing method that makes it tougher to compare prices is to split the price into components.[97] At Amazon.com, you can buy used DVDs for only $0.01, but they will cost you $4.00 once you add the $3.99 shipping and handling. The $3.99 is obviously more than what the postal services charge; it also includes the "handling." But isn't "handling" the core work of sellers? After all, sellers don't manufacture goods.

The opposite of splitting—bundling cost categories—can also work to hide fees. How much does Hotwire.com charge you for their services when you book a hotel room? That is nearly impossible to find out. Booking fees are hidden under the "taxes and fees" umbrella, and there can be many types of taxes and fees. (Moreover, if the amount looks high, customers may think it is because of the taxes rather than because of the fees.)

Another technique, mandated by some manufacturers to internet retailers, is to only reveal true prices after a consumer has placed an item into their checkout cart. The goal is simply to prevent search engines such as Google Shopping from finding out the price. This technique (of the so-called hidden prices) is still legal, at least for the moment.[98]

Even then, this is all peanuts compared to what the true

masters of nontransparency—the providers of medical services—
do. A blogger once described her long but unsuccessful quest to
discover the actual cost of an operation for a torn meniscus at an
American hospital.[99] First she had to see a doctor. The doctor
couldn't even give her a clue about the price of the procedure.
The doctor's administrative staff couldn't say much more
except that the price could depend on the patient's insurance
coverage. When the blogger kept insisting for a price quote, an
assistant assured her that it might be possible to calculate a figure,
but only after the surgery was scheduled. A billing expert then
confirmed that billing required a code, which in turn required a
scheduled surgery. The billing expert was eventually able to make
an estimate, based on the costs of a previous operation. But, as
it turned out, this was only a part of the expenses, as it did not
include the hospital's surcharge. Nobody in the hospital seemed
to be able to provide that information, but the blogger received a
toll-free number that she could call. In the end, the blogger gave
up her quest and decided to have her surgery done overseas.

This story is not an exception—it is the rule. According to a
report of the Institute of Medicine, 63 percent of patients don't
know how much their care costs until they receive the bill; 10
percent never even find out.[100] In this foggy environment, it is
no surprise that prices vary enormously.

The US spends 18 percent of its GDP on medical services—
more than any other wealthy country—and the data does not
show that US citizens are any healthier. Many explanations have
been offered for this divergence, but our framework may offer
the simplest one: rents. The US health-care system, more than in
any other country, is based on free markets (which is good), but
the markets are completely nontransparent (which is bad). *The
less transparent markets are, the higher the rents will be*—that's
what rent theory predicts. Given the degree of nontransparency,
rents must be significant.[101]

Increasing the Fog by Increasing the Number of Products

In many modern markets, the number of products is nearly infinite. Manufacturers tend to own several brands, and each brand tends to have many product lines. Each product line consists of many products—often just variants of the same product. Are you interested in buying, say, a Philips electric toothbrush? It may take you a while to figure out the differences between the multiple yet similar models.

Philips is not alone. "Versioning"—offering the same product in many variants—has become a widespread marketing practice. A common, simplified form is to offer at least three variants of the same product: the good one, the better one, and the best one. The "good" and "better" versions often stand for slimmed-down variants—products that have artificially been made worse, so to speak. The reason why slimmed-down variants are offered is not necessarily that they are cheaper to produce; very often the production cost savings are negligible. Slimmed-down variants are offered because they allow the seller to separate the "high-value" from the "low-value" consumers. The "high-value" consumers are willing to pay a higher price only if the slimmed-down variants are sufficiently worse. So, versioning has an ironic side: it suggests that profits can be increased by making products worse!

To be sure, the enormous amount of choices in the marketplace is also a benefit for consumers. If you can choose among hundreds of different products, there is an increased chance that you will find something that corresponds to your preferences. Yet at the heart of increasing the number of products there is not only the desire to satisfy consumer preferences—there is also the desire to increase fog and stifle competition by flooding the market.

Flooding the market with product variants stifles competition in a very subtle way. The more time consumers spend comparing all your versions, the less time they spend looking at the products of the competitors. It's like the foggy football field, where consumers can see only a few products, and marketers make sure consumers see only the products of their client. Suppose that the consumer is able to compare only ten products (because of time constraints). If those ten products come from ten different suppliers, there is price competition among ten suppliers. If she compares two product lines of five products each, there is price competition among two suppliers only. If these two product lines from two different brands are owned by one supplier, there is no longer price competition because the prices of the ten products are set by the same supplier. In essence, this strategy comes down to crowding out competitors' products. You put so many of your own products in the consumer's face that she is only able to look at yours.

Flooding through product lines also makes it easier to exploit behavioral shortcomings. One is the *price anchoring* effect: if the price of some products is set extremely high, the others may look like a bargain (more on that in the next chapter). Another is that a few consumers always buy the most expensive product because they believe that its quality must be significantly better—an often-mistaken belief that leads to an information rent for the supplier.

Preventing Price Comparison by Making Products Incomparable

In chapter 1, we have already seen that an often-applied technique to stop price competition is to make products incomparable. If products are different, or look different, or create the false impression that they are different, comparing them becomes like comparing apples and oranges.

Suppose there are two stores in a little city, and both offer different product lines from different brands from the same manufacturer. There will be no cutthroat price competition between those two stores, because their products are hard to compare. The point is not that it is impossible for consumers to organize comparative tests; the point is that it is very costly to do so.

One subtle technique to make price comparison of the *same* product difficult was discussed in chapter 1: Breathe Right Nasal Strips products are sold in boxes with different quantities in different shops, making them mathematically difficult to compare. Some strips are sold in boxes of 44 in one shop and in boxes of 26 in another shop. Only math wizards with excellent memories can tell you in which shop the product is cheaper. A more refined technique we have seen is to reduce comparability by bundling commercial goods with charity contributions. Alternative food giant Whole Foods has become a master at this.

A remarkably simple technique to make two similar products *appear* different is to give them different product numbers. If the dishwashers sold in one store have a different number or name than those sold in other stores, salespeople may convince customers that the ones they sell are different and better. (If they do so, they are, strictly speaking, making a fraudulent misrepresentation, which violates contract law, tort law, and consumer protection law. But as chapter 7 will show, those rules are underenforced, so that in practice businesses get away with these violations.)

A related technique is to simply not mention the product number. A plumber who gives a quote will rarely mention the product number of the sink. Product numbers make it too easy for consumers to discover that they can get the same for a lower price elsewhere. Here is an even subtler example. A few years ago, I bought a Sony TCWE475 Dual Cassette Deck for $131.51 to digitize some old cassettes. But I nearly bought a Sony cassette deck (also on Amazon) that was $25 more expensive. This cassette deck was described by the seller (not Amazon itself) as a "Sony Professional Cassette Deck." The product number was not mentioned, and the product description was slightly different though not contradictory. I first thought, "This is the better deal because for only $25 more I get a professional cassette deck." But after a while, I discovered that the "professional" cassette deck was just the same TCWE475 that was offered elsewhere for $25 less. The seller tried to receive an information rent here: she knew that what she had described as the "professional" version was just the same TCWE475, but she hoped that many buyers would not figure that out until it was too late.

Remarkably, this trade practice is perfectly legal: she did not say it was not a TCWE475, and the term "professional" is vague enough to be considered "puffery" instead of misrepresentation.[102] There is also no legal rule that requires sellers to clearly mention the product number.

Still, the hardest-to-detect way is to give similar products a different design. The mechanics inside the product may be identical, but when the design is different, consumers tend to believe that the mechanics are different. If sellers want to make consumers believe that the mechanics are also *better*, they can simply make the product more expensive—that will be enough to make many consumers believe that it *is* better.

All these strategies are perfectly legal. Nothing in the law currently prevents sellers from making their products incomparable. The law may even help sellers by granting intellectual property rights to specific designs. Such intellectual property rights make copying products illegal. In a sense, they make it illegal to transform a product into a commodity! The goal of the law is to stimulate new designs, but its unintended effect is to reduce transparency and price competition.

The Tragedy of the Brands

In most modern markets, there is a significant amount of *quality* fog. You may have experienced this the last time you bought a washer, vacuum cleaner, toothbrush, bulb, or bottle of fish oil.

At first glance, there is something that makes consumers' lives easier: brands. You may not know how good a specific TV model is, but you know that Sony generally makes good TVs. You may never figure out how good your surgeon was (unless he leaves a sponge in your abdomen!), but you know that the hospital has a good reputation. So, brands seem to be a great market remedy against quality fog. Consumers may not know the exact quality of specific products, but they learn over time which brands are most reliable. Suppliers have strong incentives to offer great quality; if they don't, their brand reputation will decline, and so will their ability to raise profit margins.

Unfortunately, brands solve one problem only by creating another. They solve the quality problem but at the same time create a pricing problem. Indeed, brand-name products are typically more expensive, and only a part of the higher price is justified by higher production costs. Brand products are sold at higher profit margins, and there is no doubt these margins partly consist of rents.

How large are these rents? That depends on how many bad products there are in the market. Suppose that you have the choice between a branded product, which is certainly good, and a nonbrand product that costs $100 and that could be equally good but also extremely bad. How much more are you willing to pay for the brand product? Suppose that there is a 99 percent chance that the nonbrand product is equally good, and only a 1 percent chance that you will have to throw it away. In this case, you are willing to pay only about 1 percent more for the brand. Now suppose that there is a 50 percent chance that the nonbrand product is bad. In that case, you are willing to pay twice the price of the nonbrand product for the brand.[103]

The rents for brand owners are further increased if we introduce uncertainty. Uncertainty is worse than risk; a risk can be calculated (as in the previous examples, where we assumed that the consumer knew that the risk was 1 percent and 50 percent, respectively), but the same can't be said for uncertainty. Psychological studies have shown that human beings have a strong distaste for uncertainty. Uncertainty is what happens when you need to cross a swamp and you have no clue whether there are crocodiles in it: you will instinctively try to avoid crossing it at all costs. So, if there is uncertainty about the quality of the nonbrand product, most consumers are willing to pay an even higher premium for the brand, translating into even higher rents for the brand owner. This explains why the owners of a brand have no incentive to demand transparency-increasing policy measures for their sector.

True, brands compete not only with nonbrands but also with other brands. Could it be that this competition eliminates all rents? In theory, it could, but in practice, that is unlikely. One reason that prevents perfect competition among brands is that human beings are limited by their own brains. We may know the reputation of a couple of vacuum cleaner brands, but how many people can tell what the reputation is of, say, fifteen brands? Moreover, once a few brands are established, there is a slow and costly process to create and market a new brand in the industry, partly because most consumers are naturally reluctant to try unknown products. If you look at a randomly chosen market at a randomly chosen point of time, the market structure is nearly always an oligopoly with only a few well-established brands.

Brands create rents in two ways. First, there is a brand premium, based on a perceived higher quality. Second, there may be a loyalty premium because consumers are inclined to stay with a familiar product. How large is the loyalty premium rent? In principle, it equals the "search cost" or "switching cost." Suppose the competing products cost $100, but the search and switching cost is $20. In this case, you are willing to pay up to $20 more for the product you currently use. The manufacturer of the current product may be able to exploit this loyalty to acquire a rent of up to $20.

What determines the search costs? The degree of transparency. The more information there is about the quality and price of each product, and the easier it is to get this information, the lower the search costs will be. So, once again, more fog means more rents.

Hiding Cost Structures behind Fixed or Percentage Fees, Avoiding Hourly Fees or Wages

Suppose you want to remodel your home. Should you pay workers a fixed fee for the whole job, or should you pay them per hour? Or should you pay them a percentage of the value? Relatedly, how should you pay a roofer, a real estate agent, a lawyer, or a doctor?

Traditionally, economists look favorably at percentage fees and fixed fees, and unfavorably at hourly fees and fixed wages. This is because most economists only look at incentives, risks, and transaction costs, and not at information rents. Indeed, if you omit the latter, percentage fees and fixed fees seem to have many advantages. First of all, they give an incentive to work fast.[104] Hourly fees and fixed wages, by contrast, give an incentive to slow down. In the case of real estate agents, for instance, hourly fees and fixed wages provide an incentive for keeping the house on the market for as long as possible (for instance, by setting the price too high or being inflexible during negotiations). Second, percentage fees give an incentive to maximize output; for instance, they give real estate agents an incentive to obtain the highest possible price for the owner.[105] Moreover, fixed fees and percentage fees do not require the principal to monitor the number of hours worked by the agent; this is a transaction cost advantage.

This is not to say that economists never recommend hourly fees (or fixed wages). Such arrangements can make sense if the monitoring costs are low (so that shirking or slacking can be kept under control) and the worker is very risk averse (so that she dislikes unpredictable income). In addition, such arrangements can make sense when output is hard to measure, or when the worker has many different tasks.[106] But generally, output-based contracts such as fixed fees or percentage fees are believed to have intrinsic advantages. This is why many economists and commentators believe that paying doctors per problem solved would be an excellent way of keeping medical expenses under control; when doctors are paid for solving a problem, they no longer have an incentive to overexamine the patient.[107]

The problem with this analysis is that it overlooks information rents. Indeed, a smart "principal" (i.e., an employer, consumer, or patient) will also try to prevent overpaying the agent (i.e., the employee, the seller, or doctor). To avoid paying information rents, the principal needs information on the cost structure.

This is where hourly fees or fixed wages suddenly get an advantage. If you pay someone an hourly fee, you receive information about how many hours it takes to do the job, and (obviously) on how much the agent receives per hour. The same applies to fixed wages, because as an employer you have the right and opportunity to monitor the number of hours spent on each project. This is different from a fixed-fee contract. If you pay a roofer $2,000 to repair your roof, you may never know how many hours a job of this nature normally takes (both on the roof and in preparation for the work), and how much you are effectively paying per hour.

But if you pay a fixed fee to a roofer, couldn't you just count the number of hours that are effectively worked and calculate afterward how much you actually paid per hour? The problem is that a fixed-fee contract also transfers the risk to the roofer. Sometimes a job takes less time than expected, sometimes it takes more time. So, if you count the number of hours the job effectively took, the roofer can always say that this is one of those jobs that went faster than planned. The roofer may, in other words, say that if he made a profit on this job, you should also consider the losses he incurred on many other jobs. To check whether the contract was really overpriced, you need statistical information on the distribution of hours for such jobs. The roofer may have this information, but he will not reveal that to you.

Here is another way of looking at this example. The roofer received an information rent from you because he had an informational advantage: he knew better than you how much work was involved in the particular job. The reason why he could keep that information advantage was that you paid him a fixed price. Fixed-price contracts make it easy to conceal overpricing. Of course, if bidding costs were zero, you could solicit bids from hundreds of roofers, and competitive forces would be strong enough to make them reveal their true costs. But since consumers typically only ask for a few bids, competitive forces are not strong enough to obtain this effect; at most, they can turn monopoly pricing into oligopoly pricing.

Still, wouldn't you get the same problem with hourly fees—if you asked only three roofers to make a bid for an hourly fee, you get oligopolistic pricing too, no? One important difference is that making a bid for an hourly fee is much cheaper than making a bid for a fixed price. As a matter of fact, making a bid for an hourly fee takes no more than a few seconds—the time to utter a number—as there is no need to study the job beforehand. Because the costs are lower, more bids can be solicited in the same amount of time, and the sheer number of bids leads to more competitive pressure. A related difference is that information on hourly fees can easily be spread by word of mouth (just ask your neighbors how much they paid per hour for the same service), while this is harder to accomplish for fixed fees (if your neighbors paid $2,750 to repair their roof, that does not say much because each repair is different). This again reduces the fog: it is as if you can see many more roofers on the football field because you can also see those who worked for your friends and neighbors.

So, in the oligopoly-caused-by-fog model, fixed fees have a

double function: they make it easier to hide information and reduce the competitive forces to reveal that information by reducing the number of bidders. Hourly fees, in this respect, have a double function too: they reveal the rents and at the same time increase the competitive forces that help to reduce the rents.

Of course, hourly fees and wages have the disadvantage that they require monitoring the number of hours and the intensity of working. And here we see again the trade-off between efficiency (monitoring less) and information rents.

This trade-off is nicely illustrated by the following anecdote. An economist I happened to know had a well-paid position at a bank. To my surprise, he decided to take six months off to help on the construction of his own house. At first sight, I thought this was absurd, because his talents were obviously used more productively at the bank than at the construction site (where he essentially worked as an unskilled worker). But he explained to me that the big advantage of being on the construction site was that he could pay construction workers per hour; he later showed me how much he had saved compared to what he would have paid for his house had he taken the lowest of three fixed-price bids. It turned out that he saved more money in six months than he could ever have made at the bank.

Rent-camouflage theory leads to the following empirical prediction: in sectors in which fixed fees or percentage fees are dominant, rents are more likely to exist. This prediction stands in contrast with the one that can be derived from the traditional analysis, which suggests that hourly fees, wages, fixed fees, or percentage fees should all lead to the same income (aside from risk premiums).

A few empirical studies have confirmed the rent-camouflage theory. For instance, lawyers who work on contingency fees (that is, who receive a percentage of the awarded damages) earn much more per hour than those who are paid per hour.[108] But the theory is also supported by other, more anecdotal evidence.

Consider the income of real estate agents. Nearly all work on percentage fees, and the most common percentage fee in the US, seems to be 6 percent of the sales price—which may have to be split among two real estate agents if both the seller and the buyer have one. For a $500,000 house, this corresponds to a $30,000 commission. This amount may seem normal, but from an economist's perspective, it is absolutely mind-boggling: $30,000 is nearly two times the yearly income of a fast-food cook! In a competitive economy, prices just reflect true costs, and it is true that costs not only include time directly spent showing homes and negotiating sales but also time spent on many other tasks. Moreover, real estate agents have to invest in a college education and bear the usual costs of operating a business (time spent by others to clean the offices, to do the bookkeeping). But even when "work" is considered broadly, does selling a single $500,000 house really require as much work as 3,200 hours of hamburger flipping?

The complexity of the work in itself cannot explain the magnitude of such a commission. Sure, real estate agents need to develop some skills in order to give expert advice such as, "Here is the bathroom," or "This is a two-car garage," or "The school district has a good reputation." (Maybe I am underestimating the years of training that are needed before such statements can be made.) Sure, real estate agents need to learn how to do all the paperwork, but this paperwork almost exclusively consists of filling out standard forms.

The point is that the percentage fee makes it easier for real estate agents to get a rent. (Obviously, many of these rents go to the companies rather than to the individual real estate agents. Remember, the principal does not like to leave rents with the agents.) Clients have no clue how many hours of work are on average required to sell a $500,000 house, and so they may not realize how much they are paying the agent by the hour. And since commissions have to cover the *average* amount of work plus the costs, real estate agents can easily claim that their average amount of work and their costs are very high—there is no way for the client to verify this, especially since real estate agents will never reveal the underlying data.

I'll admit that the rent-camouflage theory does not explain why competitive forces do not lower the percentage. If a 6 percent commission is excessive for a $500,000 house, why doesn't the market price move toward a 4 percent commission? Some economists have suggested it's because there is an implicit cartel in the sector. The fact is that the percentage is irrationally sticky—it does not change when true costs change. Consider those real estate markets in which prices in 2012 were 30 percent lower than in 2007. Since the amount of work remained constant, the market percentage for real estate agents should have gone up, but it did not.[109] Similarly, in regions in which real estate prices doubled between 2000 and 2007, economic logic dictates that the percentage for real estate agents should have been halved in that period, but it did not change. These are signs of a very seriously distorted market. My only point is that the compensation type—the percentage fee—makes it easier for these fees to remain at a distorted equilibrium.

The rent-camouflage theory may also explain the income differences among doctors. Most doctors are very well paid, but there is still a large income variation among types of doctors. The general pattern seems to be that performances that consist of "talking" (such as office visits) are lowly paid, while performances that consist of doing a technical procedure are highly paid. Within the traditional economic framework, this is puzzling. Sure, technical procedures (like doing an echography or a surgery) involve costs (buying echography or surgery equipment), but this does not explain why the doctor's time itself is so much better compensated during such procedures. Some have speculated that society values technology more than human interaction, but this explanation has no economic basis at all—it is not "society" that sets prices but markets, and in competitive markets the price is not determined by the "value" but by the costs. Many have argued that competition is distorted in the medical sector (for instance, through artificial barriers to entry in the form of excessive schooling requirements), but while this may be true, it is not clear why this would work differently for some types of performance within the same profession. It does not explain, in other words, why the same doctor receives $100 per hour for some performances and $500 for others.

Here is a better explanation: overpricing is easier when there is a technical component that makes the cost structure nontransparent. If, on the other hand, the performance consists only of talking with the patient for a thirty-minute consultation, it is difficult to overprice. If the doctor charged $500, patients would immediately see that the price is outrageous. But $2,000 for a thirty-minute surgery? That does not sound so unreasonable, because it is not clear which part of the price compensates the costs of the surgery and which part compensates for the doctor's time.

How about another robust fact—that the poorest paid labor forces tend to work for an hourly wage? The traditional explanation by economists is that these people have a low income because they don't take risks and because they lack the human capital to do more complex tasks. Rent-camouflage theory offers a different explanation: if you work for an hourly rate, it is harder to overcharge for your services. Therefore, many hourly wage workers do not capture any rents in an economy full of rents. And that's why they find themselves at the bottom of the income distribution.

A New Theory of the Firm: Businesses Are
Set Up to Hide Cost Structures

Why do firms exist? This is one of the central questions of a field in economics called "industrial organization." Many theories have been proposed to answer this question. One theory sees firms as tools to create limited liability. If your firm goes bankrupt, creditors can only take the money you put in the firm.[110] Another theory (Coase 1937) sees firms as tools to minimize transaction costs. If you outsource everything, you need to renegotiate contracts every time you want to make a change; if you have your own workers, you can simply give them a new instruction. Still another theory (Hart 1995) sees firms as tools to protect you against hold-ups. If you fear that a supplier of parts may suddenly increase prices, knowing that you have nowhere else to go in the short run, you should not outsource these parts but produce them within your own firm.[112]

I propose a new theory of the firm: firms are tools to hide cost structures and concentrate rents. The theory is based on two underlying ideas. The first is similar to the idea that it is easier to receive an information rent when you are paid a fixed fee than when you are paid a wage. Firms have overhead costs, and this makes it even harder for outsiders to find out the cost structure and, therefore, to find out whether they have been overcharged. The second is that employees have no access to the bookkeeping, and therefore have no clear view on the cost structure either. This makes it easier for business owners to capture all the rents. The fixed-wage plumbers who work in that plumbing firm may not even realize how many rents their boss receives on their services.

I once had a long conversation with a real estate appraiser. He said that since he had his own appraisal company (which employed only one person—himself), he was making more than twice what he made in the past as an employee for another company, when he did exactly the same work, and spent exactly the same number of hours. (He said he had realized his own version of the American dream and concluded that there is enough success in this country for everyone—just be entrepreneurial, get out of your lazy chair, and start up your own company. And at that time, I agreed.)

But soon I realized there was something astonishing about this case. How is it possible that the market price is more than twice the true costs? Apparently, making such an appraisal requires less work than the bank (who had ordered it) seemed to be aware of. How is this possible in an apparently competitive market? And why doesn't a failing market immediately correct itself by attracting new suppliers who push the price downward?

Maybe this particular market failed because of price and quality fog. Maybe it failed because of payer externalities: the party who orders the service (the bank) is not the same party as the one who pays for it (the client). Whatever the fundamental cause of the rent, the fact is that overpricing becomes harder to discover for the bank and the client when a fixed price is billed rather than an hourly fee.

And of course, looking at the real estate appraiser, the resulting rents went to the owner of the business. In the past, the rents went to the appraiser's boss, but since he now owns his own company, the rents go to him. And this may be the main benefit of starting up your own business: catching the information rents that are generated by your activity.

Why Is Fog Creation Legal?

Let's now shift our attention to the law. Why is it legal to deliberately make markets less transparent? If fog reduces competition, why isn't fog creation forbidden by competition law?

Well, that is a great question. The short answer is that competition law is still focused on older methods of monopolization—the tricks Rockefeller used to monopolize the oil industry in the 1880s, so to speak. The economic literature that showed the relationship between information failures and competition failures dates back to the 1970s. Apparently, it takes time before lawmakers realize the policy implications of scholarship.

Another question is why fog creation isn't forbidden under contract law. This is a harder question because contract law forbids concealment. Concealment is any active intervention that makes it harder for the other party to get informed—an investment in search obstruction, so to speak. For instance, if the seller of a house conceals termite damage by covering the floor with carpet, she faces sanctions under contract law (and may be liable under tort law as well). So why isn't refusing to publish prices on the internet considered "concealment" under contract law?

One technical difference is that prices are not hidden forever—they are revealed at a later stage of the negotiations, right before you sign the contract. In the termite example, by contrast, the information is never revealed by the seller. This is an important legal difference, because technically, you can't sue on the basis of concealment if the information was revealed before you signed the contract. Still, the result looks inconsistent: search obstruction is wrong, unless you do it only for a while.

But how about another common marketing technique—making products incomparable? If two identical products are put in a different box from a different brand with a different product number, why does this not fall under "concealment"? Here, the information is never revealed to the buyer; so, the analogy with the termites case seems complete. I am afraid I don't have a good answer here—the legal system is simply inconsistent. Courts think it is the buyers' responsibility to discover the true differences between products, even if sellers prevent them from doing so.*

Theft Is Illegal, but Overpricing Is Not: The Pickpocket Business Model

Let's now generalize a little more. What is the Achilles' heel of the legal system?

Imagine a shop in which certain goods are sold for $100— a price that corresponds to the true costs. But as consumers walk through the shop, the owner tries to steal $50 out of their pockets. If they discover it, she gives back the $50. If they do not discover it, she keeps the $50. Most consumers end up paying $150 for the good—$100 in the form of the market price and $50 in the form of stolen money.

If shops did this literally, their owners would soon end up in jail. Taking money out of someone's wallet without permission is called "theft," and theft has been considered a crime since the earliest days of law. So, owners who want to apply this "Pickpocket Business Model" must do so in a subtler form. And it's here that the law comes to help them: stealing is illegal, but overpricing is legal.

Here is the legal way to pick someone's pocket. The store prices the good at $150. If customers do not discover that they have been overcharged, the shop keeps the money. If customers find out that it costs less elsewhere, they pay just $100.

The term "Pickpocket Business Model" is not an existing term in the marketing literature. (Marketers prefer fancier terms, such as "differential pricing.") I introduce the term to illustrate how prices

---

* By the same token, designing complex pricing plans, like those for ski passes in Winter Park, is legal. Courts consider it the consumer's responsibility to discover the prices ahead of time. It is probably easier to pass a college course on rocket science than to reverse engineer the pricing structure of a randomly chosen Colorado ski resort, but still, it remains the consumer's responsibility.

are set in nontransparent markets, and to show the similarities between two rent-seeking activities: stealing and overpricing.

How does the Pickpocket Business Model work in practice? One simple way is to just charge the $150 to uninformed customers and let the informed ones buy the good at $100 elsewhere. But ideally, the shop likes to have the best of both worlds: let the uninformed pay $150 and still sell it for $100 to the informed ones. One variant we have seen is to hide Easter eggs in the form of "coupons." Those who find an Easter egg pay the low price. Those who do not (because they had no time to search) pay the high price. Another variant we have seen is offering "best-price guarantees." These guarantees promise to match prices, should a consumer discover an item is cheaper in a competing shop, but the price is lowered only for the one who discovered it.

The core of many of these techniques is the truism that *while stealing is illegal, overpricing is not.* A plumber is not allowed to steal $28 out of a customer's pocket, but it is perfectly legal for him to charge $29 for a bolt that's worth only $1.

Why does the legal system have so much trouble attacking overpricing, compared to attacking outright stealing? The problem with overpricing is that the transfer of wealth is "consensual," at least formally. Indeed, "overpriced" means that the price *in a contract* is above the true costs of the product being sold. But it remains a contract, and a contract is based on the consent of the two parties involved—including the consent of the "victim" of overpricing. Of course, you may say that it is not a *real* consent. If you pay $29 to a plumber for a $1 bolt, you did not really give permission to be overcharged. But that is true only in the philosophical sense of the word "consent," not in its formal, legal sense. Legal systems do not require true consent in a philosophical sense, but typically enforce contracts as soon as they observe some external behavior, such as when you utter the words "I agree" or when you sign a contract.

Still, the question remains why overpricing is legal. Why don't courts simply forbid excessive prices?

The question is not as absurd as it sounds. In late medieval times, courts applied the "just price" doctrine (*iustum pretium* in Latin), which required a correct price in order for a contract to be valid. If the true value was 100 coins, and the contract stipulated 150 coins, the contract was void. But the doctrine was abandoned in the seventeenth century, partly because of the theological argument (developed by Spanish neoscholastic writers) that only God can know the true price.[113] Since then, courts have usually found that they should leave price determination to the market. Economists back this up—and even more so since Hayek convinced us that centralized economies fail because bureaucrats lack the information to determine prices.[114]

Apart from this economic argument, the philosophical argument of freedom of contract supports the legality of overpricing. Freedom of contract means not only that you are never obliged to agree to a contract (freedom *from* contract), but also that you are free to ask the terms that you desire. If you put your house on the market, you have the right to ask ten times more than the market price. Chances are slim that you will sell the house, but still, if you find someone who wants to pay that amount for your house, the legal system won't stop you.

Of course, there are exceptions; price regulation exists for a few goods. For instance, apartment leasing prices are regulated in New York. Usury laws (which forbid excessive interest rates on loans) still exist in many states. In Louisiana and a few European countries, the *iustum pretium* doctrine is still applied to real estate transactions (for instance, a sale may not be valid if the price is less than half of the market price). And in a few rare cases, in which the price "shocked the conscience," American judges have reformed contracts on the basis of *price unconscionability*.[115] But these are exceptions; the general rule is that overpricing is legal. Determining the benchmark (the "just price") is simply too difficult for the courts.

This means that, to reduce rents, the legal system will have to use smarter instruments than just price regulation. More on that in chapter 9.

Why Market Forces, Consumer Organizations, or Reputation Won't Solve the Problem

Before going further, we need to answer a simple question: Do you really need the law to handle this? If publishing information on the internet is really good, why wouldn't businesses do it spontaneously? Shouldn't governments stay out of this and leave it to the market?

It is true that, under certain conditions, markets will force businesses to publish all the information that is useful to buyers. The mechanism that could make this happen is known in the literature as the Grossman mechanism.[116] The core idea behind the Grossman mechanism is that when consumers have no quality information, they assume that all sellers offer an average quality. This gives those who offer above-average quality an incentive to provide that information. Once they do that, consumers start to assume that those who remain silent offer low quality. This in turn gives sellers whose quality is below average but still okay an incentive to reveal that. This creates a chain reaction that eventually leads to full disclosure on the market.[117]

If the Grossman mechanism always worked in practice, we wouldn't need to force businesses to publish prices and quality information on the internet (although regulation wouldn't hurt either as it would only tell businesses to do what they were already doing).

Unfortunately, the Grossman mechanism does not always

work in practice—and "not always" is quite an understatement. Do you know any plumbers, sprinkler companies, or surgeons who publish their prices on the internet? Do you know hospitals who publish the success rates for all their treatments and car manufacturers who publish the defect rate? How many manufacturers finance comparative lab tests for their vacuum cleaners, batteries, or sprinkler heads?

Why doesn't the Grossman mechanism work more often? Well, the model is based on an impressive number of assumptions that all need to be fulfilled.

The first assumption is that publishing and information-processing costs are negligible. One problem of the Grossman mechanism is that it relies on indirect exposure—those who remain silent are exposed only if all the others reveal the information. Indirect exposure, however, usually requires higher transaction costs than direct disclosure. Suppose that only 1 out of 1,000 houses have termite damage. The Grossman mechanism exposes the one with termites by letting the 999 others disclose they have no termites. But this requires 999 sellers to make a communication—999 more than a simple legal rule that forces the one seller with the termites to tell this. These higher costs may prevent the spontaneous disclosure altogether: if termite damage rarely happens, those without it may not even mention it and instead use their advertising space to focus on more relevant qualities. If that is the case, the one with termite damage is no longer exposed. (Moreover, even if the Grossman mechanism worked in such a case, it would still be wasteful compared to a legal disclosure duty for the infested houses alone!)*

---

* Underneath the previous assumption (that transaction costs are negligible), there is also an implicit assumption that standardization has occurred. Indeed, standardization makes information exchange much cheaper. But, as we have seen, standardization rarely happens spontaneously on markets—and if it happens, it is usually too little too late. Markets tend to fail here because there is a public-good problem (the costs to define the standard are for the one who takes the initiative while the benefits are for everyone) in addition to a network externality problem (adopting the standard is only beneficial once the others do it too).

The second condition for the Grossman mechanism to work is that anyone who discloses information must do so honestly. In other words, those who say they offer high quality must really offer high quality. This condition implies that antifraud rules are sufficiently enforced to deter lying. We have seen, however, that this is often not the case—there are many forms of fraud that are either legal or that businesses can get away with.

Ironically, enforcing antifraud rules may require disclosure regulation. To see why, consider the Federal Trade Commission's (FTC) decision to no longer prosecute false reference prices. If a seller falsely tells that the normal price is $150 in order to make the $100 price look like a sale, the seller commits a deceptive practice under the FTC Act, but the FTC will not prosecute the seller (more on that in chapter 7). Why not? Because proving such violations is too labor intensive (as it requires proving what the normal price was at that time). But if all sellers had to publish their prices in a standardized form on the internet all the time, proving such a violation would become easy. So, here is a paradox related to the Grossman mechanism: disclosure regulation may not be necessary when antifraud rules are perfectly enforced, but to perfectly enforce antifraud rules, disclosure regulation may be needed.

The third condition for the Grossman mechanism to work is the absence of a credible excuse for refusing to publish information. I once asked a sprinkler company why they didn't publish their prices on the internet. The answer was, "Because our competitors should not be able to see how low our prices are." You may not find that a convincing excuse, but the fact is that when enough consumers believe the excuse, the market will not "unravel" a la Grossman. And you can be sure that salespeople have developed a wide range of successful excuses over time: "Our suppliers don't allow us to publish prices because we get special prices," or "We don't want to publish prices because we don't want to overcharge our customers and therefore we first need to see how much work is involved." Some of these excuses may be flat-out lies, but there comes the antifraud-disclosure paradox again: in the absence of a duty to publish information, proving fraud may be too costly.

These are just a few assumptions for the Grossman mechanism to work. I'll explain some other, more technical assumptions in an endnote.[118] The problem is that *all* assumptions need to be fulfilled before market forces are strong enough to force businesses to publish enough pricing and quality information. We simply can't expect that this will always be the case.

If businesses don't publish this information, why don't consumers or consumer organizations do it? Well, it may be hard to collect accurate information without the cooperation of the businesses. Also, for consumers, information is a "public good" (a technical term meaning that it is hard to make people pay for the benefit they receive). Sure, Consumer Reports does some tests, but their annual testing and research budget is only $27 million, or 6,700 times less than the $182 billion advertising expenditures in the US.[119] This proves how large the public-good problem is.

Why don't businesses who offer high quality publish comparative information on their competitors? As it turns out, information is a public good for businesses as well. Financing tests on competing products is costly, and once the results are published, others benefit from the information as well.

Why can't reputation solve the problem? If a plumber is overcharging for spare parts, then maybe he will get a bad reputation and have to leave the market. If a bank is overcharging for overdraft protection, then maybe the bank will get a bad reputation and lose customers. If HP is overcharging for ink cartridges, then maybe consumers will find that out and stop buying HP printers.

The least you can say about the "Reputation Will Solve

Everything Argument" is that it is empirically incorrect. The market is full of lock-in effects and subtle forms of misleading, and reputation apparently did not eliminate them. Reputation may do something, but it typically does too little and comes too late.* This is not surprising if you analyze the mechanics behind the traditional form of reputation: word of mouth. This process is based on the perceptions of some consumers who communicate with some other consumers who in turn communicate with others. The method is necessarily impressionistic, imprecise, and random. How good is a doctor? Patients may have an impression about the doctor's quality, but that impression may say more about the doctor's friendliness than about the doctor's technical skills. (The deeper problem is that a medical service is what economists call a "credence good": even after you have experienced it, you cannot evaluate it because you lack the expertise to evaluate the expert.) Moreover, how reliable is the information after it has been passed through multiple people? Remember the telephone game you played as a child? Word of mouth is similar to what lawyers call "hearsay evidence": it is based on what you and other people heard that others said.[120] Hearsay evidence is forbidden in modern litigation systems . . . because it has turned out to be too unreliable. So, why would word of mouth be more reliable when it is used in the market?[121]

Reputation also tends to come too late. How durable is a product? It may take years to find that out. By that time, the product will have been replaced by newer models. Pricing reputation (how expensive is that plumber?) may also need years (and numerous observations) before it becomes accurate, and by that time it may be outdated. That plumber who used to be cheap when he started may now be much more expensive.

---

* If reputation were perfect, we could abolish the entire legal system. No one would ever breach a contract, make a misrepresentation, exploit lock-in effects, or abuse a dominant position because all those bad things would be bad for the actor's reputation.

Reputation has even greater difficulties when used to evaluate statistical phenomena. What is the chance that a product breaks down? Will reputation reconstruct the shape of the statistical distribution? Sure, if all 10,000 customers speak extensively with each other and hire a statistician to put all the pieces of information together. In practice, this is not going to happen. The internet may facilitate communication between consumers, but in practice, only a small fraction of all consumers write product feedback, and this makes it nearly impossible to generate accurate statistical estimates.

In short, we can't rely on market mechanisms (a la Grossman), consumer organizations, or reputation to blow away the fog that is deliberately created by marketers. There are simply too many conditions for any of those mechanisms to work. And that's why the legal system needs to step in.

5

LEGAL WAYS TO ABUSE TRUST

I n a complex economy, experts play an important role. As a consumer, you cannot be specialized in warranties, motor oil, and mold prevention at the same time—you have to rely on experts. But who are these experts? They are salespeople on one hand and professionals who perform the services on the other.

The problem is that these experts often have a conflict of interest. Their income depends on the choices you make, so they may push you into the direction most profitable for them. As a result, salespeople in electronics stores may aggressively market overpriced warranties. Repair shops may aggressively recommend premium oil. And in an NBC program, the majority of the mold contractors recommended unnecessary work.[122]

Abuse of trust, as we will see, is not a small problem. Trust is abused, in subtle or plain forms, on a massive scale. It is a lucrative way to acquire information rents. The legal system forbids some forms but, unfortunately, permits many others.

Biased Expert Advice from Your Trusted Adviser

If you walk into a bank or an electronics store, you may be directed to a "trusted adviser," who is there to assist you in finding out what is best for *you*. A leading marketing textbook (by Kotler and Armstrong) presents Best Buy as the central example of a "customer-centric marketing strategy." A former CEO is cited as saying that Best Buy wants to become "that trusted adviser capable of helping customers use technology the way they dreamed. . . . We're about people. People just like you. We really mean it. Really."[123]

That's great. Let's now look at some other marketing literature. Do you know the most profitable product sold at electronics stores such as Best Buy? Warranties. While the actual markups are never published, scholars have estimated them between 60 percent and 90 percent. Scholars have also estimated that extended warranties were responsible for 50 percent of Best Buy's profits, 100 percent of Circuit City's profits, 47 percent of Dixon's profits, and 80 percent of Comet's profits.[124]

How does Best Buy succeed in selling at such high profit margins in an apparently competitive market? For starters, it's a form of upsale. Most consumers have some information on market prices for TVs (because they read the ads, or go to different shops), but they usually do not pay attention to the market prices for extended warranties.[125] This makes it easy to overprice these warranties and obtain information rents. In addition, the "trusted advisers" are there to recommend buying the (vastly overpriced) extended warranties.

But here's the scary thing: not only are warranties enormously overpriced, but it's also irrational to buy them—even if they were correctly priced. Modern insurance economics holds that buying insurance for relatively small losses such as $1,000 is irrational.

The reason is that, statistically, you always lose money when you buy insurance. If the insurance premium is for instance $300, consumers may only get $200 paid back in the form of compensation on average, as the insurance company needs the remaining $100 to cover administrative costs. Therefore, insurance is only worth it if the loss is problematic for you. This is the case for large losses, like a house that is burnt down, but not for small losses, like a TV that needs to be repaired.*

Do the warranty experts at firms like Best Buy know this economic literature? They should, though I am not sure they do because even most insurance agents (whose job it is to help their clients make rational insurance decisions) are not familiar with this literature. This makes sense because they are not in the insurance business but in the information rent business. That it is all about information rents becomes even clearer now that warranties are being offered for incredibly small amounts. I once bought a timer at RadioShack for $9.95 and was asked whether I wanted to buy an extended warranty for $3.95 in order "to protect [my] investment."

Still, what electronics stores do is peanuts compared to what the world champions of shrouded pricing—rental car companies—do. When I first rented a car in the US, I was amazed to learn that I was "highly" recommended to buy three

---

* The reason why is somewhat technical, but here is the essence. Although insurance contracts make you lose money on average, it can be rational to buy them for large risks. The core is that when you become poor (for instance, after you lose your house in a fire), a dollar has more utility to you than when you were wealthier. If the difference between the utility values is high enough, insurance is rational, even if you lose 30–50 percent on an insurance policy in mathematical terms. At what point is the difference in utility of money large enough to make up for the 30–50 percent losses? Economists have calculated that this is only the case for very large losses— for instance, the equivalent of a year's worth of income. For relatively small losses, rational individuals are nearly risk neutral. See John W. Pratt, "Risk Aversion in the Small and in the Large," *Econometrica* 32 (1964): 122–136. The practical recommendation from insurance economists is to buy insurance only for losses that you are unable to bear yourself. If your TV gets broken, will you be able to pay for the repair costs? If the answer is yes, then it is not rational to buy an extended warranty.

types of insurance. At the end of the day, insurance cost more than the car rental itself.

I remember discussing this with a colleague of mine, who was also a visiting professor in the US, and who was also working on the economics of tort law and insurance. We said, "Holy cow, tort law needs to be reformed in this country—insurance is probably so expensive because of all those punitive damages and outrageous damage awards for emotional distress!" It didn't occur to us that the product was simply overpriced. Why not? Because we thought that would be impossible in a market with so many competitors. Moreover, we learned that the other car rental companies charged a similarly high price, which seemed to prove that the price reflected the true costs. (I have to admit that, certainly at that time, "law and economics" was a field where, to say it diplomatically, the presumption that markets are efficient was quite strong. It is not that we law and economics scholars were prejudiced, because you could always come up with evidence that markets failed; but the evidence had to prove the case beyond reasonable doubt—the type of evidence burden that is required to put a criminal on death row.) For us theoretical scholars, warranties and insurances were "risk-spreading devices." For marketers, they were cash cows.

Why Is Biased Advice Legal?

The legal system currently allows salespeople to give biased advice while pretending to give honest advice. If salespeople tell their customers they are only trying to help them, while in reality, they are trying to manipulate them into buying certain products, customers have no legal remedy. It's a legal form of abuse of trust.

Why exactly is there no legal claim? It is an example of the legal system applying its principles a little too narrowly. If people promise to give honest advice, they normally have "fiduciary duties" as they have put themselves into a fiduciary relationship. Fiduciary duties mean that they have a legal obligation to give honest, unbiased advice. But when exactly is such a fiduciary relationship created? The law makes a distinction between those who automatically fall into this category and those who may fall into it if they have made specific promises. The list of those who fall into it automatically includes doctors (toward patients), attorneys (toward clients), corporate officers (toward shareholders), and employees (toward employers) but not the salespeople at your local electronics store.

All others can fall under it if they explicitly promised to become a fiduciary, or if the other party could reasonably expect they would. Now, if the salesperson in the electronics store is called a "trusted adviser" and tells you that he only wants to help you, then you may reasonably expect that he has legally promised to give honest advice, right? Well, no. Courts inexplicably believe that you may not expect this. If a consumer is so naive that he relies on what the seller says, that's the consumer's fault.

General contract law won't help consumers either. Sure, there is a rule that says that advisers who are in a relationship of "trust and confidence" cannot misrepresent their opinion. But who is considered to be in a relationship of trust and confidence? Your doctor, your lawyer, your priest, and maybe your sibling, but not the "trusted adviser" at your local electronics store or bank.[126]

If courts believe that it is irrational to rely on sales talk, why do consumers listen to it? One reason is that outside the marketplace, we tend to trust people and tend to believe what they say. Our parents taught us to be honest. Because we try to be honest, we are also inclined to believe that other people are honest most of the time. Another reason why consumers pay attention to sales talk is that even in the marketplace, many people *are* honest. They tell you what is best for you, even if that costs them money. In other words, there are not only wolves among salespeople; there are also sheep.

To use the language of economists, there are "good types" and "bad types" among sellers. The "good types" give honest advice, the "bad types" give biased advice. But the legal system does not help us to distinguish between the two because the bad types are allowed to falsely pretend that they are good types. In other words, the wolves are allowed to hide in sheep's clothing. This leads to what game theorists call a "pooling equilibrium." The result is that the "bad types" have an easy time grabbing information rents. They know better than the consumer which products offer the best value and which offer the highest markup. They exploit this informational advantage to extract more money from the sale than they normally could in a transparent market.

It gets even more tricky when salespeople misrepresent what "experts" recommend. Sellers are already the experts, and if they say what the even bigger experts say, you tend to believe it, no? Strictly speaking, a false statement about what other experts say is a misrepresentation that may lead to liability under contract law, tort law, and consumer protection law. Yet as long as the misrepresentation is not made in an ad aired on national TV, the chance of being held liable is about the same as the chance of being hit by lightning.

So, if you get an oil change, you may be told that using premium oil (and paying a premium price) is "recommended by experts" because your mileage exceeds a certain number (for instance, 75,000 miles). Such oil is apparently good for your car because it helps to prevent engine leaks. But who are those "experts"? Neutral automotive experts believe that high-mileage oil is not worth the money for the overwhelming majority of high-mileage cars.[127] Moreover, the definition of "high" mileage should presumably be different for different makes and models (so it makes little sense to use the same mileage number for all cars).

There is another reason why such forms of misleading easily fall through the cracks of the legal system. There are numerous legal rules that make a seller liable when she delivers a *worse* product than what the consumer desired. In the case of premium oil, however, consumers receive a product that is actually *better* than what they needed. In other words, there is no quality problem, only an overpricing problem. And, as we have seen, overpricing is the Achilles' heel of the legal system, because courts are reluctant to go back to the medieval "just price" doctrine.

The problem with most consumer goods is that the experts— the ones with all the product information—have a conflict of interest because they are the ones who also sell the goods. They may know that there are better products or better prices on the market, but they have no natural incentive to reveal this information. The legal system does not give them an incentive to do so either.

How Advice Became More Biased

Biased advice may be an old problem, but it likely has increased in recent decades. For starters, the higher the rents, the stronger the incentive to give biased advice. Experts deliberately recommend the wrong good only if that good is overpriced. In a perfectly competitive market, there is no incentive to give biased advice: prices reflect true costs, so if one product costs more, that only means it requires more work. It is when markets are not perfectly competitive, and prices contain a rent, that experts have an incentive to steer nonexperts to that product with the rent. Since rents have increased dramatically from 1970–2010, the incentive of many experts to give biased advice has become stronger too.

I once needed surgery due to complications of a broken nose (I wasn't paying attention during a basketball practice, turned around, and got a ball right in my face). The surgeon insisted that he remove a wisdom tooth in the same operation. Why did he absolutely want to remove that tooth? It turned out that for that one tooth, he got about the same fee from the insurer as for the complicated nose surgery.

In the US, 18 percent of the GDP goes to health costs. What is the best way to eliminate needless tests and procedures? Well, here is a simple recommendation from rent economics: make sure these procedures are not overpriced. If most rents are removed, the desire to perform needless procedures will be weaker.

A second reason why "seller's bias" has become worse is that marketers are now using "value-based pricing" instead of "cost-plus pricing." Under the good old cost-plus method, where markups were a constant percentage of the price for all products, sellers had only one type of bias: they tried to make consumers spend too much (for instance, make them spend $2,000 instead of $1,000). Within the $2,000 budget, however, the seller was neutral—so he would honestly say what was the best way to spend this amount. But with the newer "value-based pricing method," in which markups vary among goods, the seller may also give biased advice on how to spend the $2,000. In the end, the consumer spends not only too much, but also spends it on the wrong products.

The problem is not innocent. Biased advice wastes a significant share of the GDP. The waste consists not only of needless goods and services but also of consumers not knowing whom to trust anymore and therefore asking for the same advice from many "experts." And, of course, biased advice also leads to more income inequality. Biased advice is not only a consequence of rents but also a source of rents.

Legal Forms of Corruption

When we think of corruption, we usually think of public-sector corruption. A civil servant receives a bribe to award someone an undeserved license, or a police officer receives a bribe to overlook drug trafficking. But corruption can exist in the private sector as well. For instance, a bank CEO may receive a suitcase full of dollars to sign an overly expensive construction contract for new offices. Blatant private-sector corruption is obviously illegal and therefore unlikely to happen on a large scale. But marketers have discovered subtler forms of corruption that are perfectly legal.

Before we can recognize the subtler forms of corruption, we first need to understand what corruption really is. Corruption is a scheme in which a third party bribes a trusted person to abuse the trust of someone else. To use principal-agent terminology, corruption is collusion between an agent and a third party to enrich themselves at the expense of the uninformed principal, whose trust in the agent gets abused. Let's say the agent (remember, that's the party who does the work) is a civil servant, the principal (that's the party for whom the work is done) is a government, and the third party a citizen, who pays the civil servant a bribe to receive an undeserved license. The transaction makes the civil servant and the citizen better off but makes the government worse off.

Very often, there is an informational failure that keeps the mechanism alive. If the principal knows that the agent receives a bribe, she may solve the problem by removing the agent's authority to make such decisions. The informational failure is hard to fix, though, because the agent and the third party tend to be the only ones who know about the bribe, and neither of them has an incentive to inform the principal.

A nice illustration is the *credit yield spread premiums* mortgage brokers used to receive when they manipulated clients into choosing overpriced loans. Suppose that, based on a customer's credit score, the best loan that was available on the market charged $10,000 interest over a certain period. If the broker could falsely convince the customer that the best loan with that credit score charged $15,000 interest, an information rent of $5,000 was created. If this rent was split equally among the broker and the bank, the broker technically received a $2,500 "credit yield spread premium"—a fancy name that means the same as the English word "kickback." (An even more accurate name is "abuse-the-trust-of-your-customer bonus.")

It is easy to see that this kickback scheme has the same structure as corruption. In principal-agent terminology, the customer is the principal, the broker is the agent, and the bank that pays the kickback is the third party. The customer trusts the broker, the broker abuses this trust, and the loot is divided between the broker and the lender.

Kickbacks are highly problematic because they cause market failures. Markets are based on rational, self-interested decision makers. A kickback makes someone do something that is not in her own interest. A customer, for instance, no longer chooses the best loan on the market but one that is $5,000 more expensive. So, kickbacks make markets fail by causing informational distortions.

In 2010, the Dodd-Frank Act prohibited credit yield spread premiums, but only for home mortgage loans. The Dodd-Frank Act, as you may remember, is the major act Congress passed to fix Wall Street after the 2008 crisis. Congress believed that credit yield spread premiums had indirectly contributed to the financial crisis because they made loans more expensive and, therefore, made it harder to pay back these loans. This was the wrong reason to intervene, because kickbacks are much more problematic than that. The right reason would have been that kickbacks are an irrational way to pay brokers, as they reward abuse of trust.

As a result, kickbacks are still legal for many other types of loans, such as car loans, home equity loans, and student loans.[128] Why? Well, the short explanation is that some policymakers believe that kickbacks also have positive effects. So goes the argument: First, kickbacks may lower the fee the client pays to the broker. If the broker gets $2,500 kickbacks, he may pass this on to the customer and charge $2,500 less for the service itself. In that case, forbidding kickbacks could harm consumers by making fees more expensive. Second, kickbacks may give brokers an incentive to search harder. Indeed, a broker who does not search hard is unlikely to find the highest kickback.

Both arguments fail. Empirically, less than 35 percent of the kickbacks are passed on to consumers in the form of lower fees.[129] But even theoretically, kickbacks violate a fundamental axiom of rational contracting—that rational parties will never accept arrangements that reduce the joint surplus. To see why, assume in the previous example that the entire $2,500 kickback was passed on to the consumer. In the end, the consumer has paid $5,000 more for a loan (that is, $15,000 interest instead of $10,000) in order to get $2,500 passed on. That is irrational. The core problem is that the kickback arrangement also benefits the bank that offered it. This $2,500 extra profit for that bank is what economists call a "surplus leakage." Rational parties will always try to avoid surplus leakage to third parties.

Second, kickbacks may give the broker an incentive to search harder, but search harder for what? Kickbacks give an incentive to search for the wrong type of loans. Paying brokers with kickbacks is like paying police officers with bribes. Sure, police officers will get out of their chairs and hit the roads, but when they are on the roads, they may focus on the wrong things.

Another example of a subtle corruption mechanism is fee

splitting among real estate agents. As we have seen, most real estate agents work on a percentage fee, typically 6 percent of the sale price. If the buyer has a real estate agent as well, this fee is often split between both agents—so that each receives 3 percent. At first sight this seems fair. If two people do the work, shouldn't they split the pay?

But upon closer inspection, fee splitting distorts a buyer's real estate agent's incentives. Suppose you hired an agent to help you find a house. On one street, there are two houses that meet your criteria. For the first, your agent would receive 3 percent because of fee splitting. For the second, no such fee splitting is offered. Your agent may show you only the first house.

So, fee splitting has a built-in kickback mechanism. It amounts to an implicit bribe received by the buyer's agent, so long as the buyer is pushed in a certain direction. And the buyer's agent is in a good position to do the pushing, because the buyer trusts her.

But doesn't this differ from plain corruption in that the practice is generally known? That is true in the sense that the buyer could more easily do something about it. In theory, the buyer could demand that the agent passes any kickback fee received on to the buyer. In return, the buyer could promise to pay 3 percent, irrespective of whether fee splitting was offered for that particular house. As a matter of fact, the current practice is puzzling because rational buyers and agents would never agree to let the agent keep kickbacks for the reasons explained in our discussion of credit yield spread premiums. The legal system usually forbids products no rational person would buy, such as exploding toasters. So why can't it forbid kickbacks?

A final example of implicit kickbacks are the fees paid to attorneys in some class action settlements.[130] Class actions are court procedures in which the lawyer does not represent just one client but a whole group of clients. Class actions are important when many victims suffer a small loss. Suppose that a company wrongfully overcharges one million customers $30 each. Nobody would sue for $30. But a million times $30 is $30 million—an amount worth suing for. Class actions permit attorneys to sue on behalf of the entire class of one million victims.

But the problem with class actions is that the attorney is an "agent" working for one million "principals" who have no individual incentive to monitor the agent. That is different from a normal proceeding, in which the attorney works for a single, strongly motivated client. The businesses that are sued in a class action know that the attorney is a nonmonitored agent and try to exploit it by offering a "coupon settlement."

A typical coupon settlement has three components. First, the sued business declares that it did nothing wrong. Second, the consumer attorneys get a fee of a few million dollars. Third, the consumers get coupons, that is, an invitation to buy more products from the same business.

Why do courts ever approve such settlements? Formally, courts need to check whether the settlement is in the interest of the consumers. The legal system knows that class action attorneys are nonmonitored agents and thus requires courts to monitor the attorneys on behalf of the consumers. But in practice, courts tend to be lenient. One problem is that the benefits for consumers are unclear, because, in theory, coupons can be beneficial to those who use them. In practice, the settlement is structured in such a way that this benefit is minimal; for instance, the coupons are nontransferable and cannot be combined with other coupons or promotional benefits. So typically, settlement coupons offer a price reduction that most consumers would have received anyway. But it is hard to formally prove that. Moreover, attorneys fight hard to get their million-dollar fees. And so, courts give up.

The good news is that the legal system is starting to fight back. The Class Action Fairness Act of 2005 does not formally forbid coupon settlements, but it does articulate the principle that attorney fees have to be proportional to the real value to consumers, not the illusory value.[131] This makes it a little harder for businesses to split attorneys and consumers. Unfortunately, it does not fully solve the problem—the proposed settlement just has to offer consumers a little more to get approved.

How could the legal system fully solve the problem? By simply forbidding class action settlements for less than face value. So, if the attorneys claim that the harm to consumers was $30 million, the settlement must pay $30 million compensation, or the case must be brought to court. Sure, settlements can be good for society because they save litigation costs, but here we are faced with a gigantic principal-agent problem. Moreover, settling a claim for a few cents on the dollar (say, settling a $30 million claim for $2 million) is highly problematic. If businesses harm consumers by violating the law, they should pay full compensation. If they don't, they should pay nothing at all. And if the law is unclear, the case should not be settled but instead go to court, where the law can be clarified.

But for now, one-sided class action settlements are still a successful business method. They allow businesses to breach contracts or violate the law and largely get away with it. The method essentially creates a market failure by offering a subtle bribe to an agent (the attorney) so that the principal (the consumer) is undermined from within. Markets work when rational actors pursue their own interests. If actors no longer do so, markets fail. And when markets fail, rents are up for grabs.

Abusing Trust by Letting Customers Sign One-Sided Contracts

Whenever you buy a good or service, you enter into a contract. Most mass-produced goods are accompanied by standard term contracts. When you buy a TV, the warranties and other contract terms may be printed on a card in the box. When you order something on the internet, you may have to click an "I have read and accepted the contract terms" button. When you sign an old-fashioned order sheet, the standard terms may be in fine print on the back of the form.

A few decades ago, economists felt positive about standard term contracts.[132] Standard terms do have economic benefits: They create economies of scale, both in drafting and printing. They avoid that businesses need to draft individual contracts for each customer. In this respect, they are the equivalent of mass-produced goods, which make us richer because of their economies of scale.

Unfortunately, standard terms also involve a danger: hardly anybody reads them, and those who draft them know that. As a matter of fact, who does read them? Maybe a couple of law students. I know many contract law professors and they don't read them. Recent empirical research has shown that even when terms are printed just above the "I agree" button, hardly anybody reads them.[133]

Not reading standard terms makes sense because reading costs time, and even if they were read, most consumers would not understand them anyway. American courts do not seem to realize this. They say that consumers have a "duty to read."[134] Even if consumers didn't read the contract they signed, the contract terms are still binding in principle. Consumers should only blame themselves—they should have read the contracts they have signed.

The problem with not reading standard terms is that it gives sellers an incentive to draft one-sided terms. Since all sellers reason the same way, the outcome is usually that all sellers offer one-sided terms, even in the most competitive markets. Why isn't there a firm that offers better terms in return for a higher price? Because that firm will not attract new consumers when consumers do not know that better terms have been offered. After all, how can they know that if they pay no attention to contract terms?

Here is a paradox: all sellers can say that their contract terms are "very competitive." They can say that their terms are just the industry standard. Indeed, the whole industry offers biased contracts.[135]

What exactly are the biased terms you find in one-sided contracts? One common term is an arbitration clause that bars "class actions." This means that, if the business breached the contract by overbilling each of its one million customers $30, each customer has to sue separately to get the $30 back. In practice, few customers will sue for this amount, and few will even realize they have been overcharged in the first place. This means that the business will get away with a $30 million contract breach.

Other common terms reduce appealing warranties to mere skeletons in the fine print. For instance, the fine print may state that the warranty covers only parts but no labor costs, and that the repair must be done by authorized dealers. These authorized dealers can then overcharge the customer for labor in order to recoup the costs of the parts.

In a few cases, courts may strike down such skeleton warranties, for instance, when they are so extreme that the seller never has to pay anything. There are also a few rules in consumer protection law and in the Uniform Commercial Code that make it harder for the seller to disclaim what they first promised.[136] But there is no criminal penalty or tort liability for inserting one-sided terms that are later set aside by the court—so for sellers it is always worth trying. Moreover, businesses can obtain any desired result because courts don't require warranties to be 100 percent full and courts don't intervene when customers are overcharged for the elements that are not covered (such as labor costs, or the "service call" itself). Remember, theft is illegal, but when it is authorized in a contract, it is legally no longer theft but overpricing, and overpricing is legal.*

Inserting one-sided terms in unread contracts is abusing trust. This idea is clearly expressed in German law, where signing without reading is considered an act of delegation.[137] Basically, the consumer is believed to say, "I don't know anything about these terms, but I give you permission to draft them, and I trust that you will only insert reasonable terms." Unreasonable terms are not binding under German law because the signer never gave permission to draft them. Thus, German law solves the problem by giving a duty-to-draft-fairly to businesses, rather than a duty-to-read to consumers.

---

* Do one-sided contract terms lead to rents? That depends. In a perfect market, the cost savings associated with one-sided terms are passed on to the consumers. In such a market, the consumers do not pay a rent, but only get a product with inferior contract terms—and not the contract terms they would be willing to pay for if they were fully informed. As soon as the market becomes oligopolistic, however, one-sided terms generate rents for the sellers. The reason is that in an oligopolistic market, cost savings are not fully passed on to consumers (the reason why is a little technical, so I'll skip it here, but it is a generally accepted principle of microeconomics).

Why do American courts keep validating one-sided contracts? It has to do with the strength of freedom rhetoric in this country. Freedom is an important value in all societies, but if you can frame a discussion in terms of being for or against freedom in front of an American court, you will win, hands down. Who is against freedom? And who is in favor of the opposite of freedom—oppression, dictatorship, and slavery? Thus, if a one-sided contract is disputed in a legal action, American businesses argue what is at stake is the freedom of individuals in this country. They say that the contracts were freely entered into. They suggest that if these contracts are invalidated, the whole country as it was conceived of by the Founding Fathers will collapse.

This may not sound convincing. But that is only because I presented the fallacy in its most extreme form. You should realize that *rhetoric is the art of using fallacies in small doses.* When doses are small enough, most people no longer recognize the fallacy.

Lobbyists may use similar arguments the next time the government or an agency considers regulating overpriced overdraft protection fees, or overpriced ink cartridges. They may argue that regulation threatens our freedom. They may argue that the government does not know the "just price." They may tell that the government should leave this to the *free* market. (That is like a bank robber saying that the police should mind their own business; of course, bank robbery is harder to defend by appealing to personal freedom.)

A closely related argument is that the market is for grown-ups. So, plumbers may argue that if the legal system did something about overcharging for spare parts, it would treat consumers like children. They may argue that this is not respectful toward consumers—even paternalistic.

The weakness of this rhetorical strategy is that it overlooks the fact that cheating or fooling people is in itself a violation of the freedom of contract. Contracts require "consent" and true consent requires a certain baseline of information. Rules against fraud are as old as contract law itself. Just imagine a contract that stated: "Article 1. Seller has the right to increase the price by fooling the Buyer." Would a rational buyer ever sign such a contract?

Still, in practice, "freedom" remains one of the most attractive arguments because it is not only vague enough to be stretched in any direction but also because it requires some background to recognize when this important principle is turned into a caricature.

There is a remarkable relationship between this ethical rhetoric and the debate on income inequality. The rhetoric transforms what is essentially an economic problem into an ethical problem. It suggests that losing money (through the one-sidedness of contracts) is the result of an individual choice; that those who are wealthy just made better choices; and that those who are poor have only themselves to blame. It is the same line of reasoning that suggest that the solution to income inequality is teaching everyone how to make better choices or sending everyone to college, not stopping practices that are, at their core, abuses of trust.

6

LEGAL WAYS TO
MONOPOLIZE MARKETS

In principle, the legal system tries to prevent the monopolization of markets. It also tries to prevent cartels (agreements to fix prices). Yet marketers have developed techniques to achieve the same outcome in a legal way. As a result, numerous markets have been turned into monopolized or cartelized markets.

Legal Forms of Hold-Up

In the first chapter of this book, we already saw one example of a monopolized market: the market for ink cartridges. Printer companies apply the *razor-blade model* and design printers in such a way that they only work with cartridges from the same company. Consumers therefore have the choice between buying the overpriced cartridges or throwing away the printer.[138] Let's analyze now why exactly this monopolization strategy is legal.

In principle, the legal system forbids hold-ups. You cannot get a rent by telling someone, "Pay me $10,000 or I'll shoot you." You also cannot say, "Buy my overpriced cartridges or I'll destroy your printer." Yet in a less extreme form, some types of hold-up are permitted. You can legally say, "Buy my overpriced cartridges or throw away your printer because it only works with my cartridges." A software company can say, "Buy my overpriced upgrade for your software or lose your data (or build up a new administrative system from scratch)." Such lock-in effects are perfectly legal, even if they are deliberately created as part of a business plan.

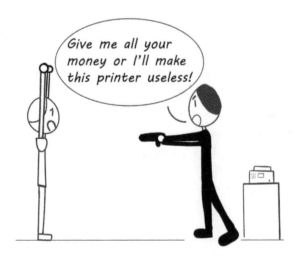

For starters, why are these lock-in strategies allowed under contract law? There is something puzzling about this because contract law attacks the exploitation of lock-in effects under "economic duress." Consider the famous case of the *Alaska Packers Assn. v. Domenico.*[139] A canning company hired fishermen from San Francisco to sail to Alaska and work there during the salmon season. Yet when the fisherman arrived in Alaska (after spending several weeks on a boat en route), they threatened to stop working unless the employer promised to pay a higher wage than originally agreed upon. The employer agreed to their demands because by the time a new crew of fishermen could be hired in San Francisco and brought to Alaska, the salmon season would be over. The court sided with the employer and decided that the renegotiated contract with the higher wage was unenforceable. In other words, the fishermen weren't allowed to keep their rents.

The fishermen in *Alaska Packers* initiated what economists call an opportunistic renegotiation. They waited until the salmon cannery was in a vulnerable position and then exploited that vulnerability by demanding higher wages. Before sailing to Alaska, the fishermen were in a highly competitive market. Once they arrived in Alaska, they were in a monopoly position because it was too late for the cannery to hire other workers.[140]

Why aren't printer companies sued on the basis of the *Alaska Packers* case? One technical difference is that in *Alaska Packers*, an existing contract was renegotiated; the court set aside the new contract with the higher wage and as a result, the old contract (with the lower wage) became binding again. In the printer example, the sale of the printer and the sale of the ink are different contracts. Technically, the printer sales contract is not renegotiated; instead, a separate sales contract (to buy ink) is offered and accepted.

A more important technical difference is that in *Alaska Packers*, the hold-up was a surprise. The fishermen did not announce beforehand that they were going to renegotiate the contract when they arrived in Alaska. Therefore, the employer met one of the conditions of economic duress—the "absence of a reasonable alternative." In the razor-blade model, by contrast, the hold-up is announced beforehand: buyers know in advance that the required ink cartridges are expensive. The ink cartridges are available in the same store. Therefore, courts may conclude that buyers had a reasonable alternative—not buying the printer.

The reason why competition law (also known as "antitrust law") does not intervene is similar. The razor-blade will usually escape antitrust scrutiny, so long as the business did not have a monopoly position in the primary market.[141] In essence (and I'm really simplifying here, because the law is more nuanced and less consistent), antitrust courts say that there is no monopoly problem because we shouldn't look at the ink market but at the printer market. This comes down to saying that consumers can defend themselves by being more careful when they buy a printer.

Rhetorically there is, of course, something fascinating about a lock-in effect in that it creates a monopoly position which the consumer voluntarily steps into. It is like a crime with a willing victim. This is very different from the monopoly position of your local water utility company, where you simply never had a choice but to buy from the utility company. In the case of a printer, you voluntarily decide to buy a product and therefore voluntarily put yourself in a situation where you can and will be exploited.

So, at the heart of a lock-in effect, there must be an informational failure. Consumers buy a printer without *fully* realizing how much they will be overcharged during the life span of the printer. But why don't they realize this? The ink cartridges are available in the same store and are clearly priced, right? One reason is that human beings are irrational. Psychological studies have shown that human beings are inclined to make certain errors of thinking. Moreover, most human beings are bad at math.

But the problem goes beyond bad math. Even if you are good

at math, you wouldn't be able to do the math. Estimating the true expenses for a printer requires knowing the future price of the cartridges, the expected life span of the printer (10,200 pages? 31,500 pages?), the expected repair costs, and the number of pages you will need to print in the future. Some of these costs (such as the future price of cartridges) depend on arbitrary decisions made by the seller (which are hard for you to predict). Other costs depend on statistical probabilities (how often does such a printer need to be repaired and what is the average repair cost? How many pages can these printers print on average before falling apart?). Sellers may have data on this, but they have no incentive to reveal it.

Don't manufacturers have to disclose the expected true ownership costs of a printer? No, they don't. The legal system believes it is the consumer's responsibility to find that out. That is not very logical because the law usually requires the "least-cost information gatherer" to disclose the information; the printer company is the least-cost information gatherer here, that is, the party that is in the best position to produce this important piece of information.

Upsell! Upsell! Upsell!
A Legal Form of Monopoly Pricing

I once entered a take-out pizza restaurant and noticed that the woman who took my order constantly looked at a sign on the wall that was angled so that customers could not read it. When she went into the kitchen, I leaned forward to read the paper. It had ten marketing instructions, but the first was printed in bold and in a huge font. It read: "Upsell! Upsell! Upsell!" Upselling is jargon for selling extras to an existing customer. "Do you want to make it an extra-large? Double the cheese?

Add breadsticks and a 2-liter soda? Maybe add some wings to really set this pizza off?"

Why was upselling so much more important than all the other instructions? Because it is a legal form of monopoly pricing. Sure, there are many pizza stores in every city, but once you have entered a store and ordered a pizza, there is no longer any competition for the extras. Suppose I find the $3.99 for the extra two inches of pizza excessive. I cannot take my baked pizza to another store and ask them to enlarge it by two inches for a more reasonable price. In some other cases, you are not even allowed to buy the extras elsewhere. If you want to drink wine in a restaurant, you are not allowed to bring in your own bottle— you must pay the restaurant's monopoly price. Why is wine often more expensive than food in restaurants? Because most consumers choose the restaurant on the basis of its food prices, not the prices of its upsold products such as wine.

Of course, if consumers were perfectly rational and informed, they would take the price of the upselling into account when they chose a restaurant. In that case, it would not help the store to have larger profit margins on upsold products than on the basic ones. But considering the prices of both the regular products and the "upsold" products really requires a lot from simple human beings like you and me.

Why is upselling a *legal* form of monopoly pricing? What upselling does is essentially exploit *natural lock-in effects*. Once consumers have decided on the main order, they are locked in for the side orders. If deliberately created lock-in effects are legal, natural lock-in effects are definitely legal. As a matter of fact, it isn't even a strategy to monopolize a market; the monopoly is there already, naturally. It doesn't have to be created—it only has to be exploited.

Natural lock-in effects also exist in the market for spare parts. I once bought a $200 vacuum cleaner. In the box, I found an order form for replacement parts. When the vacuum's hose broke a year later, I noticed that the price for a replacement hose on that form was only $49. I was perplexed that it did not cost more. Sure, it probably costs less than $10 to produce such a hose, but still, $49 is far below the monopoly price because my only alternative to buying the replacement part was to throw away the vacuum cleaner. The only logical conclusion I could come up was that this vacuum company was one of the remaining companies who had never hired a pricing consultant. Two days later I got a call—whether I wanted to continue with the order. The hose no longer cost $49 but $79. Apparently, they had hired a pricing consultant since I had bought my vacuum.

I paid $79—way above the likely production costs of this single part but still cheaper than buying a new vacuum. This is exactly what a monopolist does: charging a lot but not so much that the consumer no longer buys it. Still, why didn't I look for a cheaper alternative on the market? Well, maybe there was one, but markets are foggy. Simply finding out which hose would fit is costly. And why don't vacuum manufacturers standardize their hoses so that each hose fits all models? Well, that's asking why manufacturers don't work together to *reduce* rents.

Natural lock-in effects are not limited to the goods market. As a matter of fact, they may even be stronger in the services market because service providers tend to acquire customer-specific information, which naturally increases the cost of switching to another service provider. When you switch to another lawyer halfway through a case, the new lawyer will have to memorize the facts of your case again, which is costly to you. This gives a subtle form of market power to your lawyer, your accountant, your doctor (to the extent that prices are freely negotiable), and even to your sprinkler service company (which may be the only one that knows where all the lines are buried). Because of the switching costs, these service providers may charge a premium to existing customers—in a subtle way of course, without openly telling you that's what they're doing.

The fact that locked-in customers are gold mines has a counterintuitive implication: a company's most loyal customers pay the highest price! This is contrary to social norms; you'd expect that your best friends get the best treatment. But for businesses, letting loyal customers pay more makes sense because they are the "high-value types" and sellers can extract more value from them. From a negotiation perspective, it makes sense because these high-value customers are most attached to your products (and in this sense locked in), and therefore have more to lose than other customers when prices are renegotiated. From a search cost perspective, it makes sense as well, because loyal customers are those who have stopped searching, and therefore are least informed about market prices.

Why is it legal to charge more to your loyal customers? Here we are back to the Achilles' heel of the legal system: overpricing. Courts don't want to intervene when businesses charge too much because this would require courts to know what the "just price" is.

Legal Forms of Cartels

Cartels are agreements between businesses to fix prices at an artificially high level. In the old days, business owners came together in smoky rooms to agree on uniform prices in an industry. Cartels are economically harmful because they stop price competition. Cartels also increase income inequality by giving participating businesses an easy rent.

Obviously, explicit cartels are illegal. If authorities discover that businesspeople have gathered in a smoky room to fix prices, these businesspeople may spend some time in jail. Nonetheless, marketers have developed perfectly legal strategies to obtain the same results.

To understand these strategies, bear in mind that oligopolistic prices are naturally indeterminate because they depend on the players' strategy.* If businesses are friendly to each other and do not compete on price, oligopolistic prices may be as high as monopoly prices. If businesses are aggressive and fight price wars, oligopolistic prices may be as low as perfect market prices.

Fortunately for society, and unfortunately for businesses, two human instincts make price wars more likely than high prices. First, people tend to think in the short run. If you lower your prices, your sales volume will go up in the short run; in the long run, when your competitors have adjusted their prices as well, your profits will likely go down because of lower overall prices in the industry. If human beings would think in the long run, they would rarely start price wars; but in practice, people tend to think only one move ahead. Second, human beings tend to fight back. When you see a competitor lower her prices, your gut reaction is to lower yours even further. But this gut reaction causes a downward spiral that may eliminate all rents in the industry.

A few decades ago, when businesspeople were not formally trained to play the oligopoly game, there was a good chance that oligopolistic prices were as low as perfect market prices. But in the meantime, business schools have figured out how to play the game better.

First, business schools now teach you not to follow your gut reaction. Instead, you need to think about the likely reactions of your competitors, which will probably make you realize that a price war is not in your long-term interests. So a first principle

---

* This is not the case in perfect markets and monopolistic markets. In a perfect market, competition drives prices down until all rents are dissipated. In a monopolistic market, the monopolist sets the prices above the true costs so as to maximize rents. But in an oligopolistic market (with only two or a few competitors), prices can go either way.

you should memorize for the exam is that you should never start a "price war."[142]

Second, business schools teach you that, when a competitor is foolish enough to start a price war, you should consider other options than lowering your prices. For instance, you could try to compete on quality instead of price; warn customers about the risks associated with the cheaper products; create new products; or lower the cost of delivery or operation.[143] And if you have to lower your price, lower it only for those who are aware of the lower prices. Or lower it by creating a cheaper second brand with lower-quality products that are appealing only to price-sensitive buyers.[144]

Business schools will also tell you that if a customer claims prices are lower elsewhere, you should always double-check. Indeed, sometimes price wars are started by a single customer falsely claiming that she has been offered a better price elsewhere. If the business immediately matches the price without checking the statement, and competing businesses hear about the lower price, they may lower their prices in turn, starting a price war. So, double-checking competitors' prices is a simple little trick to prevent many price wars.[145]

Surprisingly, business schools will also teach you that, in some cases, you should do the exact opposite of the previous strategies and immediately retaliate if a competitor lowers prices by lowering yours as well.[146] At first sight, this strategy seems puzzling. If all businesses keep their finger on the trigger, price wars can be started by the slightest price change.

To understand how such a strategy may nonetheless work, note that lowering prices has a short-term advantage (a higher sales volume) and a long-term disadvantage (lower overall prices in the industry). The short-term advantage is essentially a first-mover advantage: the business that lowers its prices first has an advantage over the businesses that do it later. The longer those businesses take to react, the larger the first-mover advantage, and the more attractive it becomes to compete on price. So, if the first-mover advantage can be kept small enough by immediately responding, the incentive to be the first to lower prices can be removed. As price consultants Nagle and his colleagues write, "Why would an opportunist ever cut prices if it believed that other companies were willing to retaliate? The answer is that the opportunist's management believes that, by quietly negotiating or concealing its price cuts, it can gain sufficient sales volume to justify the move before the competitors find out.... To minimize such opportunistic behavior, competitors must identify and react to it as quickly as possible."[147] (Note that the English term "opportunist" is used here to describe someone who deviates from the implicit cartel!) The strategy works when all players are rational—when they are all trained by business schools.

Fortunately for businesses (and unfortunately for society), new technology has made it easier to reduce first-mover advantages. In the old days before the invention of the internet (that's a long time ago; I vaguely recall that dinosaurs were still alive and human beings still breathed through gills), it could take weeks for competitors to discover price cuts and even longer to implement price changes. Indeed, when price lists were still printed in yearly catalogues, it could take a full year for competitors to adjust their prices. But in the electronic age, adjusting prices has literally become a matter of days, or even milliseconds—if competitors' prices are available in electronic form, software can constantly monitor these prices and automatically lower prices in response to price cuts.

Quickly adapting prices is also a great strategy in the other direction—for price increases. The problem with price increases (from the businesses' perspective) is that the one who takes the initiative incurs a short-term loss. So, as price consultant Nagle and his coauthors note, "If competitors quickly follow price increases, the cost of leading such increases is vastly reduced.

Consequently, companies that wish to encourage responsible leadership by other firms would do well to follow their moves quickly, whether up or down."[148] (Note that the English term "responsible" is used here in a somewhat strange way, as a synonym for the English term "irresponsible.")

Why are all these strategies legal? Well, while explicit cartels are forbidden, there is no legal duty to follow a certain pricing strategy. If you follow a certain strategy, you apparently do nothing wrong—you just apply what you learned at business school. The deeper reason is that legal systems would have a hard time defining the boundaries of such an implicit-cartel doctrine. Should businesses be legally obliged to start price wars? Should they be legally obliged to lower their prices until the perfectly competitive equilibrium is reached? But how do courts know that prices are low enough? This requires them to know the "just price." And so again, this brings us to the Achilles' heel of the legal system: overpricing. Courts can ban explicit cartels because doing so only requires knowing who gathered in that smoky room and what they agreed upon (this may not always be easy to prove, but at least it is provable in theory, and the legal system can make up for this by increasing the punishment in those cases in which there was evidence or by offering rewards to whistleblowers). To throw members of a cartel in jail, courts do not need to know what the perfect market price would have been in the absence of the cartel. But to create a legal duty to lower prices until they reach the perfect market price, courts would have to know the "just price," which courts tried to do in medieval times but have since given up on.

Even Subtler Forms of Cartels

Marketers often recommend brand owners create a *flanking brand*. This is a brand created solely to prevent competitors from entering the market.[149] It is, in other words, a brand that is meant to create a barrier to entry.

Without flanking brands, markets often develop as follows. First, an innovator enters the market. Second, an imitator enters with a cheaper, lower-quality product. Once the imitator learns how to make better products, she moves up price-wise, occupying the middle. Then, a third entrant fills the gap in the market by offering cheaper, lower-quality products. Eventually, there are three businesses in the market. They all occupy a somewhat different segment but nonetheless compete on price.[150]

If these three businesses could sit together in a smoky room and fix prices, that would be great for them. But explicit cartels are illegal. Another way to obtain the same result would be to merge the three businesses. But mergers that monopolize a market are forbidden as well.

So here is a strategy to obtain the desired result without violating the law: the innovator develops flanking brands that cover the lower and middle market segments. This way, there is never an unserved market segment that competitors can use to enter the market. Eventually, there may be three brands in the market, but they are all owned by the same company. All prices are fixed in one office, but since it is just a single company exercising its legal right to set prices for its products, it is not an illegal cartel.

Flanking brands have other "benefits" as well. One is that such a brand can be "killed" at any time. For instance, if there is no immediate threat of a new entrant, products of the cheaper brand can be made "temporary unavailable" so that consumers are forced to buy the more expensive brand.[151] Very effective, and perfectly legal. (This is legal because contractual freedom also includes "freedom from contract." Parties can sign contracts, but they do not have to. So, sellers can sell products, but they are never forced to keep selling these products.)

Here is an even subtler form of an implicit cartel: Create three brands, all with three or four products. Rent an entire shelf at a local supermarket to put them on (this is a very common practice—I am not making this up). Consumers now see ten different products from three different brands. While there may be hundreds of products and dozens of brands in the market, consumers have no time to study them all and so they compare just the ten that are available, apparently preselected, in their local store. Consumers also think these products are competitively priced because, after all, they came from three different brands. But what consumers don't know is that all three brands are owned by the same company. All the prices are set at the same office.

If these three brands had three different owners and all the prices had been jointly fixed, that would have been an illegal cartel. But since all the brands that are visible to this consumer are owned by the same company, there is nothing illegal about it. It is a *perfectly legal form of a cartel*—a cartel between a business and itself, so to speak.

Once again, a marketing strategy has been developed that makes markets fail in a legal way.

Payer Externalities: Letting Someone Else Pay the Bill

Credit card companies, such as Visa and Mastercard, charge stores hefty fees for the use of credit cards by their customers. Typically, the fee is between 3 and 4 percent of the purchase price—a puzzling amount for a service that is largely done by computers. Credit card issuers argue that this price is low compared to the offered "value"; that credit cards are more convenient than cash payments or checks; and that sellers have the benefit of selling goods to consumers who wouldn't have enough money without some form of credit. So, without the credit card, there would be no sale.

This last argument is puzzling, not so much from an economic point of view but from a logical point of view. The argument basically says that a credit card can be a *necessary condition* for some buyers to buy the good. That may be true, but there are hundreds of such conditions. Shoemakers could also claim 3–4 percent on all purchases because without shoes, people would not be able to go to the store—definitely not in the winter. Raincoat manufacturers could say the same in Seattle, Ireland, and Belgium. Shopping would also not be possible without electricity, roads, light bulbs, and so on. If all those companies whose products are a necessary condition for shopping could claim 3–4 percent of the purchase price, 100 percent would not be enough to cover all claims.

The first argument, that credit cards create value, sounds logical, but it is still puzzling from an economic point of view. In a perfectly competitive market, as we have seen in chapter 1, prices depend only on costs, not on value. So, the very fact that a company can capture some of the "value" suggests there is a market failure.

But what market failure? The market failure you get when *those who decide whether to use a product are not the ones who pay for it.* I will use the new term *payer externalities* to refer to this specific type of market failure.[152]

Here is how it works. Buyers decide whether they are going to use a debit or credit card to pay. A debit card costs nearly nothing to the store, which makes sense, because the true costs are also nearly nothing.[153] A credit card costs much more—let us say 3 percent (of the purchase price) more than a debit card. But a credit card pays 1 percent back to the buyer in the form of "cash rewards," "points," or "miles." So, the buyer chooses the credit card to get the "miles." But in order to get a 1 percent reward, he causes a 3 percent cost at the store's side. The difference is a 2 percent profit for the credit card issuer.

What is puzzling about this is that the outcome violates a fundamental axiom of rational contracting: contract parties will in principle never allow one of them to do something that costs more to the other party than it benefits the first party. If a rational buyer and seller would sit together to discuss the terms of contract, they would never agree that the seller will bear a cost of 3 percent in order to give the buyer a benefit of 1 percent. Instead they would agree to pay via a debit card.

So here is a way to look at it. If the buyer would act in the joint interest of the buyer and seller, she would pay by debit card. But the buyer is bribed by the credit card company to do something that is not in the joint interest of the buyer and seller. The kickback is the 1 percent "miles."

Another way to look at it is that this business model takes a general principle of product pricing to its extremes. Open a marketing book and you will read that prices should be set higher if demand is less "elastic." And when is demand less elastic? One case is when the one who chooses the product is not the one who pays for it. This explains, for instance, why services delivered to businesses tend to be more expensive than the services delivered to consumers (the employees who order these services for their employers are not the ones who pay for it). It also explains why medical services can be so expensive (the patients who demand them are not the ones who pay for them when they have insurance). In the credit card example, it is the buyer who decides how to pay. And so, credit card issuers have to make sure that it is not the buyer who pays the bill, but the seller. Since the buyer pays zero percent of the bill, the demand is very inelastic. Therefore, the bill to the store can be sky-high.

Of course, in the long run it is the consumers who pay the bill.

All stores face the same costs, and so they may pass on these costs to the consumers. But there is a difference between the outcome for the consumers as a group and the outcome for an individual consumer. If you stop using credit cards, you will still pay the higher prices, which are needed to recoup the credit card costs caused by the other consumers. In other words, there is what economists call a *collective action problem* among consumers. If all consumers would sit together and agree, they would agree to use cheaper payment forms. But they don't.

Why doesn't the seller offer a 2 percent price reduction if the buyer does not pay by credit card? This would be an application of the famous Coase Theorem. This theorem says that in the absence of transaction costs, the initial distribution of rights does not matter to the outcome if parties can negotiate. This may sound somewhat abstract, but in this case it means that it should not matter whether credit card companies make the buyer or the seller pay. If buyers and sellers can negotiate, they will always jointly decide to use the cheaper payment form. But why does this not happen in practice? Because stores are not allowed to do this according to the contracts they have to sign with Visa and Mastercard.[154]

The success story of Visa and Mastercard is the success story of a business model. First, the business model makes sure that the one who decides is not the one who pays. Second, it makes sure that the one who decides makes the wrong choice (wrong from the perspective of the joint interest of customer and store, not wrong from the perspective of the credit card company) by receiving kickbacks in the form of miles. Third, it levers the network externalities associated with credit cards (another source of market failure) into a contractual provision that forbids the store from passing on the costs to the customer. And fourth, there is a collective action problem among consumers. Quite a powerful mix of market failures!

How could the legal system correct this? Very simply, by requiring that the decision maker pay. If that were the case, I would immediately stop using credit cards. Why would I pay 3 percent more to get 1 percent back in the form of miles? Most consumers would reason the same way. So, a simple legal rule could eliminate billions of dollars of rents.

Here is another illustration of the same type of market failure: expensive college textbooks. College textbooks have indeed become remarkably expensive over the last couple of decades. A typical casebook for first-year law students costs between $150 and $200—a lot of money for reprinting content (published cases) that is largely in the public domain.

At first glance, the market for college books has all the ingredients for healthy competition. There are many publishers, many authors, and many students. There is no price regulation and no legal barriers for entry. So, what is the market failure that prevents competition from driving down the prices?

Again, it is the market failure you get when those who decide what textbook to use are not the ones who pay for it. Professors decide what textbook to use; students pay for it.

Still, why wouldn't professors take prices into account? Well, they do, but not to the full extent. Suppose that a new textbook comes on the market that is $100 cheaper than the version a professor currently uses. The professor has 100 students. That means that the new textbook would save $10,000. But switching textbooks requires extra work for the professor—no textbook is 100 percent the same, and adapting courses requires extra time of preparation. Let's assume that the opportunity cost of the professor's time is $5,000. If the professor were required to pay for all the textbooks out of her own pocket, she would switch. But that is not the case. The extra work is internalized by the professor and the cost savings are externalized.

This incentive problem has the same structure as in the credit card example. There, the decision maker internalized the benefit of the miles but not the cost of using the card. Here, the decision maker internalizes the benefit of less work but not the cost of more expensive textbooks. So, there is a similar market failure, leading to similarly high rents for publishers.

Once again, we have to ask why the market does not solve this market failure. Why don't universities pay for the textbooks (providing them for free to the students) and raise tuition to finance the increased expenses? At first sight, this would be a zero-sum operation, and in practice it could be a win-win situation because universities would then have strong incentives to pay more attention to prices. One market failure that prevents this from happening is that students who select a university typically pay less attention to the costs of the books than to the tuition. Another market failure is that there may be "non-convexity"—a technical term meaning that the first university to do so would not benefit from it because cheaper textbooks would only enter the market if many universities would do the same.

How could the legal system cure this market failure? Very simply, by making the decision maker pay. In this case, this would mean that the legal system could make it mandatory for universities to pay for the mandatory textbooks. Sure, indirectly, the students would still pay for the textbooks in the form of higher tuition. But since the textbooks would become cheaper, there would be an overall saving for students.

This legal solution may look far-reaching, but it is nothing special, if you think about it. This is basically what the law does to remedy pollution problems. Pollution is caused by an analogous incentive mechanism as the one discussed: the decision maker, the polluter, has the benefit of the polluting activity but does not bear the cost. So, the law makes the polluter pay. This way, the decision maker internalizes not only the benefits but also the costs.

Situational Monopolies

I once traveled from the US to Brussels, and then from Brussels to Vienna. For each of these flights, I used different airlines. For the flight from the US to Brussels, I knew that the weight limit for my luggage was 50 pounds and so I made sure I had only 49 pounds. But sixty minutes before my flight to Vienna I was told that the weight limit for that airline was only 44 pounds (20 kg). I was asked whether I wanted to leave my luggage in Brussels (and in practice also miss my flight and my appointment) or pay the extra fee. I paid the extra fee because I had no reasonable alternative. I eventually paid more for those 4 extra pounds than for the entire ticket.[155]

Paying more for 4 pounds (of extra luggage) than for 204 pounds (44 pounds of luggage plus my body weight) may sound absurd, but it makes sense from a business perspective. When I ordered the ticket, I still could choose among many airlines and so I paid the competitive price. Sixty minutes before my flight, I had no choice and so I paid the monopoly price.

It is the same logic that explains why there are higher profit margins on wine than on food in restaurants, and why upselling is so profitable. But the logic is more compulsive here—there is less of a true choice.

Why doesn't the legal system step in? It does, but only when the temporary monopoly position is more extreme. Consider the classic Desert Hypothetical (a favorite of many contract law professors). You are driving through the desert in your Jeep, and you suddenly run out of gas. Since hardly anybody travels through this part of the desert, you know you have a 99 percent chance of dying. But suddenly, out of the blue, another car drives by. You ask the driver to bring you to the next town, but he will only agree to save your life if you promise to pay him $1 million for this "taxi service." You agree to the price, but later take your taxi driver to court. The court will bail you out: it will strike down the contract on the basis of "duress."[156] And this makes sense: the taxi driver's monopoly was just temporary and coincidental. There is no reason why this coincidence should make the taxi driver wealthy and you poor.

By the same logic, there is no reason why 4 extra pounds on an airplane should have such a redistributive effect. But courts are reluctant to intervene in contracts of only a couple of hundred dollars. It may be easy to say that the price is too high, but much harder to say what should have been the right price.

The Diamond Paradox: How Even Small Search Costs Can Lead to Monopoly Prices in Competitive Markets

In a 1971 paper, Peter Diamond identified one of the greatest paradoxes of nontransparent markets: that in apparently competitive markets monopoly prices may be asked, as soon as there are search costs.[157] Here is a simplified version of his model: Suppose there is a market with an infinite number of suppliers, and suppose that each of them asks the perfect market price of $100, reflecting only the true costs and leaving no rents for the supplier. But unfortunately, there are search costs on the market. Consumers cannot know the price of a supplier for sure unless they go to her (for instance, by entering into her shop) and ask for it. After they learn the price, they may decide to buy the product there or move on to the next shop, hoping to find a lower price. Suppose that each time they move to another shop they incur a cost of $20 (in the form of transport expenses and time lost).

Here is how all suppliers end up asking the monopoly price.

The owner of that first shop knows that the price elsewhere is $100. What price should she ask? She knows that if her price is, for instance, $110, the consumer (who guesses that the price elsewhere will be $100) will not move to the next shop, because in that case he would pay $100 + $20 = $120. So, the owner of the shop asks $110. But all other sellers reason along the same lines and set their prices at $110 as well. The market price is now $110. What happens in the next round of the model? The seller sets her prices at $120, because the consumer will now pay $110 + $20 if he buys it elsewhere. All sellers reason similarly and set their price at $120. The market price is now $120. The next round, all sellers increase their prices to $130, and in the following round to $140. Where does this end? Diamond showed that the equilibrium price will be the monopoly price. Why not higher? If a seller would ask more than a monopolist, too many consumers would stop buying the product and simply switch to substitute products.

The Diamond paradox has several amazing aspects. First, it is amazing that a *very small search cost* (called an "epsilon" search cost) is sufficient to transform a perfect market into one with monopoly prices. Second, the *monopoly price is the market price*! All sellers can say that they only ask the market price. *They can say that their prices are very competitive*—they are, if we compare them to the others in the industry who all ask a monopoly price, but not if we compare them to what would be the price in a perfect market. Third, *it makes no sense for consumers to search*! They can go to another shop, but the price will be the same monopoly price. Because consumers give up searching, the equilibrium is written in stone.

The Diamond equilibrium can also exacerbate lock-in effects. Suppose your $1,000 furnace is broken. You call a repair company who will charge you $80 just for the "service call" (i.e., to come to your house). Suppose the problem can immediately be repaired, at a true cost of $100, and suppose that all other firms on the market charge just $100 for the repair itself. But letting another company do the repair requires paying another $80 for the service call, and therefore it will cost $180. Letting the incumbent do the repair costs only an additional $100, because the service call has to be paid anyway. A rational repair firm will exploit this switching cost and charge, for instance, $140 for the repair, knowing that switching to a competitor would cost the consumer even more. Since all repair firms increase their prices for the same reason, the market price becomes $140. In the second round (the next year, for instance), the market price will go up to $180, and so on, until the monopoly price is reached.

Let us analyze the source of the rent more closely in the previous case. When the price is still $140 (in the first round), the rent (the overpricing of $40) was caused by a lock-in effect: once the technician was in the house and the homeowner already owed a payment for the service call, the homeowner was locked in to the repair firm (because switching to another firm would cost $80). But the price increases in the following rounds are caused by a Diamond spiral rather than by the lock-in effect, which remained constant. In short, a Diamond equilibrium needs a trigger, and this trigger can be not only a search cost but also a switching cost (the same cost that causes the lock-in effect).

Is the Diamond equilibrium a theoretical curiosum, or a phenomenon that regularly occurs in real markets? Unfortunately, it is the latter.[158] The Diamond equilibrium predicts, for instance, that you will pay monopoly prices in the appliance repair market. There may be hundreds of companies in the market, but you don't see their prices until you have paid them a "service call" or an "inspection fee." Still, is this cost significant enough to cause a Diamond spiral?

Let's do the test. I first sent a broken espresso machine (that I bought for $300) to a repairer in Texas (who advertised "reasonable fees"). How much would a monopolist charge? My guess is about 40 percent of the price of a new product. A monopolist would never charge more than 50 percent because then most consumers would rather throw away the defective product and buy a new one. As it turns out, the Texas repairer charged me about $120 (including shipping and "handling" and including $3 for a new bolt), which corresponds to 40 percent of the replacement cost. I next let a large repair company come to our home to repair a broken downdraft in the kitchen. The price was $445.95, or about 40 percent of the replacement cost (which was $999.99 plus taxes). Maybe you can do the test too?[159]

7

GETTING AWAY WITH FRAUD

A couple of years ago, a friend of mine was driving through a nearby city when he saw a giant "liquidation sale" board above a piano shop. Although he hadn't planned to buy a piano that day, he stopped to take a look inside. There, he found a digital piano that had a "regular price" of about $10,000 and was offered for only $4,000. "But hurry," said the salesman, "this is our very last weekend." My friend realized this might have been a unique opportunity to buy a great piano for a low price and wrote a $4,000 check. The piano was delivered the next day.

A few days later, he searched the internet to see how much others paid for such a piano. To his surprise, the price was nowhere higher than $4,000 and in some places several hundred dollars cheaper. Many years later, the same piano shop was still open, and the "liquidation sale" board was still hanging above its door.

My friend had been misled in two ways. First, he was made to believe that the regular price was $10,000. In reality, the market price was less than $4,000. Second, he was made to believe that there was no time to carefully compare alternative offerings on the market. In reality, there was no reason to hurry.

Was this trade practice legal? No. Misstating the regular price and misstating the period in which the sales offer will remain open are two deceptive practices that are forbidden under consumer protection regulation.[160] The Federal Trade Commission (FTC), the government agency responsible for enforcing violations of the FTC Act, clearly says so in its official "Guides." In addition, these two statements fell under the legal definition of fraudulent misrepresentation. Therefore, the seller violated contract law (and even tort law).

If this practice was illegal, why didn't my friend sue? Well, he only lost a few hundred dollars at most. The litigation costs would have been much higher. A class action wasn't possible either because the wrongdoer wasn't a large business. Even if he could have identified a few hundred buyers who had each lost a few hundred dollars, no attorney would have taken the case.

Still, if the seller violated the FTC Guides, why didn't the seller get in trouble with the FTC? For starters, the FTC has a small budget and the United States is a large country, so the chance of getting sued by the FTC is about the same as the chance of dying by having a pot of flowers fall on your head. Even worse, the FTC all but formally stopped prosecuting reference price misrepresentations in 1969.[161] The FTC concluded that these cases are too expensive to prove and that its budget could better be used to prosecute more harmful violations. State attorneys general rarely prosecute such cases either.

But the bottom line is that the seller committed fraud and got away with it.

In this chapter, I show that this anecdote is no exception. Fraud is a *massive* problem in current markets. While most of these practices are illegal, violators get away with it. And remarkably, some forms of fraud are even legal. This is one of the reasons why information rents are high in our economy.

Getting Away with False Differentiation Claims

Bayer Aspirin costs about three times more than CVS private-label generic aspirin that has the same active ingredient, dosage, and directions. Who buys Bayer Aspirin? Well, not the pharmacists themselves, as I mentioned earlier in the book. Recent empirical research shows that pharmacists, physicians, and nurses nearly always buy the generic versions for their own use.[162] Moreover, the FDA assures on its website that generic drugs are just as safe and effective as the original drugs.[163] This suggests that those who pay the brand premium are simply misinformed.

Bayer's original aspirin patent expired in 1917. Conventional economic wisdom predicts that once a patent has expired, competition will quickly drive down prices as new competitors enter the market. Yet a century later, Bayer still has market power. It can still charge premium prices, not because it has a patent, but because some buyers are misinformed.

Misinformed by whom? In the early 1980s, one could easily say that it was by Bayer. At that time, Bayer advertised on a large scale that it had "the world's best Aspirin." Literally, that statement was correct. Since all aspirin companies produce the same substance, they can all claim that they have the world's best aspirin—no one is better. In reality, most people interpret such claims to mean that Bayer Aspirin is different from other aspirins. And the law had abandoned the "literally correct" criterion several decades before. In modern law, the criterion is whether a statement effectively misleads (in contract law) or has the "capacity to mislead" (in consumer protection law). So, Bayer was sued, and believe it or not . . . they won.[164] Why?

Because the FTC considered the statement to be mere puffery—an entertaining exaggeration that nobody takes seriously. But if nobody takes Bayer's claim seriously, why do so many people pay the premium price for it?

That was thirty-five years ago. On their current website (which they named wonderdrug.com, which is literally correct because all aspirin does wonders, including Bayer Aspirin), they describe the benefits of aspirin in general and add, "No other leading brand of pain reliever can do that."[165] Literally, this is correct because Bayer is the only leading brand for aspirin. In response to the FAQ "Is aspirin safe?" they write, "Bayer Aspirin is safe and effective for pain relief when used according to label directions."[166] Again, this is literally correct, because all aspirin on the market is safe according to the FDA, including Bayer Aspirin. Yet implicitly, they suggest there is something better about Bayer's product.

In ads, Bayer tends to avoid clear statements as well. All you see are people who feel good after having taken Bayer Aspirin. Literally, these ads do not say Bayer is any different from or superior to generic aspirin. But there is an implicit *uniqueness* claim. The ads suggest that it's rational to take Bayer Aspirin. But if Bayer aspirin is no different from the generics that are three times cheaper, it would no longer be rational to buy the branded product.

Still, most of the work is done by simply putting the products on the shelf and charging three times more. If two products differ in price and the store does not state that they are identical, many consumers will believe there must be a difference.

At the end of the day, a seller receives a large rent as result of a *false differentiation claim*—a claim that a product is different from competing products when it isn't, or that the differences are larger than they really are.

Are false differentiation claims legal? Yes and no. They are legal in that courts are likely to conclude that they are legal. Courts may conclude that the differentiation is puffery, or that the seller has not made a manifestly false claim that violates advertisement regulation, or that buyers cannot reasonably rely on such implicit suggestions.

These claims are illegal, however, in that they violate many principles clearly established in the law. First, there is a contract law rule stating that there is a duty to disclose information if you are aware that the other party is under a mistaken impression.[167] Second, in consumer law, a practice is deceptive if it has the capacity to mislead a significant number of consumers acting reasonably under the circumstances. If so many consumers are paying the premium price, isn't that enough evidence that reasonable people are being misled? Third, the rule that any impression you give is okay so long as you do not make literally false statements was abandoned many decades ago. Fourth, the party that is the "least-cost producer of information" usually has to disclose that information.[168] We apply this rule for the side effects of drugs: pharmaceutical companies are in a better position to study the side effects than ordinary consumers, and therefore we force the former to disclose this information. Also here, Bayer is in the best position to know whether competing brands of aspirin are different. So, why should it be the consumers' responsibility to find that out? Fifth, putting two identical products in the shelves with only different brand names and prices may be a *subtle* form of fraud, but nothing in the law says that fraud is okay so long as it is subtle.

Still, let us ask the "so what" question. Maybe companies should be a little more careful with what they claim in ads. Maybe courts should narrow down their definition of puffery a little. Is this really a major economic problem? And is this really substantially contributing to income inequality?

For starters, it's not only Bayer. Go to a pharmacy and you

will see that, for most drugs, there are both brand-name and generic versions. If many consumers buy the brand, we are talking about a massive problem. And it's not only the drug market. False differentiation is the secret success formula behind many brand products. Many of those products don't differ from nonbranded products. Many others differ but the differences are much smaller than consumers are made to believe. From this perspective, the essence of brand marketing is to increase the number of misinformed people—who either believe there is a difference when there is no difference or believe there is a large difference when there is only a small one.

False differentiation claims may look innocent until you realize the scale at which this takes place. Consider all the products you bought last month. How much could you have saved had you had perfect information on all the branded and nonbranded products on the market? A recent study calculated that all consumers taken together could have saved 5 percent on health-related products.[169] Well, if that was the average for the entire economy, then 5 percent of the national income went to rents (or rent-seeking costs) caused by false differentiation claims. Not exactly a minor problem!

Misleading Look-No-Further Stories— Learning from Swindlers

A look-no-further story is a story meant to make people stop searching. In the previous piano shop anecdote, the "story" was that the store would close its doors the next day, and that the piano that was offered for $4,000 cost $10,000 elsewhere. This had two look-no-further elements. First, if the store closed the next day, there was apparently no time to look further. Second, if the regular price was $10,000, trying to find an even lower price than $4,000 was apparently a waste of time. The story worked. My friend looked no further and bought the piano.

Look-no-further stories play a large role in marketing. To understand how they work, we need to better understand how stories affect decisions. And to do so, we may want to study the grand masters of manipulation—swindlers!

Swindlers try to steal other people's money, but they don't use brute force to get it. Instead, they use deception to make the victim voluntarily give them the money. By the time the victim has discovered the fraud, the money is gone.

In 1976, Yale Law professor Arthur Leff wrote a book entitled *Selling and Swindling*, in which he argued that there is a remarkable similarity between these two activities.[170] For the sake of clarity, Leff did not say that all sellers are swindlers. What he did say is that all swindlers are sellers, and that swindling is the most difficult form of selling—in other words, swindlers are the Olympians of selling.

Swindling is different from ordinary stealing, because swindling is a crime that requires the initial consent of the victim. The victim voluntarily enters into an apparently fair contract, only to later find out that the contract was not fair or that the promisor never intended to keep his promise. Swindling is the most difficult form of selling because the deal being sold is completely unattractive to customers.

Thus, swindlers face the same obstacles as sellers—but their obstacles are much bigger. One obstacle is that buyers tend to be skeptical about "bargains" because in a perfect market (where everyone is a "price taker") there could be no such a thing as a bargain. Therefore, swindlers and sellers have to create explanations for why they can offer a product that's cheaper or better than what the rest of the market is selling. They need to explain how they can sell more cheaply than others, and why they are willing to do so (because they could sell the goods at the full market price and get even higher profits).

Consider an old pattern of swindling—which Leff called the "Prisoner."[171] A con man tells you that the king has been captured by the enemy and held in prison (this takes place in medieval times). A guard could be bribed for a small amount of money to release the king, and the king himself has promised that he will reward the person who helps him escape from prison with an enormous amount of money. Unfortunately, the con man himself has no cash to finance the bribe. If you could give him some money now, you will later get rich with near certainty. There are no more than a few hours to think about the proposal, and the whole plan has to remain an absolute secret. The proposal looks too good to pass, and you decide to pay the money. Later you hear that the whole story was untrue. Gone is the con man, along with your money.

There are many variations of this swindling pattern, and I'm sure you've received many similar proposals in emails that slipped through your spam filter.

If you analyze this swindling pattern (along the lines of Arthur Leff), you will see that there is something odd about the con man's proposal. The deal was that the king would pay you an enormous amount (say, $2 million) in return for a small, short-term loan (say, $20,000). Why would someone ever do that? Why doesn't the king promise to pay you back $30,000—isn't that enough? And why wouldn't the con man keep this great opportunity for himself? The proposal looks too good to be true. You would think that nobody would ever trust it.

This is why having a good story is so important. Swindlers know the facts have to be constructed so that the market looks seriously distorted. In the "Prisoner" scenario, if a war is being waged, the king has no opportunity to compare competing offers, and there can be no normal auction because it must be kept secret that a guard will be bribed. Under these circumstances, it is also clear that it is not possible to speak with the king to check the facts or discuss the details of the transaction. Moreover, the promise to pay millions of dollars apparently comes from the king. The king is not only the most trustworthy individual in the country, but he is also somewhat outside of the market. Kings do not always want to pay the lowest possible price; sometimes they are generous to those who do something important for the country.

In another archetypal example of swindling, a con man pretends to have magical powers that allow him to multiply money. He asks you to put $100 in a box, which you do only after some hesitation. Thankfully, one hour later you open the box and find $200. Next, he asks you to put $1,000 in the box, and an hour later you open it and find $2,000. Then he asks you to do the same with $100,000. You hesitate but eventually place the money in the box, and an hour later . . . you find an empty box. The con man is gone, and so is the money.

How could this trick ever work? First of all, in the past many people *did* believe in magic. And second, victims had seen with their own eyes that the money had been doubled in the first two rounds. Moreover, the magician looked like an honest person because he did not keep the newly created money but honestly delivered it to the person it belonged to.

A modern-day version of this old trick was applied by Bernie Madoff. Madoff was considered a Wall Street star; every year, he paid above-market interests to his investors. In reality, he didn't have above-market returns. Instead, he ran what is a called a "Ponzi scheme": he used the capital of new investors to pay out the high interests to existing investors. That couldn't last forever; in 2008, he ran out of money. The fraud was discovered and Madoff was sentenced to 150 years in prison. (He was 70 when he was arrested, so he will get out of jail when he is 220 years old.)

How could he convince investors to put money in his Ponzi

scheme? Modern people no longer believe in magicians, but some do believe in computer wizards. So, Madoff pretended to own an advanced econometric program that allowed him to better predict trends than his competitors. In addition, Madoff *did* pay above-market returns to his investors, year after year. Finally, Madoff may not have been the king himself, but he was apparently one of the most trustworthy people on Wall Street. He had been the Chairman of the Board of Directors of the National Association of Securities Dealers (NASD), and a prominent philanthropist. The facts of the story were also so construed that Madoff's investors understood why they couldn't examine how the program worked or ask for the details of its past performance. This was "proprietary information," and the investors knew they couldn't expect years of innovation to be publicized and placed up for grabs to competitors.

Here is another scenario to convince consumers that they're getting a bargain. The salesman tells you he had bad luck—there was a fire in his store, and now he needs to quickly sell the remaining stock below the market price, which is terrible for him but good for you. One variant of this tale involves the seller pretending to have overstock, basically saying, "I had bad luck, I made the mistake of ordering too much, and now I have to sell it to you at a loss." An even subtler pattern is the following: "I have to give you a lower price, because you are one of those smarter buyers, and I cannot fool you like the others." The buyer gets flattered, looks no further, and buys an overpriced product.

Some other stories are meant to explain why only the seller can offer such a great product. The old version of this story states that the seller owns a secret formula, the modern version . . . that he holds a patent!

Why are stories so important? In a fully transparent market they wouldn't matter: consumers could compare the price and quality of all products and would not be interested in the story behind the proposal. In a nontransparent market, however, stories become very important. Many consumers start their search process by going to a first seller, and if the price looks fair and the quality looks good, the consumer does not look any further. So, *in a sequential search process, sellers have a strong incentive to make you stop searching.* The story's function is to convince you that you won't find better deals elsewhere.

Misleading look-no-further stories may look innocent, but they are quite harmful to the economy. You should keep in mind that consumers can mistakenly buy a product for two reasons. First, they can buy product A because they have incorrect information about product A. Second, they can buy product A because they have incorrect (or no) information about product B, C, D, or E. So, consumers can make wrong decisions, even if they have perfect information about the products they eventually buy.

Of course, the deeper problem is the sequential search process. In a total-view search process, look-no-further stories are pointless. But given that most search processes are sequential, look-no-further stories make things worse. They make the inefficient sequential search process even more inefficient.

Are false look-no-further stories legal? No. First, the definition of "fraud" or "misrepresentation" in the common law has been extended over time and is now broad enough to cover all types of misstatements. Any misrepresentation that is material (something that matters for the decision) is forbidden; any deliberately made misrepresentation is fraudulent. Second, consumer protection law contains specific prohibitions. Sellers cannot lie about who endorses the product, what the price is elsewhere, or how long a sales offer will remain open.

In practice, misleading look-no-further stories are rarely attacked by the legal system. Suppose a manufacturer pays a celebrity to say that she uses a certain product. In reality, the celebrity has never used it. This clearly violates the FTC Guides concerning the Use of Endorsements and Testimonials in Advertising.[172] Even if the story is a flat-out lie, the legal risks are negligible. First, it is hard to prove that the celebrity didn't use the product. Second, the chance of being sued by the FTC is about as high as the chance of dying by tripping over a sleeping English bulldog. Third, the FTC "punishment" is usually that the violator can no longer do it in the future! No, I'm not making this up. *Cease and desist* (that's the technical term they use for "stop!") is the normal remedy for an FTC violation. It is like a school where the punishment for cheating is that the teacher tells you that you can no longer cheat in the future! Surprised there is a lot of cheating at that school?

So, making up a story is usually a violation of the law. But in practice, *story makers get away with it because the legal system underenforces its rules.* Apparently, law enforcers believe that stories play a role only in swindling, not in selling.

Look-No-Further Stories in Practice

What stories are used in practice? Let's start with the most obvious: any story that misrepresents the market price has a strong look-no-further effect. Suppose a product costs $100 elsewhere. If consumers are made to believe it costs $500 elsewhere, why would they keep on searching? In addition, it is a type of story that increases information rents in a direct way. If consumers believe it costs $500 elsewhere, they may pay $400 for your product and still think they got a bargain.

Falsely representing competitors' prices violates the law, but in practice the rules are completely underenforced. No wonder this sales technique is so widespread. The air conditioner repairer who charged $75 per pound for a gas that costs only $10 per pound also told my friend that most others charge $120—even if that is not true. The repairer will typically get away with it, and customers even think they got a great price. Maybe they give the company five stars for "price fairness" on Angie's List!

Relatedly, there is, in practice, no punishment for lying about a business's general price level. The most expensive business in town may say it has "competitive prices" or even that it has "the best prices in town." A business that systematically overcharges for spare parts may ironically initiate a "we do not overcharge" campaign.

Some highly applauded marketing techniques come down to misrepresenting competitors' prices as well. Consider *price conditioning*, a technique where the seller, before revealing his price, prepares ("conditions") the customer for an even higher price. Then, when the consumer eventually learns the seller's price, she feels relieved and thinks she got a bargain. As price consultant Jeff Berman wrote in a blog post entitled "Why Lawyers Need to Understand the Art of Price Conditioning," price conditioning is "the art of changing the perception of your service pricing."[173] What price conditioning does is to raise the price expectations. How do you do that? Here is one tip from Berman: "For instance, in a conversation with a prospective client you might mention 'Experienced firms can charge upwards of (fill in the blank with a top end price that is more than you charge) for what you need.'"

Here is the translation in simple English: sellers should first decide how much they want to charge and then tell customers that others charge even more. Making up what others charge is fraud, but in practice, sellers will never get in legal trouble for it. (Note also the manipulative nature of the term "conditioning." Just like you can condition your dog to do certain things, you can condition your customers to believe certain things.)[174]

A false story about the quality of competitors' goods is also something for which violators are rarely sued. Such stories are quite effective: if consumers become convinced that competitors have poor reputations ("Oh my gosh, are you really considering a bid from *them*?"), they may look no further. Such stories may even be told in a vague way, without telling names. Suppose you invite a roofer to submit a bid to repair your roof. The first thing he may tell you is that he just repaired a roof that was ruined by an incompetent competitor. This story conveys two messages— that there are many incompetent roofers and that he is not one of them. This story may be a plain lie, but there is no way to check this. If you believe his story, you may take his bid, even if it is more expensive than some other bid you received. After all, that other bid may have come from one of those incompetent roofers he told you about.

Many other look-no-further stories are related to the cost structure of a good or a seller's markup. Sellers may tell you they can offer lower prices because they work without middlemen, or because they have a higher sales volume, or because they are more efficient, or simply take lower profit margins. If customers believe any of these stories, they may conclude that searching further is unlikely to uncover lower prices. Relatedly, sellers may have a story ready for why a certain product is so expensive. Ask a plumber why that bolt costs $29. He may tell you with a straight face that he does not make a profit on these bolts. Such stories may be false, or just half-truths, but the legal risks are virtually nonexistent.

A subtle way to give the false impression that markups are low is to price items very precisely. For instance, if a product would cost $100 on a competitive market, a smart marketer on a foggy market will not price it at $1,000 but at the much more precise price of $982.74. Of course, this level of precision is irrational. It is like in the old joke in which someone said, "This river is 3,000,017 years old." When asked how he had come up with that number, he replied, "I read in a book that the river is 3,000,000 years old, and the book is seventeen years old." The joke is funny because this level of accuracy is absurd. Asking a price of $982.74 is equally absurd—unless the competition on the market is so extreme that all competitors ask a price in the range $980–985. By making the price so detailed, the seller suggests he does not ask a single cent more than the true costs. If the consumer believes him and stops searching, the seller has earned an $882.74 rent!

Getting Away with Contract Breach

If the legal system did not exist, breaching a contract would be one of the easiest ways to receive a rent. Suppose you pay me $1,000 to repair your roof, and I keep your money without ever repairing your roof. That's an easy $1,000 rent for me.

Now, the law is very clear about breaching contracts: you can't breach them without paying compensation, unless you have a valid excuse (such as the contract proving impossible to perform). Even if you *have* an excuse, the law will force you to give any money back you have received for the job. Moreover, if you never actually intended to perform the contract, you have committed "promissory fraud," which can even lead to punitive damages.[175]

Nevertheless, there are some legal ways to breach a contract and keep the money, even if you never intended to perform it. As we will see, all these techniques are basically versions of one specific type of fraud—fraud about what has been agreed on.

One way to get away with contract breach is to make the other party believe that you have promised something without formally promising it. An example is *slack filling*, which is selling a product in boxes that look larger than the product is. By doing this, you seem to be promising a large product, but you're actually delivering something far smaller than what the consumer thinks he's bargained for. (That bag of potato chips looks huge and full, but when you open it up, there are only eight chips inside because the bag was mainly full of air.) A variant is to reduce the content and keep the same box (an example of a *stealth price increase*). Maybe the consumer thinks there still are 32 ounces in the mayonnaise jar and doesn't suspect that you have reduced the product to only 30 ounces. Formally, this does not breach the promise because it was never formally promised that 32 ounces would be in the box. If you look at the small print on the box, you may see that it's clearly written that there are 30 ounces inside.[176]

Another legal way of breaching a contract may sound paradoxical: it consists of hiding fees in a contract and later demanding payment. I know, this may sound confusing because if a fee is written in the contract, how can it ever be a "breach" to ask that the fee be paid? The confusion is related to the concept of "contract." Most people think that a contract is the piece of paper that you sign. The modern view in contract law (which is the dominant view since medieval times!) holds, in contrast, that the contract is what the parties really agreed to—it is the "meeting of minds." A signed piece of paper may be evidence of an agreement, but it is not the contract itself. If a business lets you sign a piece of paper and sneaks in fees that were not agreed to, these fees are strictly speaking not part of the contract. Demanding payment is therefore doing something else than what was agreed to. It is breaching the contract.

In practice, however, the legal system is imperfect. For starters, courts have difficulties uncovering the true agreement. Therefore, they tend to rely on the evidence contained in that piece of paper. In addition, courts want to give parties an incentive to read contracts. As a result, they hold that there is a "duty to read" the contract that you sign. In practice, though, consumers don't read contracts. This allows businesses to sneak in one-sided terms and pretend that these terms have been agreed to.

You may remember the first time you were charged an "overdraft protection fee" of $35 by your bank when it transferred money from your savings account to compensate for an overdraft. This was probably a complete surprise to you, something the bank never discussed when you opened your account. But the legal system, imperfect as it is, assumes that this was part of the deal because you signed a document (which included the overdraft fee).

Courts may occasionally strike down a "surprise fee" when they consider it to be "unconscionable" (I know, that's a vague criterion), but statistically this is a rare occurrence.[177] One inherent difficulty with the legal concept of "surprise fees" is that if every company in the industry starts doing it, proving that the fee was a surprise becomes difficult. Were you really surprised that your bank or rental car company charged you that unexpected fee when every other company does the same thing?[178]

Another technique is making only vague promises. Sell an overpriced "natural" extract and vaguely promise that the consumer will be healthier. Or write that the fish oil comes from Norway or that the electrolyte drink mix is fortified with ionic trace minerals from the Great Salt Lake. And ask a premium price for this premium product. The health promise is too vague to be considered legally binding. Or promise world-class legal services (in return for a fee that corresponds to world-class quality) even if you deliver the same average quality as the other law firms. Not only are legal services a so-called credence good (a good that the receiver cannot evaluate objectively even after having received the service), but statements such as "world class" are vague enough to be considered puffery by the courts.

An even subtler form of contract breach can be found in advertising. A typical ad may show a picture of young, successful people drinking a certain brand of soda. The ad does not say that there is a connection between being young and successful and drinking soda, but at the subconscious level, consumers are made to believe there is. In a sense, the ad does not even suggest that if you drink soda you will become young and successful; all it suggests is that young and successful people drink that soda. This is, in essence, inverse causation: the soda does not make you young and successful, but being young and successful makes you want to drink that soda.[179] So you may want to drink that soda to implicitly show that you are one of those young and successful people. Similarly, airlines don't suggest that you will become successful if you fly first class. What they do suggest is that successful people fly first class.

The major advantage of inverse causation is that it becomes hard, from a legal point of view, to prove a breach of contract. As a matter of fact, there can be no breach of contract because advertisers have not actually promised anything. You cannot sue them if drinking soda does not make you young and successful.

Psychological Manipulation: A Legal Way to Deceive

My guess is that in the early days of psychology as a science, its goal was to make people more rational. Leave it to marketing experts to discover that you can also use these same psychological insights to make people less rational.

Human beings are less than perfectly rational, and we tend to make mathematical mistakes. Give us a complex calculation and we will make errors. Our brain was designed to be used in nature; you don't need to know what $17.99 divided by 57 is to kill a deer for dinner. Our brain is especially miserable when we need to estimate probabilities. And this makes sense again: You don't need to know the exact probability of being bitten by a crocodile in a river. You only need to know that you should stay out of the river.

The list of biases in human decision-making is long. And so is the list of marketing techniques that help businesses exploit these biases. The techniques range from what products to put at eye level and how to graphically design restaurant menus so that customers are more likely to order high-markup items, to how to make customers walk through the store (it turns out that if they walk counterclockwise, they spend $2 more on average).[180]

Or consider a marketing strategy called *anchor pricing*.[181] Marketing experts have discovered that consumers tend to use the highest-priced model as an "anchor," as a baseline for judging other products' prices. As a result, consumers can be manipulated to pay more for a product by simply putting more expensive products in the same location. In the 1960s, Budweiser was viewed as an expensive beer. Anheuser-Busch then launched an even more expensive beer: Michelob. Surprisingly, Budweiser's sales increased; Budweiser now looked less expensive, less extreme. Williams-Sonoma once unsuccessfully launched a fancy bread maker at $279. Then it added an even fancier model at $429. The latter model flopped, but the cheaper one suddenly became successful.[182] Consumers began subconsciously comparing the prices of the two products and concluded $279 was a moderate price.

Notice how subtly this marketing strategy works: the seller doesn't say a word about the prices of competing products but lets our subconsciousness do the work. This makes it hard to attack it on legal grounds. There is no such legal doctrine as "manipulation of the subconscious." There are two doctrines in contract law that prevent the exploitation of irrational people, but they only focus on more extreme cases. One is "incapacity," which protects children, demented people, and even seriously intoxicated people, but not grown-ups like you and me who make irrational choices when being manipulated. The other is "undue influence," which protects people who are manipulated by people with whom they have a special relationship (such as family members, priests, or even employers), but "special relationship" is defined quite narrowly. We don't have a special relationship with Williams-Sonoma.

Here is another subtle way to get an information rent: offer your product in different sizes and price them in a way that customers wouldn't expect. For instance, large bottles of popular sports drinks are sometimes more expensive per ounce than small bottles. This seems to violate economic logic, because making many small bottles is more expensive than making one large bottle. Why, then, are large bottles relatively more expensive? Well, price consultants have figured out that *quantity surcharges* can increase profits because many customers blindly assume that buying in large quantities is cheaper. You can extract a higher price from customers by doing something they don't expect.

You think this is an exception? In a 1996 paper, Gupta and Rominger examined prices in local stores and found quantity surcharges on the following products: Coors Beer, Cuervo Gold Tequila, Baby Magic Baby Lotion, Enfamil Baby Milk, J & J Baby Shampoo, Brach's Candy, M&M'S Candy, Snicker's Candy, Brooks Chili, Brooks Mild Chili Beans, Bumble Bee Chunk Light Tuna,

Campbell's Soup, Campbell's Veg Beef Soup, Chicken of the Sea Chunk Light Tuna, Dole Pineapple Slices, Hormel Chili, Ivory Clear Dishwashing Liquid, Liquid Plumber, Pine-Sol Household Cleaner, Purex Laundry Detergent, Maxwell House Coffee, Heinz Ketchup, Henry's French Salad Dressing, Jif Peanut Butter, Kraft Parmesan Cheese, Open Pit Barbecue Sauce, Skippy Peanut Butter, Armour Lard, Gold Medal All Purpose Flour, Wesson Vegetable Oil, Aqua Hair Spray, Salon Selectives Shampoo, Eveready Flashlight, Bic Disposable Razors, Crest Toothpaste, Dial Soap, Irish Spring Soap, Listerine Cool Mint Mouthwash, Sure Unscented Deodorant, Arm & Hammer Baking Soda, Ziploc Storage Bags, Benylin Cough Syrup, Faber-Castell Erasers, Aldi's Generic Bath Tissue, Brawny Paper Towels, Charmin Bath Tissue, Jerky Dog Treats, Meow Mix Cat Food, Milk-Bone Dog Biscuits, Jewel Mandarin Oranges, Potatoes, Mead Wireless Notebook, Pepsi, V8 Juice, Jewel Enriched Thin Spaghetti, La Preferida Enriched Rice, Miracid Plant Food, Pringles Potato Chips, Ultraslim Diet Mix Packets, Vigo Yellow Rice.[183]

Okay, that was a long list. Maybe I shouldn't have printed it all here. But I only wanted to make clear that quantity surcharges are a common practice, not an exception. Don't believe they are made by mistake.

This brings us to a more general theme. Buying in a store involves a transaction chain of at least three parties: the consumer, the store, and the manufacturer. Whose side is the store on? Is the store ultimately looking out for the customer, helping her to find the best products at the best prices? Or is the store really partnering with the manufacturer, helping her to sell products at the highest possible margins? If reputation were perfect, the store would assume the first role and take the customer's side. After all, it's the customers who have the market power in a perfect market. Customers wouldn't go to stores that announce: "We work together with manufacturers to better trick you." And they also wouldn't go to stores with the slogan: "Supermarket X, your local information rent champion."

In the real world, however, reputation mechanisms are imperfect, and this may give stores an incentive to collude with manufacturers to create information rent opportunities at the expense of the customers. This may be unfair, but it is predictable. The two most informed players work together to extract rents from the least informed player.

Some manipulation techniques are so subtle that they are hard to recognize. At gas stations, drivers usually get three choices: "regular" gas (often with 87 percent octane), "midgrade" gas (with 89 percent octane), and "premium" gas (usually with 93 percent octane). Profit margins go up as octane percentage goes up. Which variant should you choose? As it turns out, higher octane percentages provide no benefit to almost all vehicles currently on the road.*

In practice, however, premium gas is purchased much more frequently than it should be, suggesting that many drivers are misinformed.[184]

Misinformed by whom? Gas sellers will say it's not by them. They do not give any information, and thus cannot be accused of giving wrong information. They simply give consumers a choice, and whenever consumers make the wrong choice, gas sellers get a rent.

It looks the perfect crime: let the victim hurt himself and benefit from it. The wrongdoer cannot be prosecuted because the wrongdoer didn't do it.

Still, there is a difference between a free choice and a trap. A choice without the right information is not a choice at all. Think about it—animals who fall into traps had choices as well. They could have chosen to walk around the camouflaged tiger pit,

---

* More octane does not mean more energy; it only means that energy comes in a different form. But modern motors are built to work with lower octane levels. Most cars will not drive faster with premium gas, or drive more miles per gallon. So, if your motor doesn't start knocking when you use regular gas, you shouldn't buy the more expensive grade.

but they chose to step into it. But there really was no choice; the camouflage removed a key piece of information from the picture.

At its core, this marketing method is a fraud scheme. The fraud, however, is so subtle that few recognize it as fraud when they see it. Indeed, if three choices are given with no information, people decide on the basis of a gut feeling, not on the basis of objective information. Some instinctively prefer the cheapest, others the middle, and still others the most expensive.[185]

Ultimately, the choice may be irrational, but irrational behavior is more likely to occur in the absence of objective information. Therefore, such marketing always has two components. First, do not give objective information about your products so that buyers are forced to resort to gut feelings. Second, exploit the biases reflected in these gut feelings.

Is this legal? Yes, it is, in the sense that no judge has ever called it illegal. But it is puzzling that it is legal because it violates many principles of law. The law generally holds that the most informed party ought to reveal material information, which seems to make all traps illegal. Indeed, whether a trap has been set is an important ("material") piece of information for the consumer, and the one who set up the trap has more information on it than the one who falls into it. Moreover, consumer law makes trade practices illegal as soon as they have the "capacity to mislead." The law also holds that it is not the words that you utter but the impression that you give that determines your liability. Nothing in the law says that subtle fraud is not fraud.

Fortunately, consumer education is slowly solving the problem. More and more drivers know that premium gas is not necessary for most vehicles.[186] Give it another ten years and the number of mistaken automobilists may be so low that "premium gas" disappears altogether at most stations. So, isn't consumer education the answer, rather than more law?

Well, look at it from another side: it takes decades before most consumers realize something is a trap. This means that trappers receive decades' worth of significant rents. And by the time this trap no longer works, other traps will be conceived. For a whole army of marketing specialists, studying human irrationality and designing trapping mechanisms is a full-time job. Although the effectiveness of existing traps may decline over time, at any given moment, a large number of them are operating and working. Moreover, traps are always becoming more sophisticated as psychologists get better at understanding human irrationality. So, you shouldn't be surprised that markets are getting even more distorted over time.

PART III
POLICY
RECOMMENDATIONS

8

DON'T INCREASE TAXES

What is the best way to reduce income inequality? Nearly all economists believe that the best way is to increase taxes for the wealthy and redistribute the money to the poor. Even though taxes distort the economy by undermining the incentives to work hard, taxes are believed to distort less than any other measure.

In this chapter, however, I will explain why taxes are not the best instrument to redistribute income when inequality is caused by rents. Legal rules that attack the underlying market failures are much less distortive. If you want to reduce income inequality, you should not increase taxes, but change contract law, consumer protection law, antitrust law, property law, intellectual property law, and litigation law. Taxes can only treat the symptoms of a deeper problem. The legal system can attack the causes of the problem.

The Double-Distortion Argument

My viewpoint that you should use the legal system to change income inequality goes against conventional wisdom in economics, which holds that you should use income taxes instead.[187] Let's try to understand conventional wisdom first.

Suppose an accident was caused by a wealthy injurer and that the victim turns out to be poor. Should the judge make the injurer pay extra compensation because she is wealthy? Should the judge, in other words, apply the infamous Deep Pocket Rule, which states that compensation should depend on the wealth of the injurer?[188] The answer is no. First, this would not help the poor in a systematic way; only those who became victims of an accident would be helped. Second, this would distort all the good incentives tort law tries to create. It would give poor people an incentive to trigger accidents, and it would give wealthy people an incentive to avoid places where many poor people live.

Of course, income taxes distort as well, by undermining the incentive to work hard. But here is something many people don't realize: the Deep Pocket Rule undermines the incentive to work hard in the same way. It doesn't matter whether people with a higher income pay more taxes or more compensation payments (assuming the amounts are the same, so that the redistributive effect is the same). At the end of the day, increasing your income means paying more, in some form.

The current viewpoint is, therefore, that legal rules like the Deep Pocket Rule cause a *double distortion* while taxes cause a single distortion. Both distort the incentive to work hard, but legal rules also undermine, for instance, the incentive to be careful. Because it is two distortions versus one, we even don't need to know how large that second distortion is—the Deep Pocket Rule is always worse than income taxes.

That taxes are the best instrument to help the poor is considered a fundamental axiom, taught to all economics students. It is firmly grounded in economic theory. Recent economics graduates may remember that it follows from the "second theorem of welfare economics." (More on that in an endnote.)[189] Those who took some PhD courses may know that it can also be viewed as an application of the theorem that sales taxes are worse than income taxes. (More on that later.)

An implication of this theorem is that the legal system should *not* be used to change income inequality. We should not reform property law, tort law, competition law, patent law, or contract law to help the poor. The law should focus only on economic "efficiency." Reducing economic inequality is the tax system's job. So, when economists discuss tort law, they focus on incentives, transaction costs, and risk allocation, but not on whether rules make certain people poorer—helping the poor is considered a problem for tax law.

What's wrong with the double-distortion argument? In a sense, nothing—it is correct to the extent that its central assumption is correct: that all income differences are caused by differences in talent or work ethic. But they aren't; and it is incorrect for income differences that are caused by rents.

Rents Seen as Private Sales Taxes

To better understand why exactly legal rules are better, it is helpful to analogize rents to private sales taxes. Of course, legally, rents are not sales taxes but contractual payments—the money goes to a private party, not to the government. Yet economically, they work the same way.

To see the similarity between rents and taxes more generally, go back to history. Imagine you lived as a farmer and paid a part of your harvest to the king. That was a tax. But now imagine you lived in a feudal system and paid the same amount to a local lord. Legally, this was a contractual payment for the use of land to the owner of the land. (Feudal obligations, from a legal point of view, were based on lifelong contracts.) Or imagine that you had to pay a tenth to the Catholic Church. The Church is not the state but a private organization, so in our current legal definition that payment was not a tax. Notwithstanding the legal differences, the economic effect must have felt similar.

Now come back to the present and imagine that the market for potatoes and ink cartridges is perfectly competitive and that plumbers cannot obtain information rents. So, you pay $3.95 for a sack of potatoes, $5 for an XL ink cartridge, and $1 for that bolt. Now imagine that the government introduces a crazy new sales tax, which is set at 1 percent for potatoes, 500 percent for ink cartridges, and 2,800 percent for bolts sold by plumbers. As a result, potatoes now cost $3.99, ink cartridges $30, and that bolt costs $29.

In reality, the government doesn't have crazy sales taxes like those; as a matter of fact, there may not even be a sales tax in your state. But rents exist, and the rent rate varies among products. The result is that potatoes cost $3.99, ink cartridges $30, and that bolt is billed for $29.

The main difference between a rent and a tax is, of course, the one who receives it. A rent goes to a private party, a sales tax to the government. The government could, in principle, use the money to help the poor. A tax, if used well, decreases inequality. A rent, in contrast, nearly always increases inequality because the recipient typically ends up wealthier than average. This is why rents should be analogized to *regressive* taxes. In short, rents work like private, regressive sales taxes with varying tax rates— the worst type of taxes, as we will see.

Rents Discourage Hard Work, Just Like Taxes

Since Adam Smith's 1776 book, every economist on the planet knows that taxes may harm the economy.[190] Taxes may do so by "punishing" those who work hard. Indeed, the harder you work, the more taxes you pay. If you work hard, 100 percent of the effort is for you, obviously. But if marginal taxes are 40 percent, you keep only 60 percent of the benefits of your work. Because you internalize the full costs but not the full benefits, standard economic theory tells that your choice will be distorted. Usually this means that you will work less hard because of taxes.

What does that mean, "to work less hard"? It can mean that you prefer more leisure; you are not interested in doing overtime because too much goes to the government. It can also mean that you prefer more labor at home and less on the marketplace. You repair your toilet yourself and paint your home yourself, rather than work extra hours at your job and pay a professional. Economists use the general term of *labor/leisure distortions* for all these distortions. You should not always take the word "leisure" literally here, unless you consider repairing your own bathroom leisure.

Let's illustrate "working less hard" with a numerical example. Suppose you have the choice between paying a plumber $70 or repairing your bathroom yourself, which takes you a couple of hours. If you use those hours to work longer at your office, your employer pays you an extra $100. In the absence of taxes, you would hire the plumber. But if you have to pay 40 percent taxes on the $100 you make, you keep only $60. In this case, it becomes cheaper to repair your own bathroom, even if you are less good at it than the plumber.

This example was about an income tax, but the same reasoning holds for sales taxes. This time you keep the $100 you make (because there is no income tax), but the plumber must add $40 sales taxes to the $70, so that the service costs $110.[191] Again, you decide to do the repair yourself. Again, taxes distort your labor/leisure decision.

Now back to rents. Suppose you have to pay no taxes in your country, but the plumber charges $110 (the true cost of $70 plus an information rent of $40 by selling you an overpriced bolt and screw). It again becomes cheaper to repair your own bathroom. For your decision, it does not matter whether the $40 goes to the tax authorities or to the plumber. What matters is that there is an artificial expense of $40 that drives a wedge between the true costs and the final price. Rents distort the labor/leisure decision in exactly the same way as taxes.

So, if we want to know the real tax burden on an economy, we should look not only at explicit taxes but also at implicit taxes in the form of rents. In the US, (explicit) taxes are 36 percent of the economy. (This means that, on average, $36 out of $100 you produce will be spent by all kinds of governments.)[192] Of the remaining $64, 35 percent goes to rents. Overall, if you produce $100, the true purchasing power you receive is only $42. The real tax burden, broadly defined, is 58 percent, not 36 percent. If politicians are worried about taxes harming the economy, they should be worried even more about rents harming the economy.

To be fair, the picture becomes more complicated if we look at those who *receive* the rents. This is especially true when rents go up when more hours are worked, which may be the case for a surgeon who is overpaid for every single surgery.[193] Suppose that, if a surgeon truly produces $100, she receives $400 because of rents. After paying taxes and rents to others (58 percent on average, as we calculated), she still receives a true purchasing power of $168—more than her true productivity. For such a rent receiver, rents work like an implicit subsidy. This subsidy gives the surgeon an incentive to work *more* hours than optimal! Her income will be high, and she will work many hours. This may give the impression that her income is high because she works many hours. In reality, the causation runs in the other direction: she works so many hours because her hourly income is artificially high.[194]

Rents Distort Consumption Choices— Even More So Than Sales Taxes

Not all taxes are equally distortive. Economists agree that income taxes are less distortive than sales taxes (or value-added taxes, if you live in Europe). And within the category of sales taxes (which are usually called "commodity taxes" in the economic literature), those with more "neutral" rates are considered less distortive than those with widely varying rates. Unfortunately, rents look most like sales taxes with widely varying rates.

Let's try to understand first why sales taxes are worse than income taxes. In a seminal 1976 paper, Atkinson and Stiglitz gave a simple explanation: income taxes distort only once while sales taxes distort twice.[195] Here you have it again, in a different version: the double-distortion argument.

Here is why. Income taxes undermine the incentive to work hard, as Adam Smith correctly observed. But so do sales taxes. It does not matter whether 40 percent of your income goes to income taxes or to sales taxes; in both cases, you keep only 60 percent of what you produced. The labor/leisure distortion is the same.

Income taxes, however, do not distort consumption choices. It does not matter whether you spend your after-tax income on champagne or on beer—your income tax does not change. A sales tax, in contrast, typically varies from product to product. If there is only a 5 percent tax on beer and a 50 percent tax on champagne, you pay more taxes if you choose champagne. To pay less taxes, you may drink less champagne than otherwise. Your consumption choices get distorted. This is a second distortion—exclusive to sales taxes.

Higher taxes on champagne are sometimes defended on the grounds that champagne is a luxury good, mainly bought by wealthy people. Therefore, high taxes on champagne means high taxes for wealthy people, which seems to be good for income redistribution. The problem with this reasoning is that taxing the wealthy could be accomplished more systematically with an income tax. Indeed, you can make an income tax "progressive," taxing lower incomes at for instance 10 percent and higher incomes at for instance 50 percent. This is a more systematic way to obtain this effect. If you try to do the same with a sales tax, you sometimes make "mistakes," in that wealthy people sometimes buy basic products (such as potatoes) and poor people sometimes buy luxury products (such as champagne).

How much a sales tax distorts consumption depends on how much its rates vary. A sales tax with zero variance, that is, one that taxes all goods and services at exactly the same rate, would not distort consumption choices at all.[196] If the tax on beer and champagne is both 10 percent, you will not drink less champagne. In practice, however, this is rarely the case; not only do rates tend to vary, but there are also goods and services that are excluded from taxation. Still, sales tax rates never vary extremely. They may vary from 0 percent to 20 percent, but they never vary from 0 percent to 2,800 percent.

So why are rents even more distortive than most sales taxes? Because rent rates vary extremely. For goods in perfect markets, the rent rate is zero. For goods sold on highly competitive markets, the rent rate may be 1 percent. For goods sold to locked-in consumers on ex post monopoly markets (such as print cartridges), the rent rate may be 500 percent above the true costs. And for goods on which information rents can be earned (such as the $29 bolt), the rate may be 2,800 percent.

True, there is one type of rents that does not cause economic distortions: Ricardian rents. These are rents, as we have seen, that are caused by the absolute scarcity of natural resources such as land, minerals, oil, or diamonds. If diamonds are overpriced (compared to the costs of mining them), this is economically positive in the sense that this high price signals the scarcity of the diamonds.[197] Thanks to the high price, diamonds end up in the hands of those who value them most. Similarly, the fact that land is expensive in Manhattan ensures that it is used effectively. Ricardian rents lead to income inequality but they do not distort consumption choices.[198]

Outside Ricardian rents, however, rents distort more than regular sales taxes. As it turns out, overpricing is worse than overtaxing.

Why the Legal System Distorts Less When It Reduces Income Inequality

Let's summarize. Why exactly is it better to use the legal system than the tax system if we want to reduce income inequality?

Rents work like implicit private, regressive sales taxes with varying rates. They discourage hard work, just like income taxes do, and they distort consumption choices, just like sales taxes with varying rates do. If we increase taxes to cancel out some of the rents' inequality effects, what happens? The sources of rents are not attacked, and rents keep their distortive effects. They keep distorting work effort decisions and consumption decisions. But the higher taxes distort work effort decisions even more. Higher taxes increase the degree of distortion in the economy. They create new distortions in the hope of cancelling out the inequality effects of some of the existing distortions.

When we use legal rules, in contrast, we attack the sources

of rents. By reducing the amount of rents in the economy, we reduce their distortive effects. We reduce the labor/leisure distortion and the consumption choice distortion. Legal rules that attack rents do not increase the degree of distortion in the economy—they reduce it. Legal rules that *reduce* rents, therefore *reduce* labor/leisure distortion and *reduce* consumption choice distortion. Tax increases, on the other hand, *increase* labor/leisure distortion. Taxes keep the market failures alive but just add another distortion.[199]

Here is another way of looking at it. Inequality caused by rents is essentially inequality caused by economic distortions. Therefore, legal rules that remove the rents remove the distortions as well. The tax system, in contrast, tries to cancel out the effects of one distortion by creating a new distortion.

Why the Legal System Needs Less Information Than the Tax System

In our analysis so far, we made two implicit assumptions that may seem contradictory. First, we assumed that the legal system knows where there are rents. Second, we implicitly assumed that the tax authorities don't know this. Indeed, if they knew this, they could eliminate rents by introducing "rent taxes."

Rent taxes, as the name suggests, tax rents instead of income. The idea was proposed by Henry George in the 1900s; since then, tax theorists agree that perfect *rent taxes*, if they could be implemented, would be better than any other form of taxes because they would not discourage hard work. After all, rents are payments in excess of what is needed to incentivize hard work, so if you tax away the excess, the incentives are still there. In practice, however, rent taxes have never been implemented. They are considered too hard to apply because they require information on what part of someone's income consists of rents.[200]

But if tax authorities don't have the information to implement rent taxes, why would the legal authorities have the information to prevent rents? Because the legal system has informational advantages. The legal system needs information only on *aggregate rents*, while a rent tax system would need information in *individual rents*. So, it is not that those working for the legal system are smarter—they need less information to do their job.

Let me explain the difference between aggregate and individual information. The problem with tax authorities is that they can find out how high someone's income was but not *why* it was so high. Consider three plumbers, who each have twice the income of an average plumber. The first plumber simply worked eighty hours per week instead of forty hours. The second worked forty hours per week but participated in a price cartel. The third worked forty hours per week but overcharged customers for spare parts. The first plumber did not receive any rents—he just worked harder. The second and third plumbers did receive rents because price cartels and information rents would not be possible in a perfectly competitive, transparent market.

But the tax authorities can't know that. All they can see is three plumbers with the same, high income. They can't know who worked harder and who got rents. (In theory, they could try to find this out, but it would require an enormous amount of time for each individual plumber. This is why tax authorities have given up on acquiring such information in the first place.) Unfortunately, this means that the tax system has to treat all plumbers equally. It can only tax away the rents of the last two plumbers by also taxing away the same amount from the first, hard-working plumber. And here we are back at the fundamental disadvantage of taxes: they distort work incentives.

Still, doesn't the legal system have the same problem? Doesn't it have to know where there are rents in order to know where it has to intervene? That is true, but it doesn't need information on individually received rents; it only needs information on the total amount of rents in the sector ("aggregate rents"). For instance, when the legal system has to decide whether plumbers should be obliged to publish their prices on the internet, it only has to know the total magnitude of rents associated with the current situation. (And it only needs to know this to know whether legal intervention is worth the costs.) The tax authorities, in contrast, would need information on individual rents to remove the same rents through a special rent tax. They would have to know, for each individual plumber, how many rents he received.

The deeper reason why the legal system has an informational advantage is that it *intervenes at an earlier stage*. It intervenes *ex ante*, before rents are acquired. The tax system, in contrast, intervenes *ex post*, after rents have been acquired. To better understand why this matters, consider the following hypothetical. Suppose you are transporting a box with all your golden coins on an airplane, and at some point, the golden coins risk falling out of the airplane. There are two ways to prevent losing the golden coins. The first is to prevent the box from falling out of the airplane. This is an *ex ante* intervention. The second is to let the golden coins fall out of the airplane and to later pick them up where they have fallen. This is an *ex post* correction. *Ex ante* intervention requires less information: all you have to know is how many coins there are in the box, and how much effort it costs to keep the box from exiting the plane. But to get the coins back after they have fallen, you must search for your coins across 10,000 acres, and for each coin that you find, you must prove that it is yours and not a coin belonging to the owner of the land where you found it.

Now analogize the golden coins to rents. Suppose you spill a box with rents over the economy, for instance, by keeping it legal for plumbers to acquire information rents. You may roughly know how many rents are created this way, but once they are spread over so many plumbers, it is next to impossible to find out how much rent each individual plumber received. The problem is not only that you need more pieces of information (as a matter of fact, as many pieces as there are plumbers); the problem is also that, for each plumber, you have to know which part of the income is due to rents and which part is due to hard work or higher-than-average efficiency.

Moreover, the information that the legal system needs does not always need to be precise. Very often, it is sufficient to know whether the total benefits of legal intervention outweigh the total costs associated with it. In some cases, the legal system does not even need any information at all. Indeed, if equality and efficiency point in the same direction (that is, if what reduces income differences is clearly good for the economy), it does not matter how large the total rents are—just go ahead and eliminate them.

No Leaky Bucket: How Redistribution Through Law Works

If the legal system redistributes income by attacking rent sources, how exactly does the redistribution work? How exactly do the poor receive a higher income?

If we asked the same question for the tax system, the answer would be clear. The wealthy become poorer by paying a check to the IRS. The poor become wealthier by paying less (or no) taxes, or getting free goods through Medicare or public education, or even receiving cash in the form of welfare payments. You can easily visualize how the transfer from the rich to the poor goes.

But how exactly does that work when the legal system redistributes by preventing rents? Here, the legal system does not literally take money from the rich. Instead, it prevents people from getting so rich to begin with. Similarly, it does not literally give money to the poor; instead, it increases their purchasing power by lowering the prices on the goods and services that used to contain rents. The fast-food worker may still be paid $9 per hour, but his purchasing power will increase because the prices of many goods will go down. (To be fair, the purchasing power per dollar of the wealthy will also increase, but their income may effectively go down. In other words, those who used to receive more rents than they paid rents will lose overall purchasing power. Those who used to pay more rents than they received will gain overall purchasing power.)

The fact that the legal system redistributes income in a virtual, not literal, way gives it another advantage: it avoids the transaction costs associated with literal payments. The tax system requires significant transaction costs to operate. Data show that for every $100 of taxes that are collected, $10 may go to transaction costs.[201] This includes people working for the tax authorities, citizens preparing their returns, tax consultants giving advice, and banks authorizing the payments. This is one of the reasons why redistributing money through taxes is often compared to carrying water in a *leaky bucket*. If you have 10 liters when you start, you have only 9 liters left when you arrive.

The deeper reason for this transaction cost difference is that taxes are a distortion aiming to cancel out another distortion. So, there is a first transaction that causes a distortion (a rent is paid on a product, causing income inequality). Then, there is a second transaction that takes away the money from the rent receiver (the tax payment), and a third transaction that gives it back to the rent payer (the social welfare payment). The first transaction caused a problem. The second and third transaction try to fix the problem. The legal system, in contrast, solves the problem before the first transaction is made.

Our airplane hypothetical illustrates this difference. If you prevent the coins from falling out of the plane, there is no transaction. If the coins fall out of the plane, there are two transactions: the first, in which you distribute the coins over the city, and the second, in which you take back the coins. So, the reason why the legal system has a transaction cost advantage over the tax system is that it intervenes *ex ante*, before the golden coins are distributed.

Is There Really an Efficiency-Equity Trade-Off?

Economists generally believe that income inequality can be reduced only at the expense of economic welfare. They believe there is such a thing as the "efficiency-equity trade-off." (The terms "efficiency" and "equity" refer to economic optimality and income equality, respectively; and the "trade-off" essentially means that improving equality is bad for the economy.) Free markets, so goes the underlying reasoning, pay people according to their productivity. The less regulated a market is, the larger the income differences are as it becomes more painfully clear that human beings are unequally productive. The only way to help those who are less productive is to intervene in the market, either through regulation or taxation. Unfortunately, government intervention makes the market less efficient. That holds true not only for regulation, which may distort choices and stifle innovation, but also for taxes, which undermine incentives to work hard and require administrative costs. Communism in its purest form is seen as an extreme choice for economic equality: everybody receives the same income but nobody has an incentive to work hard. Most Western countries make a less extreme choice, but they also pay an economic price for reducing income inequality—so goes the standard argument.

The efficiency-equity trade-off, however, may be largely overstated. As I explained, income differences tend to be modest in highly competitive markets. To the extent that income inequality is caused by rents, equality and economic optimality usually go hand in hand. Rents are bad because they cause income inequality and they are bad because they distort the economy. If you make the economy more efficient, you make incomes more equal.[202]

That said, there is a point at which an equity-efficiency trade-off arises even in the legal system. Indeed, the law can reduce rents by aggressively fighting organized crime, corruption, consumer exploitation, and cartels, but it can only do so at an administrative cost. Therefore, an optimal legal system will tolerate a certain rate of crime, corruption, consumer misleading, and cartelization. There will always be people who buy their yachts by exploiting the imperfections of the legal system.

Now, suppose the legal system is set optimally (making a perfect balance between its administrative costs and the benefits of reduced distortions), but that there are still rents. What should you do if you want to further reduce income inequality? Should you make the law even more aggressive (again, beyond the point that is optimal from an administrative cost perspective), or should you increase income taxes?

The theoretical answer is technical, so I'll explain it in an endnote.[203] The short answer is that, in this case, both the legal system and the tax system should do a part of the work. Still, most of the work should be done by the legal system because of yet another benefit: it uses narrow instruments, while income taxes are extremely broad instruments.

Taxes Are an Overly Broad Instrument

Suppose that your finger is infected. Should you apply local antibiotics (a narrow instrument) or general antibiotics (a broad instrument)? In principle, local antibiotics are better: they bring the substance only where it is needed. Because the side effects of the drug are limited to your finger (and not extended to the rest of your body), the total side effects are lower. And because the total side effects are lower, the dose can typically be higher.

Legal rules are narrow instruments. If a rule attacks one type of fraud that generates an information rent, it attacks only this behavior and not the totality of the economy. Indeed, the rule does not affect those who do not commit this type of fraud, and the rule does not impact the million other activities in the economy in any way. So, even if the rule has side effects (for instance, in the form of administrative costs), these side effects are "local" in the economy. And because the total side effects are small (compared to the entire economy), the "dose" can be higher, that is, the law can be quite aggressive in removing the rent.

Income taxes, on the other hand, are extremely broad instruments. If you want to do something about the income inequality effects caused by a very specific type of fraud, you could at most increase general tax rates. However, these affect the incomes not only of those who committed this type of fraud but also of everyone else with an equally high income. After all, income taxes are applied to the entire economy, not only to the sectors in which there is a problem.

Here is another way to see why taxes are overbroad. Taxes take away income from rents (which in itself does not distort the economy) but also income from hard work (which does distort the economy) and compensation for risk-taking (which also distorts the economy, because it is a quasi rent, not a rent). Taxes cannot make a distinction among these three. The legal system can, and therefore it distorts less than the tax system.

Because taxes are overbroad, they can't attack new sources of income inequality so aggressively. Suppose that tax rates are set at an optimal level—say 40 percent. Then, a new type of rent appears in the economy—say, there are a few businesses that form a cartel to fix prices in their industry. How much should the tax rate increase, now that you have this additional policy goal? Not that much, maybe to 40.01 percent or maybe not at all, because, after all, the new benefits are small and the new distortions of higher taxes occur in the entire economy. Now consider what the legal system could do. Maybe it could increase the budget to prosecute cartels from $100 million to $200 million. Since the legal system works with narrower instruments, it could make larger adjustments.

Still, while the legal system should be the first instrument to reduce income inequality, it can never eliminate the last source of rents. It can never eliminate the last implicit cartel, the last form of fraud, the last information rent in the economy.[204] To remove the very last rent sources in the economy, the legal system would need perfect information, which is impossible—at least in the foreseeable future.

So, the tax system may have to play a role in reducing income inequality caused by rents, although only a backup role—when the legal system is out of inspiration.

This brings us to the question: What kind of taxes are least distortive in an economy with rents? Should taxes be progressive, that is, should tax rates be higher for higher incomes? Should capital gains be taxed at the same rate as labor income? Should they be taxed at all? Should tax rates be the same for all industries, as is now the case? There is a large economic literature on these questions, but it generally assumes away rents. How do the answers change in an economy with rents? While this question is not the focus of this book, I nonetheless offer a few suggestions, based on rent economics.

In general, rent economics suggests that tax rates should be higher for incomes that are more likely to contain rents. The reason is that taxes want to reach a goal (finance public goods, reduce inequality) while minimizing distortions. If someone's income is the product of hard work, taxes distort more than if someone's income is the result of rents. So, having lower tax rates for income that is more likely the product of hard work and higher tax rates for income that is more likely the result of rents minimizes the overall distortions of the tax system.

This general principle has three main implications. First, tax rates should be progressive, that is, they should be higher for higher incomes. Indeed, the higher the income, the higher the likelihood that the income consists of rents.

Second, taxes should be higher in certain industries than in others. If rents are higher in the oil industry than in the food industry, taxes should be higher in the former.

Third, capital gains should be taxed at a rate that reflects the likelihood of rents in capital gains. For instance, if 50 percent of the capital gains are believed to be rents, tax rates on capital gains should be 50 percent.[205] Of course, capital gains taxes should vary according to the likelihood of rents. If interests on savings accounts and government bonds do not contain rents (as is likely the case), they should not be taxed.[206]

Here is a final, surprising recommendation from rent economics: income from patents and copyrights should be tax-free; instead, their duration should be made shorter. Making them shorter has the same effect on income inequality as taxing the income they generate but distorts the economy less. (The reason is technical; I'll explain it in an endnote.)[207]

Why Sending Everybody to College Will Not Reduce Income Inequality

"Education, education, and education!" These were the three words that the British politician Tony Blair used to summarize his 1997 election campaign. Tony Blair is not alone. As a matter of fact, it is a widely held belief that sending everybody to college is a great way to reduce income inequality.

The belief, however, is based on confusing income with productivity. If there were no rents, and income really reflected true productivity, then giving everyone a college education could be a great solution (at least if all colleges improved productivity, which is a strong assumption, but let's make it nonetheless).[208] If income inequality is caused by rents, however, sending everybody to college may not do a lot, or even make things worse. Indeed, if all future business owners go to a business school, rents would probably go up. If the problem is the difference in sophistication between the seller and the buyer, making the seller even more sophisticated will exacerbate the problem.

Would it help to give consumers some general training, such as a course on financial literacy? Well, that's unlikely to be effective. A financial literacy course can never close the information gap that exists for each individual product. A consumer can at most spend a few hours to learn about a product, while a salesperson with five years of experience has spent 10,000 hours on this type of product. Giving a consumer a quick financial literacy course is like giving her a quick tennis course and hoping that she will beat a professional tennis player.

Second, even if such courses would have some positive effect, they would be intrinsically wasteful. It is like making robbery legal but trying to reduce it through self-defense courses. Such courses can make sense in extreme cases, in which the legal system has lost its battle against the wrongdoers. But in most cases, the first-best solution is going after those very wrongdoers.

Why Bringing Back Factories Will Not Reduce Income Inequality

How about President Trump's goal to bring back factories to the United States and create more well-paid jobs? Wouldn't that restore the middle class and reduce income inequality?

Unfortunately, this view is again based on a confusion of income with true productivity. In an economy full of rents, this policy may have the opposite effect.

To see why, let's try to understand the large income differences that exist among countries. The dominant viewpoint among economists is that these differences are caused by productivity differences. That is definitely a part of the explanation. American truck drivers transport 50 tons with their high-tech trucks. Some Indian farmers transport 50 kilograms with their bike. That alone is a one-thousand-fold productivity difference. Some of these productivity differences are in turn caused by the legal system. Because foreign investors do not fully trust the legal system, they are reluctant to invest, and so there is not enough capital to bring productivity up to par.

But that is only a part of the story. The other part is that those countries get fewer rents because they tend to specialize in manufacturing, which is the stage of the product cycle that generates the least rents.

Indeed, businesspeople know that there are three stages of a production process, and that some stages are more profitable than others. The first stage, the design of the product, tends to be profitable. The second stage, the manufacturing of the product, is hardly profitable. The third stage, the marketing and sale of the product, is profitable. It turns out that developing countries specialize in the second stage, while developed countries skip it. Products are designed by Americans, manufactured by Southeast Asians, and marketed by Americans. If Southeast Asians make less, it is because they focus on manufacturing.

Why are profits lower at the manufacturing stage? Rent theory offers an easy answer. At the designing stage, there are cherry-picking rents associated with intellectual property protection and first-mover advantages. At the marketing stage, there are information rents, because buyers may be nonsophisticated consumers. But at the manufacturing stage, markets are more competitive. Moreover, earning information rents is harder, because the buyers are highly sophisticated businesses.

So, letting the United States focus more on manufacturing and letting developing countries focus more on design and marketing may not help the United States. From a global perspective, it is no solution either. Someone has to do the manufacturing, so letting all countries do their fair share of manufacturing only transforms inequality among countries into inequality within countries. A better solution, again, is to remove the cause of the inequality itself and reduce the rents at the design and marketing stage. This way, income better reflects true productivity. And this is what will truly help all the hardworking and still struggling people in the United States and abroad.

Why Empowering Unions Is Not a Good Solution

Some commentators believe that giving more power to labor unions is a great way to reduce income inequality.[209] The underlying idea is that powerful labor unions can negotiate better wages for their members, many of whom are in the bottom half of the income distribution curve.[210]

Yet the fact that empowering labor unions is a partial solution does not mean it is a good solution. Labor unions correct inequality (caused by rents) by creating counterbalancing rents, which they create by forming cartels and using hold-up strategies. Still, if in the end everybody in this country receives rents in some form, isn't the balance restored?

But correcting rents by creating new rents is not only harmful for the economy, it is also nearly impossible to achieve the right balance. To illustrate, imagine there is a medieval society in which plumbers receive rents because they have a guild that restricts competition, while carpenters and bakers work in a competitive environment. As a result, all plumbers have an income of $200, while carpenters and bakers have an income of only $100, although all three work the same number of hours. A simple way to restore income inequality is to abolish the plumbers' guild; this makes their income fall back to $100. A different way to restore income inequality is to grant guilds to carpenters and bakers as well. The problem is that the balance will be restored only if these new rents are of the same magnitude as the one they try to cancel out. Yet predicting the magnitude of a rent is hard, and fine-tuning is even harder. The elasticity of the demand for the products, for instance, may be different in each profession, so that the same legal restrictions lead to an income of $350 for one profession and only $120 for another.

The best way to reduce income inequality, therefore, is not to create new sources of rents, but to make sure that the existing sources of rents disappear. Correcting one distortion by introducing another is rarely the best solution.[211]

9

MAKE MARKETS MORE COMPETITIVE THROUGH BETTER LAW

In the previous chapters, we have seen that the best way to reduce income inequality is not to raise taxes but to let the legal system attack market failures. But isn't this what the law already does? For instance, sources of market failure such as fraud, economic duress, cartels, and the abuse of dominant market positions are already forbidden by the law. What exactly should the law do that it doesn't already do?

This chapter offers a long to-do list for lawmakers and courts. It proposes major changes to antitrust law, contract law, agency law, consumer protection law, intellectual property law, real property law, oil and gas law, and zoning law. The general idea is that the legal system should target market failures more aggressively than it currently does. In addition, it should make sure that valuable resources (like oil fields or building rights) can only be acquired after a highly competitive auction.

Let's start with an extremely simple rule that could have a major impact on income inequality.

Make All Businesses Publish Their Prices on the Internet in a Standardized Form

The single most effective way to increase competition is to make businesses publish prices on the internet. Yes—it's that simple. Make stores publish the prices of all their products on the internet. Make hospitals publish the prices of all types of surgery. Make plumbers publish how much they charge for spare parts. Make cooling companies publish how much they charge for each type of repair.

There are two reasons why a simple measure like this could have such a significant impact on rents. First, price fog turns any competitive market into an oligopolistic one. If we eliminate price fog, we restore competition. Second, information rents may be prevented if consumers can easily see market prices. It would be harder for a plumber to charge $29 for a bolt if the consumer could immediately see that the same bolt costs $1 elsewhere.

Refusing to publish prices on the internet should be viewed as a form of anticompetitive behavior in antitrust law. The justification for this new principle is simple. Competition is possible only if consumers can see what is on the market; refusing to publish prices is a deliberate effort to reduce the amount of price information on the market, and therefore an effort to reduce competition.

Would a duty to publish prices in a certain format be a novelty? Well, there are a few examples, but they are typically too modest. For instance, funeral undertakers have to reveal their prices through the phone (but not on the internet). Auto mechanics have to reveal repair costs before doing the repair (but not on the internet). Hotels have to publish the prices of their rooms on the door inside the room (but these are unrealistic prices, and by the time you see them you have already booked the room).[212] If publishing prices on the internet is such a great way to increase competition, why doesn't such a duty already exist in antitrust law? The short answer is that antitrust law was designed more than a century ago when the world was a very different place. The longer and more technical answer is that the law makes a strict distinction between competition problems and information problems. Antitrust law does not deal with information problems because it assumes they are handled by contract and consumer protection law. That should change because in a modern economy, *most competition problems are caused by information problems.*

Why doesn't current contract law attack the information problems that lead to a lack of competition? The technical reason is that these information problems are not related to products that have been bought but to alternative products that *could* have been bought. If I pay too much for a product because I have insufficient information on competing products, there is technically nothing wrong with the contract I signed. Sure, the price is higher than it could have been, but that is no ground for rescission in contract law; after all, courts have insufficient information to implement a "just price" doctrine.

Also, technically, the problem with unpublished prices is not that they aren't revealed. As a matter of fact, they are— after a sales pitch or just before buying, but too late to make the process competitive. Still, because prices are known by the buyer at the time of the purchase, the initial lack of information is not a contractual problem but a precontractual problem. And precontractual liability is still underdeveloped in the legal system.

While a duty to publish prices looks simple, its implementation is complicated. Indeed, the danger is that businesses will formally comply with the law by publishing their prices, but in such a way that even search engines have a hard time finding it, so that price comparison remains a time-consuming activity. This means that there are many details that the law needs to get right in order for it to succeed.

The most important detail is that prices must be published in a standardized form so that search engines can easily find them. This means that all pieces of information need to be coded in a standardized way so that search engines can easily pick up the information and put them in the right category. Standardization starts with a duty to give all products a unique ID number; this is an essential technical condition for setting up databases. Note that such a unique ID number already exists for many products (for instance, books have an ISBN, most products in your local store have a standardized bar code, and Medicare has thousands of codes for medical services). The law should make not only stores do this, but also hospitals, plumbers, cooling companies— anyone who sells goods or services.

Another obvious detail is that the published prices need to be binding. If published prices weren't binding, price fog could easily be injected through the backdoor. Of course, sellers need protection against typographical errors and other mistakes, but contract law already has rules in place to protect them in such cases. Relatedly, published prices should reflect the *total* price. (Yes, I am looking at you, hospitals!)

Still another detail is that mentioning the official ID number should be mandatory. Remember the merchant who offered a "professional Sony cassette deck player" that turned out to be identical to the lower-priced Sony TCWE475? This deceptive practice worked by not revealing the product number. The example illustrates why using product numbers should be mandatory, not optional.

Where exactly should prices be published? In a government-run database? Many people would worry if that were the case, as governments have a shaky reputation for offering services. Fortunately, there is no need for the government to do the job. If information is published in a standardized form anywhere on the internet, competing search engines can easily assemble such databases. The only thing the government needs to do is to make sure standards get defined.

Yes, when it comes to standardization, governments have an important role to play. This does not mean that the standards themselves must be determined by civil servants in gray suits—the preparation of the standardization proposal can be outsourced to private consultants or organizations. (Compare this to highways, the construction of which is also outsourced to private companies.) But the government has to make sure standardization happens, and that it happens fast. Standardization destroys rents, so we can't rely on the industries themselves to do it voluntarily.

A system of unique product numbers is not hard to set up for mass-produced goods, but the job can be more difficult for services or custom-made goods. Suppose you need a blood test for which one laboratory charges $300 and a competing laboratory charges $500. How do you know that both labs perform the same blood test? The code can't simply be "blood test"; there needs to be tens of thousands of standard codes for all possible blood tests.

But wouldn't publishing and constantly updating all the prices in the economy cost an enormous amount of time to stores, hospitals, and plumbers, to mention just a few? Wouldn't this be another example of red tape?[213] Well, it shouldn't, because those price lists are already on the businesses' hard drives. If sharing a text or picture with Facebook, Instagram, or Flickr takes only a mouse click, why would it take more time to "share" a price list?

Create a Similar Duty for Quality Information

Publishing price information reduces price fog. But how do you reduce the other type of fog—*quality fog*? The best way is to require sellers to finance standardized tests and publish the results on the internet.

Right now, there is no such general requirement. If you want to buy a new vacuum cleaner, you go to a store and see twenty different types of many different brands. How noisy, reliable, and effective are they? You may not receive objective, comparative information at all. Or suppose you want to buy AAA batteries. Should you buy the more expensive Duracell batteries, or the cheaper alternative? Do Duracell batteries really last longer, and if so, by how much? Duracell won't give you precise information. All they do is make ads in which electric bunnies with Duracell batteries drop dead later than those powered by an undisclosed competitor. When you are at the store, you don't have five bunnies with you to do the test.[214]

Requiring standardized quality tests is nothing new. Car manufacturers must measure the miles per gallon for each car model; pharmaceutical companies must conduct rigorous scientific tests; food producers must conduct standardized nutritional tests. Requiring such tests for nearly all their products, however, involves many details that the law must get right. One is that standardized tests must be defined for most types of products. For vacuum cleaners, this implies setting standards for how to measure noise levels (at what distance from the object is the loudness measured?), suction power on hard floors (what kind of hard floors? What kind of dirt should you throw on it?), suction power on carpet (how thick should the carpet be? What material should it be made of?), the ability to remove animal hairs (what animals?), the energy consumption, the air filter's performance, the product's expected life span, and the expected yearly repair costs. For batteries, standards need to be developed for the total amount of electric energy they generate, given a certain use, before the voltage drops below a critical point.

Are such lab tests really worth the money? Won't they make products more expensive? That depends on whether the information is "material." Materiality is a well-known concept in contract law, and it means (in this context) that the information cost is lower than the information benefit—in other words, that the information is important enough to be conveyed. If too few consumers even bother about noise levels of vacuum cleaners, the information should indeed not be produced. But in that case, the information should also not be produced through other forms, such as advertising or Amazon user reviews. (Strictly speaking, advertising on these characteristics should then even be forbidden, as it would be wasteful by definition.)

If, on the other hand, information is material (and as a matter of fact, for mass-produced goods like vacuum cleaners or batteries even small details can become "material" because of the economies of scale), it should be produced and communicated. The most efficient way to do so is to produce it in a reliable, standardized way and to communicate it on the internet. The budgets needed to do this are only a tiny fraction of the marketing budgets currently used to produce misleading puffery.

Keep also in mind that a duty to reveal quality information only mimics what would happen in a perfectly competitive market. In such a market, the "Grossman mechanism" (remember chapter 4) would work. If a business would not reveal material quality information, consumers would interpret it as a signal that the business has something to hide. To be fair, being forced to reveal information is not fun for businesses. It means more work when they launch a product, more competition once the product is on the market, and fewer opportunities to acquire information rents.

Yet true innovators may like it, as it makes it much easier for them to enter markets. In our current, foggy markets, entry in an existing market requires huge marketing budgets, even for an innovator with superior products. With standardized quality testing of all products, market penetration could happen almost instantly—search engines would immediately tell consumers that a superior product has entered the market, and consumers would not need all those commercials before being convinced. Bad news for advertisement companies, but good news for truly innovating companies.

Make Sure Caveat Emptor Is Really Dead

Requiring businesses to conduct standardized quality testing for nearly all their products may sound like a major policy change. Yet it is no more than the consistent application of an existing principle of law—that the party who is in the best position to produce information should produce it. To be fair, it goes against the ancient principle of *caveat emptor*—but contrary to what many people think, that principle is all but dead in modern law.

Caveat emptor is a Latin expression that means "buyer beware." Beware, buyer, that the seller is not going to cheat you into buying a low-quality product. Beware that the seller is not going to overcharge you. Technically, caveat emptor means there is no liability for even fraudulent misrepresentation, and that there is no duty to disclose whatsoever. If caveat emptor were still the law, sellers could lie and cheat as much as they wanted—it would be the buyers' responsibility to discover the cheating.

Legal historians debate whether caveat emptor has ever existed as a legal principle.[215] The argument is that caveat emptor is not a rule but the absence of a rule. Caveat emptor means that the legal system won't protect you if someone cheated, but it is not a rule that permits cheating. Whatever the merits of this argument, it is a fact that there used to be less legal protection in ancient times (as the legal system was underdeveloped). Nonetheless, the absence of protection was less harmful in ancient times because the economy was simpler. Suppose you bought a table at an ancient market and later discovered the table was unstable. Well, a table is a simple product that you can easily inspect before buying. The same applies to the price: just walk around your small medieval town and you know the prices of all the competitors. Caveat emptor may even have been useful to keep fraudulent claims out of the courts—buyers who complained may just have been looking for a false excuse to get out of a deal.

Still, a caveat emptor regime has probably never existed in its most extreme form—in which a buyer would never have any recourse against the worst type of fraud. Even the oldest legal systems had some anti-fraud provisions; and liability for latent defects (which indirectly creates disclosure duties) has been known in civil law countries for at least 2,000 years.

That said, it is true that there was a revival of caveat emptor in the nineteenth century in American courts, when the belief became strong that contracts were based on "arms-length" negotiations between two adults, who were each responsible for their own information gathering.

In the twentieth century, however, American courts slowly removed the remaining elements of caveat emptor. Courts started to void contracts on the basis of "negligent misrepresentation" (where the seller did not lie but should have known the information was incorrect). Moreover, misrepresentation started to include concealing something or telling a half-truth (like when the seller tells the buyer that she has received leasing income from the apartments but does not reveal that she never had a zoning permit in the first place). In numerous cases, the law created explicit duties to disclose information (that is, duties to spontaneously reveal the truth even if the buyer did not ask for it—for instance, sellers received a duty to reveal termite damage even when buyers did not ask for it).

Caveat emptor was further eroded through changes in tort law, consumer protection law, and economic regulation. Modern product liability, for instance, holds manufacturers strictly liable for physical harm caused by defects, based on the argument that manufacturers know the safety risks better than their customers. Regulation requires pharmaceutical companies not only to reveal the known side effects of their drugs, but also to conduct research to discover them. Car manufacturers must reveal the miles per gallon of their cars and food manufacturers must disclose nutritional information.

So, the principle that best describes the current law is the *least-cost information gatherer* principle. This principle states that the party that is in the best position to acquire material information should acquire and communicate it. Who knows best whether a house for sale is infested with termites—the seller or the buyer? Obviously, the seller, because she has acquired this information as a by-product of living in the house. Therefore, American common law makes the seller disclose this information. Who is in the best position to acquire information on drugs—the pharmaceutical company that sells them or the patient? Obviously, the pharmaceutical company, and therefore the FDA makes drug companies perform extensive trials before the drug can be sold on the market. If caveat emptor were still alive, it would be the responsibility of the patient to run these trials.

If caveat emptor no longer exists, why do so many people think it still exists? The reason is that there is a gap between the law on the books and the law in action. On paper, caveat emptor is no longer a legal principle. But in practice, the law is not consistently applied and enforced, so that consumers still experience caveat emptor on a daily basis. They know that if they buy an overpriced or inferior product, the legal system will usually not bail them out. It is time to make sure that caveat emptor is really dead.

Create a Duty to Reveal the Actuarial Cost of Insurance and Warranties

When you buy a lottery ticket, a part of the money (for instance, 70 percent) goes to prizes, and the rest (for instance, 30 percent) goes to administration, marketing, and profits. This 70 percent (the "actuarial cost") has to be disclosed in many countries and states.

Similarly, when you buy insurance, a part (for instance, 70 percent) goes to paying compensation and the rest (for instance, 30 percent) to administration, marketing, and profits. Do insurance companies have to reveal the actuarial cost? They don't. But if we want to reduce information rents in the insurance industry, they should.

Revealing the actuarial cost is indirectly revealing the markup. Revealing the markup feels like an invasion of privacy. Isn't it your own business how much you make on a transaction? Yet privacy is not an excuse when your house is infested with termites. If you sell the house, you have to disclose it because it is "material information." For insurance products, the actuarial cost is material information. Indeed, as we have seen in chapter 5, you need to know the actuarial cost before you can even determine whether it is rational to buy insurance. Moreover, you need to know the actuarial cost to compare competing insurance products. After all, insurance companies offer different terms and tend to differ in the ease with which they pay out.

But shouldn't the consumer know *her own* risk? The problem is that it is hard for the consumer to know this as it requires statistical data. What is the chance that I will fly off the road and land my car in a dunghill? I don't know. My friends say it's higher than average, but they don't know the average either. The insurer is clearly the least-cost information gatherer, as she obtained this data as a by-product of processing insurance claims. In addition, forcing insurers to publish the data does not destroy their incentive to collect the data precisely because they are automatically produced as a by-product of processing claims.

A legal duty to disclose the actuarial cost is even more urgent when you realize how the insurance industry obtains information rents by making products incomparable. I once got a quote for life insurance that was nearly three times as expensive as the quote a competing insurer had given me. When I mentioned this, the insurance agent replied that her quote included many extra benefits—for instance, my kids would receive an additional payment if I were to die while they were in college. When I asked what was the statistical chance that this would happen (so that I could estimate the value of these extra benefits), I only got the answer, "More than you think." At the end of the day, it was nearly impossible to determine which life insurance offered more value. I might have taken the more expensive one if I had not read all those marketing books.

What this life insurance company did was to turn a commodity into a unique product by bundling the core product with other benefits. It tried to prevent price competition by making its products incomparable with the insurance policies of other companies. What can the legal system do against such practices? Well, imposing a duty to disclose actuarial costs, not only for the total product but also for the unique components of the product, would be a good start. Maybe I would then have learned that the expected value of the kids-in-college provision was negligible. This would have made it clear that the higher price was just a rent.

A similar disclosure duty should apply to insurance-like products, like extended warranties. (Sellers of these warranties hasten to say that warranties are, from a legal point of view, not insurance. But from an economic point of view, they are no different: they transfer the financial risk of defects, so the law should not treat them differently.) Warranties are an information rent paradise because consumers tend to overestimate statistical repair costs. How much of the warranty premium that you pay in your local electronics store is effectively needed to cover repair costs? Recent scholarship suggests that if you knew, you would never buy such warranties again.[216]

A similar duty should be created for goods that are bundled with charity or environmental benefits. Whole Foods should tell us how much of the price, on average, goes to these noble purposes. Again, such a duty is less revolutionary than it may seem. In many legal systems, charities must reveal what percentage of a gift goes to the charitable project itself and what percentage goes to administrative costs. So, why not make businesses reveal the percentage that goes to charity?

Create a Duty to Disclose Statistical Information Related to Quality and Pricing

Knowing a product's true price or quality sometimes requires statistical information. How expensive is a car, if you take repairs into account? That depends on how often certain repairs are needed as well as the price of the repair and the parts needed in each of those cases. How expensive is a plumber? That varies from case to case, depending on which spare parts are needed and how much the plumber charges for each spare part.

Sellers are the least-cost information gatherers of such information. Not only are they the experts but they usually also acquire this information as a by-product of their activities. They know how many of their products are returned for repair, or how many spare components are ordered by repair shops. Consumer organizations may try to reverse engineer all this by organizing surveys, but such surveys draw a less accurate picture than what the seller already has. They are also intrinsically wasteful because they reproduce information that is already in the possession of someone else.

One difficulty is that, in some cases, the data is spread over many sellers and service providers, so that information needs to be collected. A single car can be repaired in many garages over its life span. To know how often a used car was repaired requires collecting data from many garages. Similarly, postsurgical complications may not always appear in a surgeon's own files because patients who lose confidence in their surgeon may seek help from other doctors. This holds true even more so for the long-term effects of a treatment. So, to determine how good a doctor is, or how effective a medical treatment is, data needs to be collected from many sources. Once more, this may be a piece of cake if data is stored in a standardized format but a nightmare when it is stored in different formats.

Wouldn't publishing this information be very costly to businesses? That is what they will argue. But that is only the case if information exchange standards aren't defined (or the software they use isn't adapted yet to these standards). Remember, businesses don't have to produce this information; they already have it somewhere on a hard drive. All they have to do is share it.

After millions of years, mankind has made it technically possible to share pictures on Facebook or Instagram with the click of a mouse. Do you think mankind can't achieve the same for data that destroys information rents?

Make Wholesale Prices Transparent

A duty to reveal markups goes against our instincts. A markup is sometimes seen as something intimate, something that no consumer has any business knowing. But from a principal-agent perspective, there is nothing special about revealing markups. After all, the seller works for the consumer, and the consumer "pays" the seller in the form of a markup. Why wouldn't the consumer be allowed to know how much she paid the seller for her work?

I once visited a warehouse with an interior designer to select the piece of granite that would be used for a countertop in our kitchen. When I asked the sales representative how much the granite we had selected would cost, he said: "None of your business!" Okay, I am being a little imprecise here: "None of your business" was what the salesman *thought* but not what he *said*. The words he actually uttered were: "I'm sorry, but I can't give you the price." What he meant was that he would give a price to the granite installer, who would then add an undisclosed markup and reveal this to the designer, who would add another undisclosed markup and give us the final price. How much did we pay for the services of the installer and the interior designer? I have no clue. Thus, a more honest answer the sales representative could have given me is: "I do not want to tell you the price structure because your interior designer, the installer, and I are in the information rent business and if we made pricing more transparent, our information rents would disappear."

Think about it—if all markets (and therefore also all wholesale markets) were fully transparent, consumers could easily check the wholesale prices. A legal duty to reveal wholesale prices therefore only mimics what would happen anyway in perfect markets.[217]

Forbid Dynamic Pricing and Price Discrimination Based on Fog or Hurdles

Price discrimination means that consumers pay different prices for the same good. If you are reading this book on an airplane, there is a good chance that the person sitting next to you paid a different price for his seat than you did. Price discrimination can be economically justified in some cases, such as when there is unused capacity. But the type of price discrimination that is becoming dominant in modern markets is totally different. It consists of charging more to consumers who are uninformed about the market price of competing goods. There is no economic justification for this type of price discrimination; it is a straightforward application of the Pickpocket Business Model—try to steal the wallets of customers who do not notice it.

Price discrimination is legal, except for in truly exceptional cases, such as when it amounts to racial or gender discrimination.[218] It should be forbidden whenever it is based on *informational differences*. It should become illegal to charge more for a car to naive buyers than to sophisticated buyers. After all, this is a type of discrimination that would not even be possible in perfectly competitive markets.

If price discrimination based on informational differences becomes illegal, an implication is that "best-price guarantees" should lower the price for *all* buyers of the good, not only the ones who discovered the lower prices elsewhere. As we have seen, this is not what best-price guarantees are currently doing. They apply only to the informed customers and therefore treat informed and noninformed consumers differently. Since they are a form of price discrimination based on informational differences, they should be forbidden in their current form.

Another form of price discrimination that should be forbidden is the one based on so-called hurdles. Hurdles are artificial little jobs that a consumer needs to do before qualifying for a rebate. Mail-in rebates are an example: you only get them if you perfectly fill out a long form and cut out the serial number from the box. In 2005, only 50,000 of the 104,000 eligible customers filed for TiVo's $100 mail-in rebate, many being too distracted during the Christmas shopping season.[219] The $5 million windfall allowed TiVo to surprise Wall Street with better-than-expected financial results. Congratulations to the CEO who implemented this; he deserves a large bonus!

Price discrimination based on hurdles is economically harmful for two reasons. First, it is usually no more than an exploitation of consumers' irrationality—they plan to fill out that form and then forget it. Second, the time and energy to jump over the "hurdles" and the business's costs to process the rebates are intrinsically wasteful. They do not make the country richer; they are just rent-seeking costs.

One commonly heard justification for hurdles is that they allow sellers to identify "low-value users," who are only willing to buy the product when the price is low. Yet whether a consumer mails in her rebate form does not say anything about how much she values the good—it only says something about how much she values her own time. A more refined justification is that those who mail in the rebate have a lower opportunity cost of time, and therefore may be poorer and therefore may have a lower willingness-to-pay. This is a clever rhetorical argument; after all, helping the poor is good, isn't it? But mailing in a form is a weak proxy for income. For starters, it also says something about an individual's administrative efficiency, a skill that may be correlated with higher wealth. More importantly, businesses can find much better proxies for wealth—even zip codes. This proves that the core of the business model is not the identification of low-value users, but the exploitation of human irrationality.

This brings us to the hidden Easter eggs of modern times— coupons! Coupons are a combination of price discrimination based on informational barriers and price discrimination based on hurdles. Neither of these two is economically justifiable, so the two united into one package can't be justifiable either. Or do you think that all the energy spent on searching coupons makes the country richer?

Relatedly, most forms of *dynamic pricing* should be forbidden. Dynamic pricing, as we have seen in chapter 4, allows businesses to "optimize" prices by changing them from day to day, from moment to moment, or from customer to customer. In reality, dynamic pricing increases fog by making it dramatically more expensive to find current prices. It also takes price discrimination of uninformed buyers to its extreme by letting prices depend on the degree to which buyers are informed. In some other cases, dynamic pricing is a method to enforce implicit cartels, by responding immediately whenever a competitor lowers prices so that lowering prices no longer has any advantage at all. In sum, "dynamic pricing" is usually just a fancy name for a fraud, fog, or cartel scheme. Antitrust law should forbid it, unless it is based on true production cost changes.

Stop Granting Trademark Protection on Product Names

When consumers compare products, they can make two types of mistakes. First, they can believe that the products are the same when they are different (Type 1 confusion). Second, they can believe that the products are different when they are the same (Type 2 confusion).

Trademark law is designed to prevent Type 1 confusion. If any smartphone manufacturer could print "Apple" on it, consumers could mistakenly believe that this phone has the same quality and features as the one produced by Apple. Thanks to trademark law's protection of Apple's brand, consumers are better informed.

Unfortunately, trademark law sometimes causes Type 2 confusion. If your doctor tells you to buy Tylenol and you go to a pharmacy, you may see boxes with "Tylenol" on them and boxes with "acetaminophen" on them. You may conclude that the two are different and pay a premium price for Tylenol. In reality, the substances are the same, but trademark law forbids other manufacturers from using the name "Tylenol." Because of your confusion, Johnson & Johnson (the owner of the Tylenol brand) receives an information rent. But it is trademark law that helped Johnson & Johnson sustain the confusion.

The law rewards the inventors of a drug by giving them twenty years of patent protection. Yet unintentionally, trademark law adds a second reward by granting an eternal marketing advantage. Indeed, inventors can pick an easy name for themselves (such as "Viagra") and force competitors to use an unspeakable name (such as "sildenafil"). Imagine if we were to do the same for pizza: one restaurant in the whole city may use the name "pizza" and the other restaurants have to use "carbohydrotomafromatis,"—the easiest name the scientists of the USAN Council could come up with.[220] Wouldn't many consumers pay the premium price for the thing named "pizza," erroneously believing that the thing with the longer name is something else?

How do we reform trademark law so that it no longer creates Type 2 confusion, while still preventing Type 1 confusion? Very simply: give trademark protection only to the manufacturer's name (Johnson & Johnson) but not to the product name (Tylenol). In other words: generalize the system we have for pizza. You have pizza from Papa John's, Pizza Hut, and Domino's, but they can all call it "pizza." So, let all manufacturers of acetaminophen call it "Tylenol" (since this is how the product is known in the US). Type 1 confusion will be avoided because only Johnson & Johnson can add "made by Johnson & Johnson" on the box.

Impose a Fiduciary Duty on All Salespeople Who Pretend to Give Honest Advice

The law currently allows salespeople to give biased advice while pretending to give honest advice. Wolves are allowed to hide in sheep clothes. The solution is very simple: create a legal duty for salespeople to act like what they pretend to be. Technically, this means creating a fiduciary duty to all salespeople who pretend to give honest advice. If salespeople still want to give biased advice, that is fine, but then they should openly reveal that, for instance by saying, "Do not always believe what I say. I am committed to giving biased advice. My goal is not to help you but to help my own bank account."

A duty to give honest advice is nothing revolutionary; it already exists in many forms in the law. CEOs have a "fiduciary duty" toward shareholders, which means that they must always do what they honestly believe to be in the best interests of the shareholders. Such a fiduciary duty also exists for anyone who falls under the definition of "agent"—a huge category that includes all employees in their relationship with their employer. Moreover, under contract law there are similar duties for anyone who is in "a relationship of trust and confidence." For unclear reasons, however, this "relationship of trust and confidence" is still defined somewhat narrowly. It covers your doctor, your lawyer, and your relatives, but it does not cover the "trusted advisers" at your local bank or electronics store; it also does not cover your insurance broker, your mortgage broker, your car dealer, or any other expert who makes a living of collecting information rents by pretending to be on your side.[221]

True, it is not always easy to prove that someone gave dishonest advice. In some cases, this may require reading the salesperson's mind, which is impossible. But most stores are now owned by large corporations who give detailed instructions to their sales staff, either in written form or orally. The fact that the instructions are communicated to many people at the same time makes it much easier to find legal evidence, both for FTC prosecutors and for attorneys.

Still, given these evidence issues, corporate law teaches us that a duty of loyalty (one of the components of a fiduciary duty) is best accompanied by a duty to reveal conflicts of interests. If CEOs own stock of the companies they are doing business with, corporate law makes them reveal that to their employer (in practice, the board of directors). If we apply this principle to salespeople who pretend to give honest advice, this means that they should reveal it when they recommend products that have higher-than-average markups.

I can very well imagine that many salespeople won't like this proposal. But for the good-faith type of sellers it would be an improvement, because they would receive an easy weapon for defeating manipulative competitors: legally enforced honesty.

Fight Implicit Cartels through Bertrand Post-and-Hold Regulation

Oligopoly markets can go two ways, depending on how businesses play the game. If they compete aggressively on price, the price can be as low as under perfect competition; this is called "Bertrand competition." If they are nice to each other and do not compete on price, the price can be as high as under a monopoly; this could be called an "implicit cartel."

Which outcome is more likely? That partly depends on how large the first-mover advantage is of the one who starts lowering the price. In the good old days, when prices were printed in annual catalogues, the first-mover advantage could last a full year. This created a strong incentive to lower prices. In the modern computer era, however, this first-mover advantage is sometimes no longer than a few milliseconds—that is all it takes software to adjust prices and communicate the change. As a result, Bertrand equilibria have become less likely and implicit cartels more likely—especially since the players of the game have now been trained by business schools.

What could the legal system do to bring oligopoly markets to Bertrand equilibria? The legal solution is what I will call *Bertrand post-and-hold regulation*. This is regulation that forces oligopolists to publish their prices ("post") and keep them unchanged ("hold") for a certain period of time. (I use the term "Bertrand" because it is designed to lead to a Bertrand equilibrium.) It is important, though, that they "post" simultaneously, before they have seen each other's prices. How do you do this in practice? By requiring them to submit prices in a (virtual or real) sealed envelope, similar to what is done in sealed-envelope auctions; all envelopes are then opened at the same time, by publishing them in standardized form on the internet.

Bertrand post-and-hold regulation works by creating a Prisoners' Dilemma. In a Prisoners' Dilemma, two prisoners are interrogated in a separate room. They have to decide whether to talk to the police without knowing what the other prisoner is doing. If one of them talks, that one is rewarded and the other one gets the full punishment. If both of them talk, they share the punishment. The best outcome for them would be that no one talks. In practice, however, they will betray each other, either to get the reward (if the other one does not talk) or to get a lower punishment (if the other one talks). The Prisoners' Dilemma only works, however, if the two prisoners are not in the same room. If you put them in the same room, they will not talk because they know the other one will immediately retaliate by talking as well.

Bertrand post-and-hold regulation makes oligopolists "betray" each other by taking a final position (that is why there is the "hold") before they can see their competitors' prices (that's why they have to post it simultaneously in a sealed envelope). "Betraying" here means starting a cutthroat price competition instead of respecting the implicit cartel price.

Just like in the original Prisoners' Game, the reward for lowering the price (the equivalent of "talking") should be large enough. So, it is crucial that the duration of the "hold" is long enough to make the "first-mover advantage" (of the one who posts the lowest price) large enough. How long should this be? One month? One year? That should vary from industry to industry.

Remarkably, Bertrand post-and-hold regulation could even be used in monopolized industries. The problem in those industries is that, at first glance, there is never any form of price competition. After all, there is only one monopolist in the market who does not have to compete with anyone else. A well-known economist, Baumol, has argued, however, that monopolists may have to compete with *potential* competitors if the market is *contestable*. (In other words, monopolists may have to ask low prices because otherwise competitors would enter the market.) Unfortunately, many markets aren't very contestable in practice. Competitors may be reluctant to enter a monopolized market because they fear that the monopolist would immediately lower his prices to drive them out of the market. (Keep in mind that new entrants often have higher costs than incumbents because they have to invest in marketing; as a result, incumbents can still make a profit at a price where entrants make a loss.)

Bertrand post-and-hold regulation could make monopolized markets contestable by forbidding the monopolist to lower his prices in response to new entrants. If new entrants could earn a large enough first-mover advantage, monopolists may have to keep their prices low.

Do Bertrand post-and-hold rules exist in the real world? Well, a variant is used in some states for the alcohol industry. For instance, New York requires alcohol wholesalers to post their prices for the following month by the 5th of each month. On the 15th of each month, wholesalers can see each other's future prices; then, they have three days to lower their prices to the level of the lowest posted price. The first day of the next month, all prices become binding for a month.

Cooper and (former FTC commissioner) Wright found that post-and-hold regulation *increased* prices![222] How is this possible? Well, the devil is in the details. Alcohol wholesalers can observe each other's prices before taking a final position. This is like organizing a Prisoners' Dilemma and forgetting to put the prisoners in separate rooms: of course, no one will start talking if the other can immediately retaliate by talking as well. Ironically, poorly designed post-and-hold laws make it easier to enforce implicit cartels. But well-designed post-and-hold laws, that is, Bertrand post-and-hold laws, are powerful instruments to restore competition in oligopolistic markets.

Expand Anti-Lock-In Rules

Lock-in effects (like the ones created by the razor-blade model) create monopoly power in an aftermarket. For ink cartridges, you pay a monopoly price because you are locked in once you have bought a certain type of printer. Lock-in effects are widespread in modern markets; the "razor-blade" model is taught at business schools and massively applied by marketers.[223] A marketer who now forgets to create lock-in effects in the form of razor-blade effects or loyalty cards is nearly committing malpractice. Surprisingly, the legal system has left these monopolies largely untouched.

What could the legal system do to reduce lock-in effects? To answer this question, we should keep in mind that there are two ways to look at lock-in problems. From an ex post perspective (after you have bought a printer), they are monopoly problems (you can only buy the manufacturer's cartridges). From an ex ante perspective (before you bought the printer), they are information problems (you have great difficulties comparing the true costs of printers). Therefore, there are two ways to reduce lock-in effects: reducing switching costs ex post or reducing information costs ex ante.

At first glance, providing better information to consumers seems like the least invasive solution. Unfortunately, the amount of information that is needed to correct the problem is enormous because the information is of a statistical nature. How much will it cost to print a page? This requires information on the expected life span of the printer and the number of pages that will be printed. How much will a car cost if the repair expenses are taken into account? This requires statistical information on the likelihood that certain parts will need to be replaced over the life span of a car. To make matters worse, calculating the lifetime cost of a product also requires knowing the *future* prices of ink cartridges and car replacement parts, and these future prices can be changed at will by manufacturers. Put this all together, and you will see that we shouldn't expect too much from informational remedies.*

A better solution, therefore, is to attack lock-in effects directly at the source. For starters, the legal system could stop giving patent protection to lock-in technology. (The legal system could even go a step further and grant competitors free compulsory licensing rights on the cartridge technology.) Next, the legal system could restrict termination fees (to make switching easier) and limit the duration of certain contracts (which was the problem in the Austrian propane market example, where consumers had to buy propane gas from one specific company

---

* Certification might also work when cheaper, equally good printer cartridges are on the market, but most consumers don't dare to buy them because of quality fog. If the quality of these products could be officially certified, fewer customers would continue to buy the overpriced cartridges. Of course, printer manufacturers would quickly respond by protecting all cartridges with patents.

over decades). Loyalty programs, consumer friendly as they look, should be forbidden as well; they hurt consumers as a group by distorting competition. One-Click-Switching is another great solution. One-Click-Switching means that customers should be able to switch to competitors with a single mouse click. Imagine that all bank account holders had a One-Click-Switching opportunity, so that a single mouse click would be sufficient to transfer their money, transaction history, automatic payments, and even account number to a competing bank if they became dissatisfied with their original bank. (Such a switching opportunity obviously requires standardization of the form in which some data are kept, so that's an important task for the government.) A One-Click-Switching opportunity could also increase competitiveness in the insurance sector by allowing consumers to seamlessly change insurance providers. Even Facebook's market power could be reduced if users could move their profile and data to a competitor's social media website with a single mouse click. Businesses obviously have no incentive to offer One-Click-Switching, so the legal system should step in and make it mandatory.

Reduce Market Power Caused by Network Externalities

We have seen that many (quasi-)monopolies are caused by network externalities. Nearly everyone uses Windows, Word, and Excel because nearly everyone else is using it. Nearly everyone chooses Facebook and Twitter because that is what nearly everyone is on.* Nearly everyone uses Google because it does the best job sorting the most useful sites. But Google can only do this because nearly everyone uses Google, giving Google more information on search behavior than any other search engine. And large hospital groups often have market power because they use an internal, integrated patient data system. If you go to a competing hospital, doctors can no longer easily see your records. (Sure, if they really want them, they can contact all your previous doctors and get some of the records faxed a few days later. But that is a time-consuming activity, which doctors within the same hospital don't have to undertake.)

Although network externalities are a serious threat to competition, antitrust law doesn't take them seriously.[224] Antitrust law has no general policy to fight network externalities. To make matters worse, intellectual property law (a body of law that *grants* monopoly rights) has no special rules for network externalities either, so it may unintentionally create network externality problems by granting patents to certain standards.

How can we reduce rents caused by network externalities? Since network externalities and lock-in effects are analytically related, the solutions largely coincide. For instance, giving consumers a legal right to One-Click-Switching (as explained earlier in this chapter) would definitely decrease the market power of companies such as Facebook and Microsoft. One-Click-Switching would mean that Facebook users could effortlessly switch to another social network, automatically taking everything they have uploaded on Facebook with them. It would also mean that Microsoft Word users could switch to competing software products without having to spend time

---

* Mark Zuckerberg's story is similar to Bill Gates'—becoming a billionaire by making a product with network externalities. Why is nearly everybody on Facebook and not on a competing social network site? It is a great site, sure, but that is only one part of the story. The larger part is that everybody is on Facebook because everybody else is on Facebook. These network externalities give Facebook its dominant position.

exporting all their files in a different format or losing some layout instructions in the process. In the case of hospitals, it would mean that patients can move their entire medical record with a single mouse click to a competing hospital. (In essence, it would mean that medical records are kept in a standardized form and owned by the patients.)

Intellectual property protection could reduce network externalities by simply refusing to protect technology with network externalities. This would mean that information storage formats (such as the MS Word or Excel format) can never be owned by a private company. Would this mean less innovation in formats? No, it would mean that incentives must be given in a different form than through property rights. For instance, federal agencies could pay private companies to develop them, or give grants to universities to do so. Compare storage formats to interstate highways: just because they won't be privately owned doesn't mean they're never built. But the government does have to pay private companies to build them.

Fight Payer Externalities by Making the Decider Pay

Payer externalities is not an existing term. I have introduced the term to label the special type of market failure that occurs when the decision maker for an expense is not the one who pays for the expense. College books are so expensive because professors are the ones who choose them and students are the ones who pay for them. We have also seen that credit card companies can charge stores 3 percent or more because it is the buyers who decide whether to use them (and those buyers even get bribed with a 1 percent kickback in the form of miles or rewards) and the stores who pay for them.

It is time for antitrust law to take payer externalities seriously. Fixing the problem is incredibly easy: make the decision maker pay the bill. If consumers are the ones who choose how to pay, they should pay all expenses related to their credit cards. And universities should pay for the college books they prescribe. It is as simple as that.

Reform Property Law and Oil and Gas Law

Both property law and oil and gas law determine who gets the rents related to natural resources. Rent economics postulates that natural resources rents do not cause economic inequality if competition for the resources is perfect. In most American states, however, the owner of the surface automatically owns everything below it, which means that oil and mineral rights are given away for free. Instead, these rights should go to those who bid most for them in a competitive auction.

Take oil wells. In civil law countries, such as Norway, the property rights on the surface and everything that is below it are split. The owner of land does not automatically own the mining rights below it. About 15 percent of the Norwegian GDP consists of oil and gas rents, but that hasn't increased income inequality in that country.[225] Most of the oil rents go to a public pension fund, set up for the benefit of all Norwegians.

In most American states, in contrast, the owner of the surface automatically owns everything below it. Remember how the Texas Gulf Sulphur mining company discovered the Kidd Creek mineral deposit in Ontario and then tricked the landowner into selling it for 10 percent of the market value? The problem here, from an income inequality perspective, was not that landowner had been tricked into selling something below its true value. The problem was that property law gave billions of dollars away to that landowner, who just happened to own land at a certain location. Seen from a different angle, the problem was that Texas Gulf Sulphur never had to participate in an auction and eventually got a billion-dollar windfall.

In the 1980s, the famous TV show *Dallas* portrayed Texas oil millionaires. Why do you have these oil millionaires in Texas? Because Texas property law gives away oil wells for free. Those who can acquire them receive a windfall.[226]

So, what exactly should be changed? For starters, ownership of land should be limited to the surface. The rights on the oil or minerals under the surface should initially go to the state. Incentives to discover oil and minerals should be given by paying companies fees to conduct surveys, not by giving property rights to the finder. Once oil wells have been discovered, ownership should either stay with the government or go to the oil companies who bid most for them in a competitive auction.

Of course, auctions must be carefully designed. In 1933, the king of Saudi Arabia gave away the oil rights for sixty-six years on an area larger than Texas to Standard Oil of California. The price he received for this concession was about $250,000. At that time, nobody had a clue about how much oil was in the ground. So, the king ran afoul of a principle of auction theory that says that prices get higher when there is less uncertainty. (This is one reason why Christie's carefully examines the true painter of a masterpiece.) Auctioning rights at too early a stage is like if they had organized an initial public offering (IPO) for Facebook when it had only twenty users. No American entrepreneur would ever make that mistake. Arabic countries no longer make the mistake either—they no longer use classic concessions.

Unfortunately, a country that still auctions oil rights at an early stage when quantities are uncertain is the US. Indeed, oil leases on federal land are typically granted at a stage when it is still unknown whether and how much oil will be found.[227]

No wonder the oil industry is lobbying so hard for fracking permissions. Lobbying costs are rent-seeking costs. Rent-seeking costs are only made when rents are in sight, which are only possible if oil fields are given away for less than they are worth. Remember, if auctions are perfectly designed, the good is sold for its full market price, and all rents go to the former generation of owners (the government in this case) instead of leaking to the second generation (the oil companies). If auctions are held at too early a stage, however, rents are leaked and inequality is increased.

Auction New Building Rights Created by Rezoning

Zoning law is the biggest lottery organizer in the world. Whenever agricultural land is turned into building land (or into another, higher-value type of land), the price per square meter explodes. The rent goes to the one who happens to own the agricultural land.

There is something remarkable about this from a property rights perspective. Lawyers see ownership as a basket of rights. The owner of the agricultural land had the right to use the land for agricultural purposes in her basket, but not the more valuable right to build on it. So, what happens with rezoning is that the owner receives a new property right that is much more valuable than the rights that were already in her basket, and she receives this for free. Indeed, she does not have to participate in an auction to get that new right.

Zoning law's goal is to make sure land is optimally used. Its goal was never to increase inequality—this is truly an unintended side effect. So, how do we remove this side effect?

We remove it by applying the same principle that we should

apply for oil and mineral deposits: grant new building rights only after a carefully designed auction. This means that, whenever new building rights on land are created, these should go to the one who pays the most for it.

But don't we run into a major practical problem if we apply this to rezoning? If Donald had the agricultural rights, and Mary wins the building rights auction, don't we end up with two owners, each with different rights to the same good?

Having two owners with incompatible rights to the same good is indeed a problem, known in property law for ages. And so we apply the standard property law solution in such cases, that is, let Mary become the full owner by "taking" Donald's property rights in return for compensation at the market rate for agricultural land. A more practical solution to obtain the same result would be the following: Whenever agricultural land is rezoned into building land, the government takes the agricultural land under eminent domain in return for compensation (at the going rate for agricultural land). The government then sells the building land on the market. (A softer version would be for the government to receive a right of first refusal whenever Mary sells her agricultural land.)[229]

The same should apply when the right to build two floors is turned into the right to build a skyscraper. The government in that case should take the two-floor building under eminent domain in return for compensation at the market rate for two-floor buildings. Then, it should sell the right to construct the skyscraper on the land to the highest bidder.

Of course, this method does not remove the rents that owners receive when land prices go up for other reasons. The price of a two-floor building land can simply increase because of a higher demand. While there is nothing the legal system can do about this in a direct way, it can indirectly reduce land prices by relaxing the zoning restrictions in the region, thus increasing the amount of building land. Another way to look at this strategy is to realize that building land rents are not pure Ricardian rents: while the government can't increase the amount of oil and mineral deposits, the government can increase the amount of building land. Therefore, a great way to reduce the inequality effects caused by rising building land prices is to rezone and make sure that more building land is available.

Don't Make Patents More Generous Than Strictly Needed

Patents and copyrights are artificial monopoly rights created by the law. The law's goal is to stimulate new inventions or artistic works. The law's goal is not to create rents. Unfortunately, it is hard to grant intellectual property rights without also giving away cherry-picking rents. We have seen that the reason, in principal-agent terminology, is that the agent (the innovator) has more information on how much work it takes to produce a piece of technology than the principal (the legal system). Therefore, the principal may have to overpay the agent to get a certain job done. It is like the owner of the orchard who overpays the cherry pickers per bucket to make sure they also pick the high-hanging cherries.

But wait—is overgenerosity really a problem? Isn't the desire to receive rents and become a billionaire what motivates many innovators? Literally, the argument is incorrect: rents are payments in excess of what is needed to make people do something—so by definition they are not needed to make people innovate. A slightly different argument, often made by economists, is that overgenerosity may be a good thing because the more you overpay for an invention, the more likely it is that someone will invent it. Relatedly, the long-run benefits of innovation are believed to be so huge that overgenerosity is never a big deal in the greater scheme of things. If occasionally, an inventor gets $1 billion through the patent system for an invention that can be made for $1 million, that is not something to worry about as long as the invention is made and mankind keeps on making progress—so goes the argument.

What the argument overlooks, though, is that *overpaying leads to less bang for the buck*. Imagine society has an "innovation budget" of $1 billion for a given year. By paying $1 billion instead of $1 million, the whole innovation budget is used up. At the end of the day, 1,000 times more inventions could have been made for the same budget.[230]

Although intellectual property law can't be designed in such a way that it never gives away rents (as this would require a perfectly informed government), it can nonetheless do a much better job at preventing unintended rents.

For starters, it can do a better job at letting the patent duration depend on the innovation costs. There is no reason to give twenty years of patent protection to just any type of invention. The law can try harder to identify categories of technology for which a shorter protection will be enough. A good way to proceed is to reduce the standard protection to three years, but to give longer protection when the innovator comes up with evidence that a longer protection is required to recoup this kind of investment. To be fair, an adjustable patent system is costlier to operate than a simple system with a fixed term of twenty years. Still, these higher administrative costs should be balanced against the social costs of the rents. Given the fact that we are talking about billion-dollar industries, it is worth trying a little harder to prevent spilling rents.

Next, patent protection should never be granted to innovation that would likely have been produced without patent protection. Indeed, innovators typically have a first-mover advantage, and sometimes this is enough to create incentives, especially when innovation costs are modest. Yet there is no "modest innovation costs" exception in current patent law, although there is the somewhat related "obviousness" exception. If an invention was obvious, it probably did not cost much to make. But "obviousness" is defined in a philosophical way (was the invention surprising? Did it require some creativity?), not in an economic way, as it should be (how much work did it take to develop the technology? Will the first-mover advantage be sufficient to recoup the investment?).

Another reform to reduce rents is to stop granting retroactive intellectual property rights. (A retroactive extension means that after the work has been created, Congress extends the protection.) This extra protection is by definition a rent. You should bear in mind that copyright protection is in essence a contract with the government: if you do X, you get Y years of protection. Disney was happy to create Steamboat Willy in 1928 (which introduced Mickey Mouse) in return for fifty-six years of protection (the maximum duration of copyright protection at that time). This means that anything more than fifty-six years is an overpayment.[231] So, when in 1998 Congress retroactively increased copyright protection to extend Disney's copyrights on old Mickey Mouse movies for another twenty years, economic experts were stunned.[232]

To see how absurd retroactive extensions are, suppose that the government agrees to pay a construction company $10 million for a new building. Ten years after the building has been delivered and the full price had been paid, the government sends another $20 million check as a Christmas gift (perhaps even delivered by Santa Claus through the chimney). Wouldn't this be a huge political scandal? And rightly so. But this is what intellectual property law regularly does.

The Mickey Mouse Act is an easy example of a retroactive

extension.[233] An example that is a little harder to recognize is a *geographical* extension of existing rights. The TRIPS Agreement forced developing countries to adopt the intellectual property laws of developed countries.[234] The idea was that, if those countries wanted to use Western technology, they also had to pay for it. This sounds fair, but the way this idea was implemented was puzzling from an economic point of view. If TRIPS would have applied only to *future* inventions and creations, then it would have made some sense. And even then, it only would have made sense if the TRIPS Agreement at the same time reduced the duration of protection. Indeed, if twenty years of patent protection is needed when the market consists only of the US and the EU, ten years may be sufficient when the market is the rest of the world. But that is not what TRIPS did. Instead, TRIPS kept the term constant and applied the geographic extension to *existing* patents and copyright. Such a retroactive extension cannot possibly have incentivized innovation—giving people unexpected rewards for what they have done in the past cannot change anything in the past. So, all the extension did was create rents.

An even harder-to-recognize but still real retroactive extension is given when new pricing methods allow existing patent holders to recoup their investment faster, and the legal system nonetheless keeps the term constant. In 2007, the price of two EpiPens (epinephrine auto-injectors for patients with severe allergic reactions) was $100. After Mylan acquired the rights to market the product, the price raised to $265 in 2013, to $461 in 2015, and to $609 in 2016, leading to such a public outcry that CEO Heather Bresch had to testify before a congressional committee.[235] Why did the price increase? Mylan's CEO came up with several "reasons," but let me tell you the true one: Mylan's price experts calculated that the "optimal" monopoly price was much higher than $100. Call it progress in the field of marketing—pricing experts innovate too. But twenty years of protection was given by the legal system on the argument that such a long period was needed to recoup the investment. If new pricing methods make it possible to recoup the investment in a much shorter period, the patent period should be shortened as well. Keeping it at twenty years, under those circumstances, is a subtle, retroactive Christmas present.

Put Time Limits on Trade Secrets

Innovators can now choose between patent protection and trade secret protection. Patent protection prohibits reverse engineering but requires holders to make the technology public and expires after twenty years. Trade secret protection does not prevent others from reverse engineering the technology but does not require holders to make it public. Moreover, it lasts until someone reverse engineers the technology or until an insider reveals the secret without being caught!

Pharmaceutical companies typically choose patent protection. Coca-Cola instead relied on trade secrets. As a result, the Coca-Cola formula is still a secret after more than 120 years. Apparently, nobody has ever reverse engineered it.

At first glance, granting trade secret protection makes sense. Competitors should not be allowed to free ride on someone else's investment, and innovators should be rewarded. But from a rent economics perspective, trade secret protection is a puzzling instrument to achieve that goal.

For starters, the effective duration of trade secret protection is not set in a rational way. How long should protection last, ideally? That should be based on balancing the costs of monopoly power (which the law helps to prolong) and the benefits of additional innovation. Remarkably, trade secret duration is not based on any form of balancing at all. As a matter of fact, the duration depends on coincidence (it lasts until someone reverse engineers it or leaks the secret). This means that, from a theoretical perspective, trade secret protection can be too short, but it can also be too long.

Coca-Cola provides an example of trade secret protection lasting too long. It lasts already more than a century and it may last for another century. Do you really think pharmacist John Stith Pemberton would not have invented the formula if the protection had been shorter?

Standard economic theory predicts that a company with trade secrets, such as Coca-Cola, will only receive a temporary first-mover advantage. After a few years, competitors reverse engineer the product and start to compete on price. Very soon, the rents disappear. But this is not how it works for an astonishing number of products. Heinz Ketchup, KFC chicken coating, Mrs. Fields Chocolate Cookies . . . just go to your supermarket and see how long first-mover advantages last—nearly forever. This is what you get when the legal system generously offers protection without balancing the costs and benefits.

So, what is the solution? For starters, limit trade secret protection in time. Second, require that trade secrets be made public at the expiration date. Indeed, once the innovator has benefited enough to recoup the innovation costs, competition on the market should be restored.

The bottom line is that intellectual property law should be designed more carefully. It should be just generous enough, but not overly generous. Its goal is to stimulate innovation, not to increase income inequality by giving away rents.

CONCLUSION

In a prestigious office building, well-dressed people meet to discuss a marketing strategy. At the end of the workday, they step into high-end cars. Some go to play golf, others to check the water temperature of their swimming pool. A few blocks away, men and women flip hamburgers. At the end of their workday, they drive home in cheap cars to small houses in a poor neighborhood.

These are familiar pictures. The familiar explanation, so far, is that those who own more expensive cars and houses work harder or are more talented. They are more productive, and therefore earn more money. If only everyone could become as productive as those marketers in that prestigious building, our society would become so much wealthier. Everybody would live in a huge house, drive a Lexus, and own property in Aspen.

In this book, I have challenged this view. Work ethic may explain some of the smaller income differences, but it can't explain most of the larger ones. If your neighbor makes twenty times more than you, it is unlikely she worked twenty times harder. She usually just captures more rents than you do. Rents, as we have seen, are artificial profits made possible by market failures.

The idea that there can be such a thing as a "rent" is nothing new. What this book has tried to show is that rents are much more widespread in the economy than generally believed. Most products and services you buy contain a rent; they are more expensive than they would have been in a perfectly transparent, competitive market. I have estimated that, on average, $35 of every $100 you spend goes to rents.

How exactly do rents increase income inequality? In two ways. First, fast-food cooks do not receive any rents, but they may pay rents whenever they buy something with their yearly income of $19,000. If rents are 35 percent of the economy, that means that, statistically, $6,650 of their $19,000 yearly income goes to rents. This $19,000 has a true purchasing power of only $12,350.[236] That is indeed how much the same goods and services would have cost in an economy without rents. Thus, rents impoverish those who pay rents but don't receive rents.

Second, rents enrich those who receive the rents. Who are they? Well, the people with offices in those prestigious buildings. For the largest part, it is the business owners (including stockholders), the people who work for them and to whom some rents are leaked (such as pricing consultants and corporate officers), and the owners of land and other natural resources.

Why did income inequality increase since the 1970s? Because the total amount of rents in the economy increased. In 1970, about $20 out of every $100 that people spent went to rents. By 2010, that amount had increased to $35 out of every $100.

There are two reasons why rents have increased. One is that society has become more complex, with more product types and product variants. This has made it easier for experts (like salespeople) to exploit asymmetric information. In addition, the complexity has made it easier to transform competitive markets into foggy, oligopolistic ones.

But the more fundamental reason is that the economy has

become less competitive as marketing methods have become more sophisticated. Well-trained business economists are now simply better at creating market failures and at extracting rents out of them. And so far, their insights have been applied on a larger scale in the US than in Europe. This helps to explain why income inequality has grown faster in the US.

Building Political Consensus on How to Fight Income Inequality

Income inequality is a hot political topic. Unfortunately, there is no consensus on what to do about it.

The fundamental reason for this lack of consensus, in my view, is that policymakers focus on the wrong instrument—taxes. Taxes are an easy way to reduce income inequality, but they also have serious economic side effects. They discourage hard work and innovation; they sometimes distort prices and consumer choices; and they entail significant administrative costs. If taxes are buckets that bring money from the rich to the poor, they are leaky buckets. Therefore, taxes present politicians a tragic choice: Do we want equality or economic efficiency? Politicians on the left tend to give more weight to the former; those on the right tend to give more weight to the latter. It is hard to say who is right. The lack of consensus can be attributed to different empirical estimates on the true costs of inequality and the true costs of tax distortions.[237]

The analysis and proposals in this book may help deblock the political discussion. If rents are the real culprit, it may be possible to find common ground on how to fight income inequality. Indeed, rents cause not only inequality but they also distort the economy. Rents distort the economy even more than taxes. If politicians on the right are worried about taxes harming the economy, they should be worried even more about rents harming the economy.

Rents are also hard to defend from an ethical point of view. They are not the result of hard work, but the result of strategies such as exploiting information asymmetries (that is, not being honest), creating lock-in effects (using traps), using subtle cartels (cheating the game), or being overrewarded by the legal system (picking up golden eggs that should not have been laid there by the government).

The proposals of chapter 9 may fit well into a new cultural wave that is emerging. People are tired of the lack of ethics in the economy and the lack of fairness in the income distribution. This book has shown how the two are related, and how the two can be solved at the same time.

This is why the solutions offered in this book may be *politically* more *feasible* than existing proposals. It is hard to reach consensus on increasing taxes and even harder to stop lobbyists from lobbying. Most proposals in this book are much easier to agree upon—they come down to more honesty and more competition. And many are much easier to realize—they are legal rules that can be implemented by courts without being blocked by political gridlock in Washington, DC.

Do We Need More Regulation or More Market?

In chapter 9, I have proposed legal changes that could drastically reduce rents. One question that may arise, however, is whether these proposals come down to having more regulation, that is, more government intervention in the economy. Do we really need more red tape?

Well, I fully share the concern of red tape. I once was laying on an operating table in my hospital gown when the surgeon came to me. I thought: he is here either to explain the procedure or simply to assure me that everything is all right. Instead, he uttered three words: "Please sign here." I could hardly reach the iPad he was holding because my body was connected with tubes and wires to fluids and machines that said "Beep!" Nor did I have my glasses with me, so I had no clue what the form said. But I signed, and sixty seconds later I was in a deep sleep.

This anecdote is not an outlier. Ben-Shahar and Schneider have documented how pervasive disclosure requirements have become, and how ineffective and wasteful they tend to be.[238]

But the proposals I have made in this book are different. They are all rules that make market forces stronger. They are not rules that reduce competition but rules that increase competition.

The point that some legal rules do not "regulate" the market but rather make the market possible was made by Coase (1959) in a paper that discussed the Federal Communications Commission's intervention on radio frequencies.[239] Before 1927, no radio station could own a specific radio frequency. Stations with a stronger transmitter could simply blow away the signal of competitors. The Federal Radio Commission (the forerunner to the Federal Communications Commission, or FCC) stepped in and gave radio stations their own radio frequency. As a result, new entrants had to buy radio frequencies from existing stations, rather than taking someone's frequency by blowing the station's signal away. Commentators at that time considered this a prime illustration that government regulation was needed to bring order on a chaotic, failing market. Coase argued instead that the chaos couldn't be called a market failure because there wasn't even a market. Only after the FCC created (largely) transferable property rights could a market exist. And it worked well.

When is the law not regulation, but just the establishment of a market? Coase (1959) mentioned property rights. In another paper, he suggested rules that make contracts binding as another example (how can there be markets if the legal system does not enforce contracts?).[240] We can easily extend this to rules that forbid fraud (how can markets be "free" when lying and cheating is permitted?) and rules that forbid cartels (how can there be price competition if competitors can fix prices?).

The proposals in chapter 9 are essentially of that nature. They forbid forms of fraud, cartels, and duress that are now falling through the cracks of the legal system. They make sure that markets are transparent. They make sure that competitive auctions take place whenever mining and building rights are given away. And they reduce intellectual property protection—a government-installed system of monopoly rights. The only case where the government has to take over a job from the market is standardization. Standards are public goods with network externalities, which is why markets aren't good at producing them.*

Competitive markets are formidable mechanisms to

---

* Don't terms like "markets" or "regulation" then become just words? Can't you frame all forms of regulation as "rules that create more markets"? No, you can't. Regulation, in its proper definition, means rules that reduce the role of market mechanisms. Regulation makes markets do less and the government do more. A legal barrier to entry, for instance, reduces market competition. Price regulation lets the government set prices instead of the market. Having government-owned enterprises, with a communist economy as its extreme form, means giving up markets altogether in favor of another organizational form. All these types of government intervention are regulation in its proper sense.

achieve both economic efficiency and income equality. All the government has to do is write down the laws that make it happen.

Rent Economics

Although the economic literature on rents started in 1817 with David Ricardo, it is still underresearched today. Economic analysis of law is traditionally based on only three pillars: incentive analysis, risk analysis, and transaction cost analysis. To evaluate a legal rule, economists look at its incentive effects, its risk allocation, and its transaction costs (a broad category that includes enforcement costs). That's it.

Why isn't rent analysis a fourth pillar? A first reason is that, so far, rents have been considered economically harmless. Rents are believed to affect, at most, who gets the economic pie, but not how large the pie is. I have shown, however, that this is incorrect. Rents distort the economy even more than poorly designed taxes.

A second reason why rents have largely been ignored is that, even if rents increased income inequality, taxes were believed to be the best instrument to fix these distributive distortions. This book has shown that this does not hold when inequality is caused by rents. Legal rules are the best instrument in that case because they can fix the market failures that cause the rents in the first place.

A final reason why rents have largely been ignored by economists so far is that rents were believed to be small. Rents were seen, at most, as temporary problems because whenever rents appear, there are market forces that make them disappear. This book has shown, however, that rents are 35 percent of the national income. Not exactly a minor problem.

This has major implications for the cost-benefit analysis of legal rules. Inequality costs should become a part of the equation when we design legal rules that affect rents. The result will usually be that the law will have to be more aggressive against market failures—even more aggressive than it should be on pure market efficiency grounds.

Here is another way of looking at it. Go back to the 1950s, when pollution costs were disregarded by policymakers. Take a time machine up to the present, when we realize that pollution has a cost. As a result, we now add pollution costs to the equation when we discuss legal changes, and we fight pollution more aggressively. By the same token, if we realize that income inequality is a serious problem that should largely be addressed in the legal system, we should add those costs to the equation and fight market failures more aggressively.

The lack of interest in rents may be similar to the lack of interest in transaction costs before the 1960s. Transaction costs are, in a sense, also temporary: whenever they arise, there are market forces at work that make them decrease. If drafting a contract takes one hundred hours, there is room for innovators to sell model contracts. If finding a certain piece of information takes one hundred hours, there is room for an innovative app that does the same in a few minutes.

For transaction costs, just as for rents, there are forces at work that make them smaller over time. But at the same time, there are forces at work that create new sources. The result is that, at any given moment, transaction costs may be significant, just like rents.[241]

But until today, economists have underestimated the impact of rents. It is time to correct this mistake. It is time to take rents seriously.

ACKNOWLEDGMENTS

This book is the result of many years of research and of countless discussions with colleagues and students. I am grateful to Adam Badawi, Douglas Baird, Scott Baker, Omri Ben-Shahar, Marcus Berliant, Clemens Cool, Giuseppe Dari-Mattiacci, Ben Depoorter, Dhammika Dharmapala, John Drobak, Frank Easterbrook, Dan Epps, Brian Galle, Michael Greenfield, John den Hertog, Mitja Kovac, William Larson, M. Todd Henderson, David Levine, Saul Levmore, Goldburn P. Maynard Jr., Danielle d'Onfro, Barak Y. Orbach, David Pervin, Robert Pollak, Katie Pratt, Alex Raskolnikov, Adam Rosenzweig, Chris Sanchirico, Theodore Seto, Jacques Siegers, Jeffrey Stake, Andrew Tuch, and Roger Van den Bergh for insightful comments on parts of the project.

Earlier drafts of chapters have been presented at workshops and conferences at the University of Chicago, Columbia Law School, Duke University, Vanderbilt University, Indiana University, Ghent University, Saint Louis University, Washington University, Notre Dame University, St. Thomas University, Loyola University (LA), and the University of Toronto. I thank the participants for helpful feedback. Over the years, I have also benefited from comments made by my law students, graduate students in economics, and MBA students.

I greatly benefited from the work of my research assistants Lauren Abbott, Caleb Brown, Mark Edlund, Richard Espenschied, Jacob Franchek, Alberto Ghiani, Mark Gum, Ethan Hatch, Philip Lenertz, Haiming Li, Mark Lipscomb, Anthony McLaughlin, Thomas Parker, Caleb Shreves, Kevin Simpson, Melissa Thevenot, Addison Thiel, Sarah Walton, Amy Xu. Special thanks go to Lauren Abbott, Caleb Shreves, and Addison Thiel for their many significant contributions. I also thank my copyeditor Christina Roth, book cover and interior designer Leah McDowell, illustrator Madeline De Geest, marketing expert Alaina Waagner, and publicist Lucas Jones. I have received research support, in different forms, from Washington University School of Law and the Coase-Sandor Institute for Law and Economics at the University of Chicago.

I would like to thank my late father, an economist, for countless discussions on economic policy. I am indebted to Boudewijn Bouckaert for the broad intellectual training I received at earlier stages of my career at Ghent University.

Finally, I am grateful to my wife, Christine Vandenabeele, for her critical perspective on economic theory. This book aims to bring law and economics closer to the empirical reality of modern markets, and Christine played a major role in shaping my thoughts in this respect.

NOTES

[1] There is an extensive literature on inequality. A first strand of literature is based on the standard economic view that income differences in free markets reflect productivity differences, which may, in turn, reflect risk-taking or educational differences. The standard solution is to use the tax system, possibly to subsidize new education programs. Recent books in this tradition are Edward Conard, *The Upside of Inequality: How Good Intentions Undermine the Middle Class* (Portfolio, 2016, arguing that technology has caused the widening income gap, and that the top 1 percent are those who contribute most to innovation); Don Watkins and Yaron Brook, *Equal Is Unfair: America's Misguided Fight Against Income Inequality* (St. Martin's Press, 2016, arguing that more equality could harm the economy by discouraging the most successful members in society); David Smick, *The Great Equalizer: How Main Street Capitalism Can Create an Economy for Everyone* (PublicAffairs, 2017, arguing that entrepreneurship related to technology is the ultimate solution for America's economic issues); Ruchir Sharma, *The Rise and Fall of Nations: Forces of Change in the Post-Crisis World* (W.W. Norton, 2016, distinguishing between "good billionaires," who improve the economy, and "bad billionaires," who harm society); Robert D. Putman, *Our Kids: The American Dream in Crisis* (Simon and Schuster, 2015, explaining how inequality puts poor kids in a vicious cycle by limiting their access to education); James M. Stone, *Five Easy Theses: Commonsense Solutions to America's Greatest Economic Challenges* (Houghton Mifflin Harcourt, 2016, criticizing the "aristocracy of wealth"). Some other books focus on how taxes could be increased, or how tax money should be spent. See, for instance, Gabriel Zucman, *The Hidden Wealth of Nations: The Scourge of Tax Havens* (University of Chicago Press, 2015, stressing the importance of eliminating tax havens); Philippe Van Parijs and Yannick Vanderborght, *Basic Income: A Radical Proposal for a Free Society and a Sane Economy* (Harvard University Press, 2017, defending the idea of a basic income); Stewart Lansley, *A Sharing Economy: How Social Wealth Funds Can Reduce Inequality and Help Balance the Books* (Policy Press, 2016, proposing to let the government create "social wealth funds" to make sure that the profits no longer go to just a happy few);

Anthony Atkinson, *Inequality: What Can Be Done?* (Harvard University Press, 2015, arguing that reducing inequality in the UK requires not only taxes on the wealthy but also fresh ideas with respect to technology, employment, social security, and the sharing of capital). A second strand of literature is written by macroeconomists or historians, who see long-term historical patterns. The best-known example is Thomas Piketty, *Capital in the Twenty-First Century* (Harvard University Press, 2014). In Piketty's view, the cause of growing inequality is that interest on capital tends to be higher than the growth rate ($r > g$). For instance, if the average return on capital is 4–6 percent, whereas the economic growth is only 1–2 percent, capital owners become 4–6 percent richer each year while the population as a whole becomes only 1–2 percent richer. In the long run, this inevitably leads to the accumulation of wealth. Piketty does not explain why $r > g$ but considers it a historical fact. (My book could explain this fact—rents are most likely to be picked up by capital owners—but Piketty's model does not take rents into account.) In Piketty's view, only (wealth) taxes can reverse the trend (outside of major economic crises and wars). See also Walter Scheidel, *The Great Leveler: Violence and the History of Inequality from the Stone Age to the Twenty-First Century* (Princeton University Press, 2017, showing that only catastrophic events have significantly reduced inequality throughout history); Robert Gordon, *The Rise and Fall of American Growth: The U.S. Standard of Living Since the Civil War* (Princeton University Press, 2016, taking a pessimistic view toward future growth); Branko Milanovic, *Global Inequality: A New Approach for the Age of Globalization* (Harvard University Press, 2016, arguing that inequality rises, falls, and then rises again, perhaps endlessly, in "Kuznets waves"). See also François Bourguignon, *The Globalization of Inequality* (Princeton University Press, 2015). Other authors offer a broad historical and international perspective and conclude that many factors affect inequality. See, for instance, Peter H. Lindert and Jeffrey G. Williamson, *Unequal Gains: American Growth and Inequality Since 1700* (Princeton University Press, 2016) and Thomas Sowell, *Wealth, Poverty and Politics: An International Perspective,* 2nd ed. (Basic Books, 2016). A somewhat different argument— that inequality, in turn, may have macroeconomic effects—is developed by Matthew Drennan, *Income Inequality: Why It Matters and Why Most Economists Didn't Notice* (Yale University Press, 2015, arguing that unsustainable debt taken on by the impoverished middle class caused the Great Recession of 2009). A third strand of literature follows the tradition of political economy, showing that some income differences may be attributed to political rent seeking. This strand has been revived by Joseph Stiglitz, *The Price of Inequality: How Today's Divided Society Endangers Our Future* (W.W. Norton, 2012). Stiglitz argues that politics shapes the market and that politics has been pro-wealthy. Stiglitz gives examples of political lobbying in tax law (lowering taxes for the wealthy), labor law (lowering wages by weakening unions), corporate and bankruptcy law (permitting high CEO bonuses), bankruptcy law (bailing out banks), and procurement law (letting the government overpay for military contracts). Along the same lines, Robert B. Reich, *Saving Capitalism: For the Many, Not the Few* (Penguin Random House, 2015) argues that a "free market" cannot exist independently of government and that large corporations, Wall Street, and very wealthy individuals have shaped the rules in their favor. Reich gives examples from property law, contract law, bankruptcy law, and antitrust law.

The fundamental solution, in his view, is to restore democracy. Other proposals include reducing CEO pay and creating a basic income. See also Bernie Sanders, *Our Revolution: A Future to Believe In* (Thomas Dunne, 2016); Jeremy Gantz and Bernie Sanders, *The Age of Inequality: Corporate America's War on Working People* (Penguin Random House, 2017, mentioning political favoritism, the decline of manufacturing, the deregulation of the financial industry, and privatization as causes of increasing inequality). A related literature focuses on the diminished political power of unions. See, for instance, Andrew Glyn, *Capitalism Unleashed: Finance, Globalization, and Welfare* (Oxford University Press, 2006, relating inequality to globalization and de-unionization); Jake Rosenfeld, *What Unions No Longer Do* (Harvard University Press, 2014, arguing that unions reduced inequality also in indirect ways, by shaping cultural understandings of fairness). In addition to these three economic strands, there is some other (usually noneconomic) literature that analyzes the broader societal implications of inequality. See, for instance, Richard Wilkinson and Kate Pickett, *The Spirit Level: Why Greater Equality Makes Societies Stronger* (Bloomsbury Press, 2010, arguing that inequality harms society in many indirect ways); David Cay Johnston, ed., *Divided: The Perils of Our Growing Inequality* (The New Press, 2015, discussing the implications of inequality on education, justice, health care, social mobility, and political representation). See also Simon Reid-Henry, *The Political Origins of Inequality: Why a More Equal World Is Better for Us All* (University of Chicago Press, 2016, linking inequality to the limited role of public concerns in modern political discourse); Ganesh Sitaraman, *The Crisis of the Middle-Class Constitution: Why Economic Inequality Threatens Our Republic* (Knopf, 2017, arguing that economic inequality threatens the American constitutional system, which assumes a flourishing middle class). There is also some literature that criticizes manipulative marketing practices, without making the link to inequality, or without offering a general theory of marketing. See, for instance, Bob Sullivan, *Stop Getting Ripped Off: Why Consumers Get Screwed, and How You Can Always Get a Fair Deal* (Ballantine Books, 2009, written from a consumer self- help perspective); William Poundstone, *Priceless: The Myth of Fair Value (and How to Take Advantage of It)* (Hill and Wang, 2010, telling the story of the growing impact of marketing); Oren Bar-Gill, *Seduction by Contract: Law, Economics, and Psychology in Consumer Markets* (Oxford University Press, 2012, showing how certain marketing practices exploit behavioral biases of consumers, and proposing legal changes).

Rents differs from each of these strands of literature. The book differs from the first strand of literature (the standard view among economists), both in terms of explanation (I disagree that most income differences are caused by productivity differences) and solution (I disagree that taxes are the best way to redistribute income). The book differs from the second strand of literature (written by macroeconomists), both with respect to methodology (I believe that microeconomics is more useful than macroeconomics to identify the causes of economic trends) and with respect to the results (I believe there is nothing wrong with capitalism per se, as long as the law keeps markets competitive). The book has one element in common with the third strand of literature (written by political economists): it uses the concept of rents. However, the book uses the term "rents" in a much broader meaning than just political rents. As a matter of fact, I argue that the rents caused by political lobbying are small compared to the rents generated by distorted markets and that rents are nearly everywhere in the economy, in varying doses. The book offers a new explanation of income inequality (income inequality has increased because markets have become less competitive, which is caused by more sophisticated marketing) and a new solution to reduce it (don't raise taxes but change the law to make markets more competitive).

This book also makes several other contributions to the literature. It develops a new theory of marketing (trying to change the way you look at shopping) and a new way to look at income differences (trying to change how you look at income differences around you), and it is the first to show the connection between marketing, law, and income inequality (connecting what you experience as a consumer with what you experience as an income earner). Rents also makes several technical contributions to economics. It challenges a generally accepted fundamental theorem of welfare economics (and law and economics), that taxes are the least distortive way to redistribute income. It develops a new method for estimating rents in the overall economy, which is at the same time a new method for estimating the level of competitiveness of the overall economy. It develops a more general theory of rent economics. It proposes several new concepts, such as radiation rents, cherry-picking rents, payer externalities, and productive versus rent capital. It offers a new theory of the firm. It is the first to apply the *efficiency versus information rents trade-off* (an insight developed in specialized principal-agent theory) to the inequality debate, and to the law more generally. It identifies the technical reason why economic analysis of law should not only look at incentives, risks, and transaction costs but should also include a rent analysis. Methodologically, *Rents* differs from other books because its analysis is not based on political economy, macroeconomics, or general welfare economics but on microeconomics, advanced principal-agent theory, and law and economics.

[2] Rafi Mohammed, *The 1% Windfall: How Successful Companies Use Price to Profit and Grow* (HarperCollins, 2010), 104.

[3] Lock-in effects have been extensively studied in the economic literature, often under the term "unequal relation-specific investments." Seminal books are Oliver E. Williamson, *Markets and Hierarchies: Analysis and Antitrust Implications* (Free Press, 1975); Oliver Hart, *Firms, Contracts, and Financial Structure* (Oxford University Press, 1995).

[4] See, for instance, Jean-Jacques Laffont and Jean Tirole, *A Theory of Incentives in Procurement and Regulation* (MIT Press, 1993), 663–65; Patrick Bolton and Mathias Dewatripont, *Contract Theory* (MIT Press, 2005), 259–61.

[5] In reality, the process is more complex, because the assumption that there are on average three bidders is not the same as the assumption that there are always three bidders. This variance, however, may even drive up prices, as bidders may focus their strategies on the higher profits in the state of the world in which there are only one or two bids.

[6] Antoine A. Cournot, *Recherches sur les Principes Mathematiques de la Theorie des Richesses* (1838). The Cournot model is based on several assumptions that are not always realistic (all suppliers produce a commodity; they decide only on the quantity they will produce and not on the price they will ask; they move simultaneously and cannot adjust their choices based on what others do). Nonetheless, the Cournot model makes intuitive sense as it depicts what is naturally expected to happen: the more firms compete, the closer the price approximates the perfect market price; the fewer firms that compete, the closer the price approximates the monopoly price.

[7] If we assume a linear demand curve and constant average costs, the formula is $4n/(n + 1)^2$, where n is the number of firms. Here is the math. Assume for mathematical simplicity that the true costs are $0 (i.e., there are neither variable nor fixed costs). Therefore, the price p equals the rent per unit. Normalize the maximum output when the price equals the costs ($0 in this case) to 1 and let p^{max} denote the highest individual willingness-to-pay. Assume a linear demand curve, $p = p^{max}(1 - q)$. A monopolist has the following objective function: Max pq subject to the binding constraint $p = p^{max}(1 - q)$. The solution is $q = \frac{1}{2}$. Indeed, the first order condition is $p^{max}(1 - 2q) = 0$ and the second order condition is -2 (meaning the function is concave). With n competitors, it can be shown that the total output $q = n/(n + 1)$, since $p^{max}(1 - q - q/n) = 0$. From this, it can be calculated that $p = p^{max}/(n + 1)$. The total rent in the industry is $R = qp = p^{max}n/(n + 1)^2$. The total output in the industry compared to the monopoly output is $2n/(n + 1)$. The rent per unit compared to the monopoly rent per unit is $2/(n + 1)$. The total rents in the industry compared to total monopoly rents are $4n/(n + 1)^2$.

[8] In the Bertrand model, all competitors must decide simultaneously on the price they will charge. There is no communication between them, there is no time to "retaliate" by matching prices, and all competitors perfectly know each others' cost structures. The best strategy in this model is for the one with the best cost structure to set the price one dollar below the true costs of the one with the second-best cost structure. If all competitors have the same cost structure, they will all ask the perfectly competitive price (which reflects the true costs and no rent at all).

[9] Mohammed, *The 1% Windfall,* 104 ("Printer refill cartridges are brimming with profits. . . . It is estimated that 70 percent of Hewlett-Packard's operating profits are from its imaging and printing division, most of which comes from printer supplies such as toner refills." Thomas T. Nagle, John E. Hogan, and Joseph Zale, *The Strategy and Tactics of Pricing: A Guide to Growing More Profitably* (Prentice Hall, 2011), 61 ("This tie-in strategy enables HP's inkjet division to maintain a 50 percent market share and profit per dollar sales ratio that is twice that of the company in general").

[10] Ellen Byron, "101 Brand Names, 1 Manufacturer: The Mass Pet-Food Recall Reveals a Widespread Practice: Many Competing Products Come from the Same Factory," *Wall Street Journal,* May 9, 2007.

[11] That modern markets are far from perfect is taken for granted in the marketing literature. See, for instance, Elliot B. Ross, "Making Money with Proactive Pricing," *Harvard Business Review* on Pricing (2008, originally published 1984), 176–77 ("In the perfect market that theoretical economists envision, of course, pricing freedom doesn't exist. . . . However, successful industrial marketers have understood and exploited the fact that a multitude of imperfections in the marketplace affect the dynamics of supply and demand in the real world of industrial products . . . the existence of this price band in virtually every industrial market results from variations or imperfections in both demand and supply factors. . . . In contrast, in industries where price visibility is low, the price band is usually wide").

[12] Evidence of the steadily increasing degree of implementation of the new pricing methods can be found in marketing books. For instance, pricing books in the 1990s mentioned that, at that time, most companies did not use the new pricing methods yet. For instance, Robert J. Dolan and Hermann Simon, *Power*

Pricing: How Managing Price Transforms the Bottom Line (Free Press, 1996), 4 ("A 1994 survey found only 12% of firms doing 'any serious pricing research' and one-third of these had no strategy for using the research results. Our general experience squares with these survey findings").

[13] Simon-Kucher & Partners was founded in Bonn in 1985 by business professor Hermann Simon and two of his doctoral students. William Poundstone, *Priceless: The Myth of Fair Value* (and How to Take Advantage of It) (Hill and Wang, 2010), 5–6.

[14] Like all structural analyses, the new version doesn't draw a precise picture. That is why in antitrust litigation, emphasis is put on more precise techniques, such as price elasticity analysis. Unfortunately, there is no data on elasticities across the entire economy. (For a rare attempt, see Matthew D. Shapiro, "Measuring Market Power in U.S. Industry," Cowles Foundation Discussion Paper No. 828, April 1987.)

[15] See, for instance, Albert Wesley Frey, ed., *Marketing Handbook* (Ronald Press, 1965), chapter 8 (focusing on price theory, competitive constraints, and cost-plus pricing, and devoting only eleven lines to psychological pricing); Richard Buskirk, *Principles of Marketing: The Management View* (Holt, Reinhart and Winston, 1966), 421 ("It should not be automatically assumed that the marketing manager is completely free to establish whatever prices he desires on his wares; this is simply not so. The price- setting procedure is usually encompassed by many restrictions.... Often they may establish certain bounds, and at other times they actually set the price. . . . In many industries traditional prices are so well established that the producer must abide by them. . . . In many industries the executive must meet a fairly well-recognized market price for his product.")

[16] See, for instance, Dolan and Simon, *Power Pricing.*

[17] I thank Gerhard Ölsinger, a former executive MBA student, whose term paper inspired this section. See also https://www.bwb.gv.at/de/kartelle_marktmachtmissbrauch/entscheidungen/detail/news/bwbm_180_fluessigg as/.

[18] Steinmetz and Brooks, *How to Sell at Margins Higher Than Your Competitors,* 108.

[19] Ibid., 26; Reed K. Holden and Mark R. Burton, *Pricing with Confidence: 10 Ways to Stop Leaving Money on the Table* (John Wiley, 2008), 111.

[20] Hal Varian, "A Model of Sales," *American Economic Review* 70 (1980): 651–59.

[21] For instance, Einer Elhauge and Abraham L. Wickelgren. "Robust Exclusion and Market Division through Loyalty Discounts," *International Journal of Industrial Organization* 43 (2015): 111–22.

[22] *Occupational Employment Statistics* (OES) Survey, May 2015, Bureau of Labor Statistics, http://www.bls.gov/oes. $19,610 (or $9.43 hourly) is the average. The median is $19,080 (or $9.17 hourly), and the 10th percentile $16,510 (or $7.94 hourly). The assumption in these statistics is that 2,080 hours per year are worked, which corresponds to forty hours per week times fifty-two weeks. (In other words, the assumption is that no vacation is taken at all.) The 10th percentile of all occupations is $18,870. Note that the minimum wage under the Federal Fair Wages Act is $7.25; jobs that are exempt can be covered by state or local minimum wages, which can be higher or lower than the federal amount. For an overview by state, see http://www.dol.gov/whd/minwage/america.htm.

[23] In 2013, CEOs of the Standard & Poor's (S&P) 500 Index companies received, on average, $11.7 million in total compensation, according to the AFL-CIO's analysis of available data from 350 companies (http://www.aflcio.org/Corporate-Watch/CEO-Pay-and-You). In 2013 the CEO-to-average-worker

pay ratio was 331:1 (compared to 42:1 in 1982), and the CEO-to-minimum-wage-worker pay ratio was 774:1. Note that these ratios are much larger than in Japan and Europe. See, for instance, Glyn, *Capitalism Unleashed,* 58 (mentioning ratios in the 10–25 range in Japan and Europe).

[24] *OES Survey.*

[25] In 2013, the average profit per partner of the top 100 American law firms was $1,470,022. See http://www.americanlawyer.com/id=1202651706887.

[26] Teachers receive a *wage* that is 20 percent above the average in the *OES Survey* (elementary and middle school teachers made on average $58,060 and secondary school teachers on average $60,270; the average of all occupations in this database was $48,320). Yet the *income* of teachers (assuming they have no other major sources of income) is below the *average income.* In 2015, the national income per active member of the workforce was over $100,000; since the national income per capita (which includes children) was around $48,000, the national income per adult exceeded the average teacher wage. (National income and total population estimates based on BEA 2015 data; active population estimates based on 2010 Census Data.) A major cause of the divergence between the average wage and income is the magnitude of the capital share, as explained in chapter 3.

[27] The calculation is simplified, for instance, by not adding a risk aversion premium to the equation. Yet adding more nuance would not alter the qualitative conclusions. (Also, if failed business owners do not live in complete poverty but just have a below- average income, there should be even more than nine failed business owners for each successful one to make the example work.)

[28] David Ricardo, *On the Principles of Political Economy and Taxation* (1817). The concept itself has early traces in Adam Smith, *An Inquiry into the Nature and Causes of the Wealth of Nations* (1776).

[29] Todd G. Buchholz, *New Ideas from Dead Economists: An Introduction to Modern Economic Thought* (Plume, 2007), 14.

[30] Some economists define rents as anything that exceeds the "opportunity costs" of the seller. That, however, is incorrect if there is more than one source of rents in the economy. Suppose that both doctors and dentists earn rents and that both jobs require the same type of talent. Then, a doctor who makes $300,000 per year could say, "I don't receive any rents because if I hadn't become a doctor, I would have become a dentist and made the same money." This shows that the baseline for whether a rent exists shouldn't be the person's alternatives (which may include another rent source), but the price that would have been paid in a perfect market.

[31] John Stuart Mill, chapter 16, in *The Principles of Political Economy* (1848).

[32] The "actuarially fair price," or "actuarial cost," is the expected cost of the coverage. For instance, for a 1 percent chance to receive $100,000, the actuarial cost is $1,000. (The term "fair" should not be taken literally because insurance companies and lottery organizers have to receive compensation for the administrative costs on top of that.)

[33] Ricardo's finding seems to be well understood by successful entrepreneurs. See, for instance, Felix Dennis, *How to Get Rich: One of the World's Greatest Entrepreneurs Shares His Secrets* (Portfolio, 2009, explaining that absolute ownership is a necessary condition to get wealthy).

[34] The equity premium was estimated 6.18 percent for 1889–2000 in the seminal paper of Rajnish Mehra and Edward C. Prescott, "The Equity Premium: A

Puzzle," *Journal of Monetary Economy* 15 (1985): 145–61. Empirical estimates vary greatly, depending on the methodology. See Pablo Fernandez, "The Equity Premium in 150 Textbooks" (SSRN research paper, November 18, 2015), http://ssrn.com/abstract=1473225. There is an extensive literature that tries to "explain" the equity premium. From a theoretical perspective, the equity premium is puzzling because it seems inconsistent with the most fundamental theorem in corporate finance—the Modigliani-Miller Theorem. Franco Modigliani and Merton Miller, "The Cost of Capital, Corporation Finance and the Theory of Investment," *American Economic Review* 48 (1958): 261–97. The Modigliani-Miller Theorem holds that, in a perfect market, the value of a company will not be affected by whether it is financed through stock (shares) or bonds (loans). Although the Modigliani-Miller Theorem looks at decisions made by businesses, it indirectly also has implications for investors. Risk aversion itself—the fact that human beings dislike variance—cannot explain the equity premium either, because smart investors reduce variance by not laying all their eggs in one basket. Other common "explanations," such as psychological biases, borrowing constraints, liquidity constraints, or tax biases, do not explain the equity premium either.

[35] Gordon Tullock, "The Transitional Gains Trap," *Bell Journal of Economics* 6 (1975): 671–78. The idea has been applied more broadly in the economic literature on property rights, for instance, in its analysis of open access regimes and first possession rules. See Dean Lueck and Thomas J. Miceli, "Property Rights and Property Law," in *Handbook of Law and Economics*, ed. A. Mitchell Polinsky and Steven Shavell, vol. 1 (Elsevier, 2007), 183–257.

[36] In some cases, the opposite of leakage occurs: second-generation owners overpay and incur losses. This may happen when shareholders buy stock at the height of a bubble. In that case, the first generation of shareholders will receive more than the value of all the future rents.

[37] The economic literature has identified other reasons why employees may be paid rents. In the "efficiency wages" theory, overpaying is the cheapest way to discourage "shirking" (that is, breaching the contract). For instance, in a country with a tradition of corruption, judges may be overpaid to deter them from accepting bribes. This makes corruption less attractive because corrupt judges now not only face criminal sanctions but also risk losing an overpaid job. See Gary Becker and George Stigler, "Law Enforcement, Malfeasance, and the Compensation of Enforcers," *Journal of Legal Studies* 3 (1974): 1–19; Carl Shapiro and Joseph E. Stiglitz, "Equilibrium Unemployment as a Worker Discipline Device," *American Economic Review* 74 (1984): 433–44.

Employees may also receive "hold-up" rents, for instance when they have learnt the know-how of the company and may threaten to start working for a competitor. See Benjamin Klein, Robert G. Crawford, and Armen A. Alchian, "Vertical Integration, Appropriable Rents, and the Competitive Contracting Process," *Journal of Law and Economics* 21 (1978): 297–326; Hart, *Firms, Contracts, and Financial Structure*. The employer may try to prevent this by requiring the employee to sign a non-compete clause or a confidentiality agreement, but there are often legal restrictions on these techniques, and even legal ones may be hard to enforce. On the limitations of legal protections against hold-ups, see Orly Lobel, chapter 3, in *Talent Wants to Be Free: Why We Should Learn to Love Leaks, Raids, and Free Riding* (Yale University Press, 2013).

[38] See also Mark J. Roe, "Rents and Their Corporate Consequences," *Stanford Law Review* 53 (2001): 1463–94.

³⁹ Greg Smith, "Viewpoint: How Wall Street Rigs the Game," *Time*, October 22, 2012. See also Greg Smith, Why I Left Goldman Sachs: A Wall Street Story (Grand Central, 2012).

⁴⁰ See, for instance, Tony Ellery and Neal Hansen, *Pharmaceutical Lifecycle Management Making the Most of Each and Every Brand* (John Wiley, 2012).

⁴¹ See William H. Page and John E. Lopatka, "Network Externalities," in *Encyclopedia of Law and Economics*, ed. Boudewijn Bouckaert and Gerrit De Geest, vol. 1 (Edward Elgar, 2000), 952–80.

⁴² See also Peter S. Menell, "Tailoring Legal Protection for Computer Software," *Stanford Law Review* 39 (1987): 1329–72.

⁴³ Let's theorize a little more. An obvious condition for radiation rents is that those who receive them must possess the skills to enter the rent-receiving market. In the case of medical professors, this seems obvious: medical professors have the qualifications to become doctors. Can't medical schools avoid paying radiation rents by hiring those who are just a little underqualified? Probably not, because medical students want to learn from the best doctors, not from the worst. A second condition is that there is a net rent to be earned in the other sector, after we deduct entry costs. In other words, there must be a rent, not a quasi rent. This condition is easily met in the case of the medical profession, where doctors don't have to buy a license from someone who retires.

⁴⁴ Here's how. Suppose that there is only one type of talent and that all individuals in a society can be ranked from the least talented to the most talented on a scale of 100, which also reflects their income in equilibrium. Suppose that those higher on this scale can always do a job better than the less talented. (This assumption means that a surgeon would be a better car seller than individuals who are currently selling cars.) Start from the equilibrium without rents. Then suppose that, for whatever reason, rents are paid to one profession (for instance, car selling) that requires a talent of 50, so that the payment for this job becomes 90. In this case, and under some additional conditions, all those with a talent above 50 and below 90 may need to be paid at least 90 as they can all threaten to become a car salesperson.

⁴⁵ This is an application of the broader principle that first-generation owners receive all rents, where society, or the government, is the first-generation owner. A perfectly designed auction with full information makes sure that no rents leak to the second generation.

⁴⁶ Morton Shulman, *The Billion Dollar Windfall* (McGraw Hill, 1969). See also Anthony T. Kronman, "Mistake, Disclosure, Information, and the Law of Contracts," *Journal of Legal Studies* 7 (1978): 1–34.

⁴⁷ Richard Posner, "The Social Costs of Monopoly and Regulation," *Journal of Political Economy* 83 (1975): 807–27. Tullock argued that rent-seeking costs may even exceed the rents under some conditions. Gordon Tullock, "Efficient Rent Seeking," in *Toward a Theory of the Rent-Seeking Society*, ed. James M. Buchanan, Robert D. Tollison, and Gordon Tullock (Texas A&M University Press, 1980): 97–112. Recent scholarship, however, has shown that the conditions for this to happen will rarely be fulfilled. Giuseppe Dari-Mattiacci and Francesco Parisi, "Rents, Dissipation, and Lost Treasures: Rethinking Tullock's Paradox," *Public Choice* 124 (2005): 411–22.

⁴⁸ Joseph A. Schumpeter, *Capitalism, Socialism and Democracy* (Harper, 1975) [orig. pub. 1942].

⁴⁹ Raquel Meyer Alexander, Stephen W. Mazza, and Susan Scholz, "Measuring Rates of Return for Lobbying Expenditures: An Empirical Case Study of Tax Breaks for

Multinational Corporations," *Journal of Law and Politics* 25 (2009): 401–57.

[50] See endnote 9.

[51] A negative price would also destroy the lock-in effect.

[52] The economic literature frequently uses the term "endowment" instead of "talent" to refer to intrinsic potential.

[53] Steinmetz and Brooks, *How to Sell at Margins Higher Than Your Competitors,* 103.

[54] Another reason is that data on "national accounts" (data on the US economy, collected by agencies like the Bureau of Economic Analysis, or BEA) are based on tax data. Because there is no such thing as a rent tax, rent data cannot be derived from tax returns. The more fundamental reason, however, is that rents are hard to measure. After all, that is why the government doesn't even try to tax rents. From a different perspective, the absence of data is remarkable because Ricardo, the founding father of rent analysis, also happens to be the founding father of national income analysis. Since Ricardo (1817), the national income is traditionally divided into wages (for employees), profits (for capital owners), and rents. Ricardo, On the Principles of Political Economy and Taxation. The BEA does collect data on "rents," but this refers to what tenants pay to landlords (an amount that only partly consists of true rents). Note that the categories "wages" and "profits" also partly consist of rents.

[55] The following table summarizes my estimates:

All data in comparison to US national income	1970	2010
Capital share	21	29
True private capital	237	282
Market interest rate (percent)	2	1
Capital share in perfectly competitive economy	5	3
Rent in capital share	16	26
Rent in labor share	6	12
Total rents (estimated via national accounts)	22	38
Natural resources rents	1	5
Land rents (incl. agricultural)	2	3
Ricardian rents (estimated via World Bank and real estate data)	3	8
Persuasion costs/2	11	15
All rent-seeking expenditures (incl. rents in rent-seeking industry) if = (persuasion costs/2) + 50 percent	16	23
Non-Ricardian rents (excl. rents in rent-seeking industry) if 50 percent of these rents get dissipated	16	23
Rents in rent-seeking industry (if same rents as in other industries at that time)	3	7
Non-Ricardian rents (estimated via rent-seeking data)	19	30
Total rents (estimated via Ricardian and non-Ricardian rents)	22	38
Pure rent-seeking costs	13	16
Total rents + pure rent-seeking costs	35	54

⁵⁶ Thomas Piketty, *Capital in the Twenty-First Century* (Harvard University Press, 2014), table S4.2. Private capital was 410 percent, but net foreign capital was minus 25 percent, meaning that foreigners owned more assets in the US economy than Americans in the rest of the world. Therefore, the private capital in the US economy was 435 percent.

For Germany, the national private capital in 2010 was 412 percent of the NI, but that number includes 39 percent net foreign capital, owned by Germans abroad (Piketty, table S4.1). For France, the national private capital was 574.5 percent in 2010 (Piketty, table S5.1), but there was a minus 12.7 percent difference between foreign assets and foreign liabilities (Piketty, table S5.9), meaning that foreigners owned more assets in the French economy than vice versa.

⁵⁷ The GDP is usually 10–20 percent higher than the national income. For instance, in 2015, the US GDP was $17.7 trillion, or 18.3 percent higher than the national income, which was $15.2 trillion (data Bureau Economic Analysis, June 24, 2015). The reason why the GDP is higher is that it overestimates the true production by not taking into account capital depreciation. The net domestic product (NDP) does take depreciation into account, and more or less equals the national income. (The NDP may differ from the NI, for instance, when Americans make more money abroad than foreigners make in the US economy; but the difference between the NDP and NI tends to be small, and some statistics [for instance, Piketty's] are in comparison to the NI.)

Although the NDP and NI are more accurate measures, the GDP is used more because there is no international convention on how to calculate depreciation, which makes the NDP less suitable for international comparisons. While the GDP may be a good enough proxy for the NDP to study economic growth, it is too inaccurate to study income distribution.

⁵⁸ I am simplifying the math here by assuming away discounting costs.

⁵⁹ I am again simplifying the math.

⁶⁰ Piketty, *Capital in the Twenty-First Century*, table S4.2. Note that in France, agricultural land was worth 337 percent of the national income in 1780 (table S4.4).

⁶¹ See, for instance, ibid., 209 ("the annual rental value of housing . . . is generally 3–4 percent of the value of the property").

⁶² For those of you who like math, the formula becomes $C^R = R^C d/2$, where the symbol C^R stands for the total amount of rent capital in the economy (in other words, the capitalization of all appropriated future rents), R^C stands for the total amount of rents in the economy that goes to capital owners each year (remember, another part goes to workers), and $d/2$ stands for the remaining duration (in years) halfway through the life cycle. The simplifying assumption that all rent sources are, on average, halfway through their life cycle seems plausible for an entire economy, with new sources of rents constantly popping up.

⁶³ See also Piketty, *Capital in the Twenty-First Century,* 281–84. Capital gains are more likely to be underreported than labor income because profits are more malleable and more transferable to tax havens. In addition, capital gains are typically only taxed when they are "realized." (This is a technical term; the idea is that you only pay taxes at the time you cash in the money.) Although these gains will show up in the statistics one day, when they are realized, it still means that the data shows a delayed picture of reality. If the capital share is growing

over time, this means that it is underestimated at any given point of time. Also, gains from private home sales are often nontaxable (your parents didn't have to pay taxes when they sold the family home for three times the price they bought it for) and therefore do not show up in the data either.

[64] Piketty, table S4.2.

[65] Here is how I estimated this number. "Housing," which includes building land plus buildings, equaled 182 percent of the NI (Piketty, table S4.2). The value of the land represented 30.5 percent of the value of residential real estate, averaging CSW-based and FHFA-based estimates, with data used in Morris A. Davis and Jonathan Heathcote, "The Price and Quantity of Residential Land in the United States," *Journal of Monetary Economics* 54 (2007): 2595–620 (updated data at http://www.lincolninst.edu/resources/). Note that 56 percent of the NI is a conservative estimate, as recent estimates using hedonic regression suggest higher values; see William Larson, "New Estimates of Value of Land of the United States" (working paper, Bureau of Economic Analysis, April 2015).

[66] The stock market capitalization of US companies was 108.3 percent of the GDP (https://fred.stlouisfed.org/series/DDDM01USA156NWDB), which corresponds to 128.4 percent of the NI.

[67] Piketty, table S4.1. The German national private capital equaled 412 percent of the NI, but that included 39 percent net foreign assets. Housing (incl. building land) represented 231 percent, or 235 percent including agricultural land, and other domestic capital assets (a category that includes corporate capital) was 138 percent (or 141 percent minus 3 percent public capital).

[68] To be fair, there is also a downside risk for the second-generation rent source owners: they may overestimate how many rents the company will receive in the future and therefore overpay for the shares and eventually incur losses. This risk may, in theory, have a negative effect on the market valuation of the companies (and thus reduce the illusory capital in the economy). In that case, the "return on investment" may appear even higher. However, this phenomenon does not affect the rent part in the capital share. Therefore, it cannot explain why the capital share is so high.

[69] If we look at the ten-year US government bonds issued over the last decade (2006–2015), we find an average interest rate of 3.12 percent. These calculations are based on data collected by the US Department of the Treasury https://www.treasury.gov/resource-center/data-chart-center/interest-rates/Pages/default.aspx. That number, however, includes compensation for inflation. The average inflation rate in the same period was 1.95 percent. The difference is a *net interest of 1.17 percent.* (In the period 2008–2012, the average was 1.01 percent.) Using the same methodology, we find an interest of 0.33 percent for 5-year bonds, 1.78 percent for 20-year bonds, and 1.80 percent for 30-year bonds.

This methodology, however, assumes that the inflation rate in a given year also reflects the inflation expectations in the longer run. Since the inflation was at historically low levels in this period, investors may have expected inflation to go up at some point in the future—which may explain the higher interest rates for 20- and 30-year bonds. How can we disentangle inflation expectations (which matter only for nominal instruments like government bonds) and net interest demands (which matter for all long-term investments)? Fortunately, the government has issued inflation-adjusted bonds since 2003. If you buy these, you will receive a fixed interest (for instance, 1 percent) plus whatever the inflation will be each year (for instance, if the inflation turns out to be 3 percent, the government will pay you 1 percent + 3 percent = 4 percent). The average fixed interest (so, without the inflation part) in 2006–2015 was *1.04 percent for 10-year* bonds, 0.51 percent for 5-year bonds, and 1.48 percent for 20- year bonds. The average interest for the 30-year bonds (which are only issued since 2011) in 2011–2015 was *1.06 percent.*

[70] Here are the calculations for 1970 using the same data sources. Agricultural land was 19 percent and building land 31 percent of the NI. The capitalization of the stock market was about 80 percent of the NI (about 70 percent of the GDP). If we assume the illusory part was one-half, we find that 40 of the 80 percent was illusory. Therefore, the sum of the illusory capital was 90 percent (19 percent + 31 percent + 40 percent). This means that the *real domestic private capital was 237 percent of the NI* (as the domestic private capital was 327 percent).
Note that it is not clear whether the illusory part was lower in 1970 than in 2010. On the one hand, concentration and leveraging strategies were less frequently implemented than in 2010, so corporations owned a higher percentage of their buildings, machines, trucks, and inventory. On the other hand, the capitalization of the stock market declined to about 48 percent of the NI (40 percent of the GDP) in the period 1975–1984, which suggests that more than half of the market value of companies in 1970 must have been illusory capital.
In 1970, the inflation-adjusted *pure market interest on capital can be estimated at about 1.75 percent.* Note that at that time, inflation-adjusted government bonds were not yet issued. The difference between the nominal interest for 10-year government bonds and the inflation rate in the year they were issued was 1.71 percent in the period 1968– 1972, and 1.79 percent in the period 1965–1972. The following years were atypical because of the oil crisis.

[71] Piketty, *Capital in the Twenty-First Century,* 299, fig. 8.7.

[72] In France, 27.6 percent went to the top decile in 1968–1972, and 27.1 percent in 2006–2010 (Piketty, table S8.1). In the US, 25.7 percent went to the top decile in 1968–1972, versus 34.75 percent in 2006–2010 (Piketty, fig. 8.7). Data for 1970 and 2010 were 25.67 percent and 34.47 percent, respectively. From 1970 to 2010, the share of the top percentile increased from 5 percent to 11 percent (Piketty, table S8.2).

[73] To the extent that a small part of the 10 percent corresponds to true productivity increases at the top, this is easily offset by the assumption, made in this estimate, that there is no rent increase in the regions below the top decile.

[74] Assume that the 90 percent lowest wages contain no rents at all and that everything paid above the cutoff wage of $121,457 for the 90th percentile are rents. (In other words, we are making two unrealistic assumptions that may cancel each other out.) Since the average wage in the top 10 percent is $226,257, we find that the average rent per worker is $10,480. So, we find that 16 percent of the wages are rents, which corresponds to 11.5 percent of the national income—very close to the number of 12 percent.
It is possible, however, that the rents in the labor share are way higher than the 12 percent. Indeed, this 12 percent of the NI corresponds to about 16 percent of the wage mass. This would mean that the remaining 84 percent of the wage mass contains no rents at all and is strictly paid according to true productivity.

But the bottom half of the workers receive only 13 percent of the wage mass, leaving 70 percent to compensate the upper half for their productivity. This would imply that the upper half is more than five times as "productive." Since almost all do a job that is needed (someone needs to cook hamburgers), it is hard to visualize what five times more "productive" would mean. Note that if the upper half is just three times as productive as the lower half, we explain only 52 percent of the wage mass. In that case, rents would be 48 percent of the wage mass, or nearly three times as high as I estimated.

[75] "Rents" in this dataset are correctly defined as the difference between the market price for the resources and the true production costs (including capital expenses). See "World Development Indicators," http://data.worldbank.org/ (accessed on August 10, 2016).

[76] Most rents are related to energy (oil 2.91 percent, natural gas 0.73 percent, coal 0.30 percent). Mineral rents are responsible for 0.66 percent and forest resource rents for 0.32 percent of the world GDP. The last three decades, energy expenditures averaged about 8 percent of the GDP See US Energy Information Administration, *Monthly Energy Review May 2018,* figure 1.7, http://www. eia.gov/totalenergy/data/monthly/pdf/sec1_16.pdf. Obviously, not all these expenditures are rents (for instance, oil needs to be pumped, refined, and transported, and electricity plants need workers). The World Bank data suggest that over the past decade, about 3.66 of the 8 percent were rents. This does not include rents on uranium or alternative energy sources. Calculations based on 2010–2014 do not significantly alter the results.

[77] EIA, *Petroleum Consumption (in Barrels Per Day),* https://www.eia.gov/ cfapps/ipdbproject/IEDIndex3.cfm?tid=5&pid=5&aid=2; EIA, *Dry Natural Gas Consumption (Billion Cubic Feet),* https://www.eia.gov/cfapps/ ipdbproject/IEDIndex3.cfm?tid =3&pid=26&aid=2; EIA, *Coal Consumption (Thousand Short Tons),* https://www.eia.gov/cfapps/ipdbproject/IEDIndex3. cfm?tid=1&pid=1&aid=2. Note that I took the average of 2010–2014 to estimate the US consumption in comparison to its relative GDP. There is no reason to assume the results would have been significantly different in the longer period 2005–2014. As it turns out, oil and natural gas consumption in the US is nearly identical to the relative GDP. Americans consumed 21.12 percent of all oil and 21.36 percent of all natural gas, while the US GDP was 21.96 percent of the world GDP. Coal consumption in the US (11.71 percent), on the other hand, was only about half of the relative GDP. Data on the relative consumption of all minerals taken together or the relative consumption of forest resources are not available. To be conservative, I assumed that the US mineral consumption is only half, and the forest resource consumption only two-thirds of its relative GDP. Overall, I find that in 1970, 0.96 percent of the US GDP went to natural resources rents, versus 4.21 percent in the period 2005–2014. When these numbers are compared to the national income (which is lower than the GDP), they become 1.11 percent and 4.97 percent, respectively.

[78] A way to measure *land rents plus their local inflation effect* is to estimate the cost of living in a certain area. Such data are available for American cities, even for small cities, although not for rural areas. In those data, 100 represents the average cost of living in the US. Manhattan (New York) has an index of 217, which means that life is more than twice as expensive there as in the average American city. Urban (metropolitan) areas: table 728. Cost of Living

Index—Selected Urban Areas, Annual Average: 2010, https://www2.census. gov/library/publications/2011/compendia/statab/131ed/tab les/prices.pdf. What are the cheapest places? Some smaller cities in the South and Midwest, for instance, Harlingen, TX (82.8), Pryor Creek, OK (84.5), Pueblo, CO (85.6), Cookeville, TN (85.7), and Springfield, IL (85.8). Of the larger cities, Louisville, KY, has the lowest cost-of-living index (87.7).

Now, let's assume that the cheapest cities are those in which land rents equal zero. The cost-of-living index in the cheaper places is about 85, that is, 15 percent cheaper than average. This suggests that 15 percent of the US national income is spent on land rents plus their local inflation effect. Indeed, if you spend $100 in the average American city, that would have cost only $85 if land wasn't scarce.

Note, however, that this estimate is based on numerous shortcuts, and that it may either under- or overestimate the true number. Land rents may be overestimated if those cheaper areas are cheaper by some random other factor— such as access to cheaper electricity, or a local, temporary disequilibrium in a services market. Yet, this is unlikely to be the case in all these cities. Moreover, there are also entire states with a cost of living that is much below the average (Mississippi 87.5, Kentucky 89.0, Tennessee 89.8). On the other hand, the methodology may underestimate the outcome because land rents are likely to be higher than zero in those regions. Moreover, the regions with the lowest land prices are not even in the data—those are the rural areas. Also, in the absence of Ricardian rents, life would be cheaper in New York than in Kentucky because the geographic concentration of resources leads to economies of scale (as a matter of fact, the very reason why economic factors tend to concentrate geographically is these efficiency gains). A final reason why this methodology may underestimate the results is that a part of the Ricardian rents in New York are paid by consumers from elsewhere.

The more difficult question is what part of the 15 percent is the local inflation caused by rents and what part is the rents. The inflation effect depends on how many goods and services bought by New Yorkers are locally produced (where local is defined as "the whole region where life is more expensive"). For instance, if a cup of coffee becomes more expensive in New York, that makes life more expensive for locals only, causing local inflation. But if a good that is produced in New York for the entire US market becomes more expensive, this doesn't make life relatively more expensive in New York. (If you move from New York to Kentucky, you still buy these goods.)

In a very simple model, with only two regions, and the same rent level within each region, it can be shown that the inflation rate is $1/(1 - L)$. For instance, if the local rate L equals 80 percent in the US (that is, if 80 percent of what people consume is produced for the local market), then the local inflation effect explains 12 percent (of the 15 percent), so that the pure land rents are 3 percent of the US economy.

Unfortunately, the reality is much more complicated, as "local" itself is not an all-or- nothing notion but a continuum. (As you walk away from Wall Street, life and land slowly get less expensive.) This makes it mathematically complicated to even design a model. Moreover, the data to plug into such a complicated model are not available. This is why other methods need to be used to estimate land rents.

Still, it is important to realize that the local inflation effect caused by land rents needs to be ignored when measuring true income inequality. To understand why, just ask who receives this 15 percent. Well, to a large extent it is those who work in the expensive areas. A New York office worker may receive more than a Kentucky office worker for the same work, but life in New York is more expensive than in Kentucky, so that the New York worker is in reality not better off. She may have a higher income on paper, but not in real terms. In a broad sense, these inflation effects may be a form of Ricardian rents, but they are not the ones that cause real income inequality.

[79] Data from https://fred.stlouisfed.org/release/tables?rid=53&eid=44183&od =2010-01-01; in 1970, housing expenditures were $91 billion (https://fred. stlouisfed. org/series/DHSGRC1A027NBEA).

[80] Indeed, they are estimates of "imputed rental income," based on a questionnaire that asks owners the following question: "If someone were to rent your home today, how much do you think it would rent for monthly, unfurnished and without utilities?" See Bureau of Labor Statistics, "How the CPI Measures Price Change of Owners' Equivalent Rent of Primary Residence (OER) and Rent of Primary Residence (Rent)," https://www.bls.gov/cpi/factsheets/ owners-equivalent-rent-and-rent.pdf. I estimate property taxes to be 3.29 percent of the national income for residential housing. Property taxes were 3.74 percent of the national income (data US Census Bureau, T01). Assuming that the ratio of Case (2007) also applies to property taxes, 3.29 percent were related to residential land.) I assume financing and transaction costs to be 20 percent of the rental income. Note that a mortgage interest being 1 percent above the government bond interest on a thirty-year loan corresponds to about 15 percent. Transaction costs includes not only the time spent to finding new tenants, but also the time during the rental period. (This estimate may also include losses caused by nonpayment and nonverifiable moral hazard.) The 2005 value of residential and commercial land has been estimated at $9.5 trillion and $1.3 trillion, or 88 percent and 12 percent of the total land rents, respectively. Karl E. Case, "The Value of Land in the United States: 1975–2000," in Proceedings of the 2006 Land Policy Conference: Land Policies and Their Outcomes (Lincoln Institute of Land Policy Press, 2007), 127–47.

[81] For 1970, I am making the same assumption of costs that need to be deducted as in 2010.

[82] I assume that the ratio for yearly rents is the same as for capitalized rents in the form of real estate values. In theory, the depreciation rate for land and structures may differ, though it is not clear which one depreciates faster.

[83] Based on the ratio between residential and commercial land in Case (2007), and assuming proportional costs, I find that commercial land rents were 0.26 percent in 2010 (0.13 percent in 1970). If we assume that yearly agricultural land rents equal 2 percent of the agricultural land value, we find that agricultural land rents were 0.24 percent of the NI (0.38 percent in 1970).

[84] Deirdre N. McCloskey and Arjo Klamer, "One Quarter of GDP Is Persuasion," American Economic Review 85 (1995): 191–95. McCloskey and Klamer frame it as 26 percent of the GDP, but since they measure working hours rather than money spent, their results are better interpreted as referring to the NI, which closely follows the NDP and therefore does not overestimate true production as the GDP does.

[85] McCloskey and Klamer use data from the Census Bureau. Before 1983 and after

2003, however, the Census Bureau used different categorizations of professions. Trying to get as close as possible to McCloskey and Klamer's methodology, Antioch calculated that persuasion costs had increased to 30 percent in 2009. See Gerry Antioch, "Persuasion Is Now 30 Per Cent of US GDP: Revisiting McCloskey and Klamer after a Quarter of a Century," *Economic Roundup Issue (Australian Government Treasury)* 1 (2013).

To estimate persuasion costs in 1970, the proxy that seems to be most strongly correlated with persuasion costs over the period 1983–2009 is the share of managerial positions in the US economy. Its slower growth in the 1970s suggests that the growth of persuasion costs may have been in the range of about 1 percent per decade rather than about 3 percent per decade as was the case in the 1980s and 1990s. This suggests that persuasion costs may have been around 22 percent in 1970.

Persuasion costs	Managers and administrators
1970 22% (estimated)	10.54%
1983 23% (McCloskey and Klamer)	11.02% (in 1984)
1993 26.26% (McCloskey and Klamer, Antioch)	3.76% (in 1995)
2003 29.11% (Antioch)	14.53% (in 2004)
2009 30.01% (Antioch)	15.06% (in 2010)

Note that McCloskey and Klamer estimate the number of persuasion jobs rather than their monetary valuation. Depending on how much persuasion jobs are paid compared to other jobs, persuasion costs may have been higher or lower than 30 percent of the GDP.

[86] I mentioned that rent-seeking costs also exist on the buyers' side. Most of these, however, should not be counted when we calculate what part of the NI consists of rent-seeking costs. The reason is that the time devoted to shopping does not show up in the national accounts in the first place. Indeed, the NI incorporates only the paid labor on the market, not the unpaid labor at home or as a consumer. Still, some buyers spend this time as a part of their job (as is the case when your employer asks you to order a printer for your office). So, rent-seeking costs get higher than the 15 percent when we also include search costs and listening-to-persuasion costs.

[87] I am rounding down in 1970 and rounding up in 2010 because product differentiation costs have likely increased disproportionally in this period.

[88] For starters, we may assume that nearly all these rent-seeking costs are related to *non-Ricardian rents*. For Ricardian rents (land, oil, minerals, forest, agricultural land), rent-seeking costs are probably trivial compared to the national income. Most landowners do not have to do anything to capture the rents of rising land prices. Some need to engage in political lobbying, but as we have seen, political rent-seeking costs tend to be small compared to the rent at stake. Acquiring oil wells or mines may require geological research, but these expenses are not always wasteful and also do not fall under the "persuasion costs" of McCloskey and Klamer. Thus, we may assume for simplicity that the 23 percent rent-seeking costs are related to non-Ricardian rents. How large are the rents compared to the rent-seeking costs? In other words, how much of the rents gets dissipated in the form of rent-seeking costs at any given moment in the life span of a rent? Initially, when a new source of rents is created, there

tends to be little dissipation. Over time, rent-seeking costs increase. Yet, it is not sure that there will ever be a point at which the rents are fully dissipated as competition may eliminate the rents before they get fully dissipated. Rents can also be dissipated in the form of cross-subsidization of "razors" in the razor-blade model, which does not fall under the definition of "wasteful rent-seeking costs" either (as they are just transfer payments). Thus, it seems reasonable to assume that, at any given moment, half of all rents are dissipated on average in the form of wasteful rent-seeking costs. If wasteful rent-seeking costs for non-Ricardian rents are 23 percent of the NI, this implies that the nondissipated non-Ricardian rents are also 23 percent.

But here comes the tricky thing: a part of the 23 percent rent-seeking costs are in turn . . . rents! Indeed, businesses specializing in rent-seeking services (such as advertising companies and consultancy firms) and individuals performing rent-seeking activities for their employers may receive rents as well. How high are these rents? In the absence of data, the most reasonable assumption is that they are the same as the non-Ricardian rents in the rest of the economy.

The previously made estimate that non-Ricardian rents are 30 percent is consistent with the estimate that rent-seeking costs are 23 percent. If these rents are 30 percent, then of the 23 percent that initially went to the rent-seeking service industry, 16 percent are true rent-seeking costs and 7 percent are rents. If you add the 23 percent direct non-Ricardian rents to the 7 percent non-Ricardian rents in the rent-seeking industry, you find that non-Ricardian rents were 30 percent of the NI (23 percent + 7 percent) in 2010. For 1970, similar calculations give 19 percent.

[89] For another way to realize how much business schools can increase rents, let's look at just one type of rents—information rents—and create a brand-new test, which I'll call the *Information Rent Potential* test. This test measures how much information rents sellers of goods or services could acquire if they really wanted to. For instance, how much could plumbers overcharge for spare parts if they really wanted to? To what extent could electronics salespeople manipulate consumers to buy low-value, high- markup items such as extended warranties if they really wanted to? To what extent could Goldman Sachs make clients underestimate risks associated with certain financial products if they really wanted to?

The test does not tell if people do exploit asymmetric information to acquire information rents. It only says that they could do so if they wanted to. The test measures the opportunities that exist, not those that are taken.

For the test, just imagine that the consumers (and employers) were perfectly informed about prices and quality so that there were no information rents in the economy. Suppose that under these circumstances, the price of a product was $100. Now enter the current reality in which consumers are poorly informed, and some are better informed than others. How much could an individual plumber or electronics salesperson increase the price by exploiting asymmetric information? If on average, throughout the entire economy, prices could be increased by 10 percent, the Information Rent Potential is 10 percent.

What is the average Information Rent Potential in the economy? No data are available, which is not so surprising as this is a newly proposed test. But it is obvious that the average Information Rent Potential has increased over the past decades. The number of products has exponentially increased, making choices more complex. As Ben- Shahar and Schneider wrote, "Only a few decades ago, you made fewer choices about fewer things. You got a black telephone from AT&T. . . . Today, phones come in landline, cell, and VOIP versions from many manufacturers making many models for many service providers offering many plans." Omri Ben-Shahar and Carl E. Schneider, *More Than You Wanted to Know: The Failure of Mandated Disclosure* (Princeton University Press, 2014), 4–5. Ben-Shahar and Schneider use this example to argue that the legal system should do less as it can't reduce natural complexity; I use it to argue that information rents have increased and that the legal system should do more. Note that marketers have added to the complexity by recommending product versioning and complicated price menus.

Still, the Information Rent Potential rate doesn't say that sellers will do this. It only says they could do it. So, the next question is how likely it is that they would do it. This is a function of two factors. First, are they sophisticated enough to see the opportunities? Second, do they see business as a game, so that they don't feel guilty if they do it? And here we are back to the role of marketers and business consultants. They increase the sophistication of sellers. In addition, they help them see business as a game.

[90] Traditional marketplaces, where people could see the entire market by walking 200 feet, made a quasi-total-view search possible, at least if prices were clearly indicated. Price haggling, on the other hand, suggests that not all of these markets were transparent.

[91] See also Glen Ellison and Sara Fisher Ellison, "Search, Obfuscation, and Price Elasticities on the Internet," *Econometrica* 77 (2009): 427–52.

[92] Mohammed, *The 1% Windfall*, 85–86: "Fifteen minutes of research yielded prices ranging from $136 to $358.80 per night for the same hotel. . . . 'It's common for a full-service hotel to offer as many as five-hundred possible room rates,' Bjorn Hanson, Ph.D., a professor at New York University, told me."

[93] Walter Baker, Michael V. Marn, and Craig Zawada, "Pricing Smarter on the Net," *Harvard Business Review* (February 2001): 155.

[94] Ibid., 165.

[95] Jagmohan Raju and Z. John Zhang, Smart Pricing: How Google, Priceline, and Leading Businesses Use Pricing Innovation for Profitability (Wharton School Publishing, 2010), 135.

[96] Varian, "A Model of Sales," 651–59.

[97] Raju and Zhang, *Smart Pricing*, 146 on shipping fees: "Others have tried to make it a profit, assuming that the 'sticker' price on the website or the catalog is usually the one about which the consumer is most aware. Generally, a correct assumption."

[98] See Brad Stone, "The Fight Over Who Sets Prices at the Online Mall," *New York Times,* February 7, 2010. Amazon openly criticizes this practice (required by some manufacturers), arguing it decreases transparency and raises consumer prices.

[99] Eric Lespin, "The Quest for Price Transparency," healthcareblog.com, May 7, 2011.

[100] See Institute of Medicine, *Best Care at Lower Cost: The Path to Continuously Learning Health Care in America* (The National Academies Press, 2012).

[101] Data on the magnitude of the rents in the health-care system are not available. The fact that the average income of doctors is high may be one indication. The fact that hedge funds are buying hospitals may be another (after all, Wall Street's core business is to detect rent opportunities).

[102] Puffery is an exaggerated, promotional statement that no reasonable person would take seriously. For the best puffery article ever, see David A. Hoffman, "The Best Puffery Article Ever," *Iowa Law Review* 91 (2006): 1395–448.

[103] Mathematically, denote p^B and pN as the price of the brand product and nonbrand product respectively, and L as the chance the nonbrand product will have to be thrown away and replaced by the brand product. In this case, $p^B = p^N/(1-L)$. The brand premium increases in L.

[104] Note that the incentive to work fast is not optimal as there is an incentive to work too fast (shirking on quality).

[105] An incentive, but not a perfect incentive, because the real estate agent receives only 3 percent of the higher price but incurs 100 percent of the extra effort costs. See Steven Levitt and Stephen J. Dubner, *Freakonomics: A Rogue Economist Explores the Hidden Side of Everything* (William Morrow, 2005), 68–73.

[106] See Bengt Holstrom and Paul Milgrom, "Multitask Principal-Agent Analyses: Incentive Contracts, Asset Ownership, and Job Design," *Journal of Law, Economics, and Organization* 7 (1991): 24–52.

[107] Fixed fees, however, may give an incentive to underexamine the patient, since they give an incentive to work as little as possible for the money. Medical malpractice may counterbalance some of these incentives. See also Gerrit De Geest, "Who Should Be Immune from Tort Liability?" *Journal of Legal Studies* 41 (2012): 291–319.

[108] Lester Brickman, "Effective Hourly Rates of Contingency-Fee Lawyers: Competing Data and Non-Competitive Fees," *Washington University Law Quarterly* 81 (2003): 653–736.

[109] Suppose, for instance, that a house in 2007 cost $500,000 and that it really involved $30,000 work for the real estate agents. In 2012, the market price has decreased to $350,000, so that the real estate agents only get $21,000. How can they survive if there was really $30,000 work involved?

[110] Limited liability makes it easier to raise capital. If liability were unlimited, wealthy investors would risk losing more, and therefore would demand compensation for that; this in turn would require investors to check each other's wealth. For a review of the economic literature, see Nicolai J. Foss, Henrik Lando, and Steen Thomson, "The Theory of the Firm," in *Encyclopedia of Law and Economics,* ed. Boudewijn Bouckaert and Gerrit De Geest, vol. 3 (Edward Elgar, 2000), 631–58; William J. Carney, "Limited Liability," in Encyclopedia of Law and Economics, vol. 3, 659–91.

[111] Ronald H. Coase, "The Nature of the Firm," *Economica* 4 (1937): 386–405.

[112] Hart, *Firms, Contracts, and Financial Structure.*

[113] Juan de Lugo, *Disputationes de Iustitia et Iure,* vol. 2 (Lyon, 1642), d. 26, s. 4, n. 40, p. 312 (arguing that the price equilibrium depends on so many elements that only God is able to know it: "Pretium iustum mathematicum licet soli Deo notum"). On the history of iustum pretium and the related doctrine of laesio enormis, see Reinhard Zimmermann, *The Law of Obligations: Roman Foundations of the Civilian Tradition* (Oxford University Press, 1996), 255–70.

[114] Friedrich A. Hayek, "Economics and Knowledge," *Economica* 4 (1937): 33–54; Friedrich A. Hayek, "The Use of Knowledge in Society," *American Economic Review* 35 (1945): 519–30.

[115] On price unconscionability in the US, see Edward A. Farnsworth, *Farnsworth on Contracts,* 3rd ed., vol. 1 (Aspen, 2004): 596–98. ("Courts have been

more reluctant to pass judgment on the fairness of the price term . . . it is not surprising that courts have tended to avoid square holdings that an excessive price without more is unconscionable . . . most of the cases in which price has been stressed as an element of unconscionability have emphasized elements of procedural unconscionability.") Price unconscionability is also mentioned in the Uniform Consumer Credit Code §5.108 ("gross disparity between the price of the property or services obtained on credit"). A leading case on price unconscionability is Jones v. Star Credit Corp., 298 N.Y.S.2d 264 (Sup. Ct. 1969) ($1,234.80 for a freezer that cost approximately $300 elsewhere was unconscionable).

[116] Sanford J. Grossman, "The Informational Role of Warranties and Private Disclosure about Product Quality," *Journal of Law and Economics* 24 (1981): 461–83.

[117] To illustrate, suppose there are many sellers offering products of varying quality, ranging from 9 (very good) to 1 (very bad). Consumers don't know the quality and therefore assume (for better or worse) that all products have the same average quality of 5. In this case, the businesses who offer a quality that is higher than 5 (that is, those who offer 6, 7, 8, or 9) have an incentive to disclose this information. If they do so, consumers start to assume that businesses who did not disclose anything (and whose quality now must be 5 or lower) offer an average quality of only 3. This gives the businesses who offer 4 or 5 an incentive to reveal the quality of their products. Then, consumers start to assume that those who still remain silent offer an average quality of only 2, which gives the businesses that offer 3 an incentive to reveal this. The process goes on until all businesses—except for the one with the lowest quality—have revealed the quality of their products. But the last one (that did not say anything because its quality is so bad) is exposed by all the others—consumers rightly assume that the one who remains silent has something to hide.

The same mechanism applies to price information. Suppose that some plumbers are cheap and others are expensive. If consumers don't see these prices before hiring a plumber, they will rationally assume that all plumbers charge an average rate. This gives the cheaper plumbers an incentive to publish their prices on the internet. Once the cheaper ones have published their prices, consumers start to think that those who don't do this are quite expensive, and this again gives some other plumbers at the margin an incentive to publish their prices. This process goes on until all plumbers except for the most expensive one have published their prices. And the most expensive one is exposed by all the others: consumers assume he must be the most expensive plumber—what other reason could he have for not publishing his prices?

[118] The fourth condition is that there is "convexity." This technical term basically tells that there must be an incentive to be the first to publish information. There may be several reasons why there is no convexity. First, information is often only useful when it allows consumers to compare products. For instance, 28 miles per gallon for a car does not mean much until we know the miles per gallon of competing cars. Moreover (and here comes the standardization issue again), 28 miles per gallon does not say much if every car company uses a different test. Second, even the one with the best quality may not dare to reveal the numbers if consumers have unrealistically high beliefs about quality. Suppose that patients believe that only 2 percent of them will have complications after a medical procedure, when even the best hospital has a 4 percent rate. In this

case, even the best hospital will not disclose its complication rate. The fifth condition is that there are no implicit cartels in the industry. If all businesses realize that publishing prices will only start a "price war" (that's the term they use to denote "price competition"), no one will publish first. As we have seen before, implicit cartels are perfectly legal under current antitrust law. And this brings us back to a previous point: that a duty to publish information should be seen, first and foremost, as a measure to restore competition.

[119] Data on advertising expenditures can be found at www.zenithoptimedia.com (estimate in text based on forecasts March 2016).

[120] The traditional legal definition of hearsay is: "hearsay. (16c) 1. Traditionally, testimony that is given by a witness who relates not what he or she knows personally, but what others have said, and that is therefore dependent on the credibility of someone other than the witness. Such testimony is generally inadmissible under the rules of evidence." Bryan E. Garner, ed. *Black's Law Dictionary* (West, 2009).

[121] Other factors may play a role. One is the free-rider problem associated with all public goods: many people don't bother to share their experiences. Reputation is also easy to fog or manipulate ("All banks have the same type of issues and complaints; it's just the way it works when you're a big business").

[122] Jeff Rossen and Robert Powell, "Are Mold Contractors Charging for Unneeded Work? Hidden Cameras Reveal Some Want Big Bucks for Repairs Experts Say Aren't Necessary," *Today*, May 4, 2012, https://www.today.com/news/news/rossen-reports/rossen-reports-are-mold-contractors-charging-unneeded-work-2689406.

[123] Philip Kotler and Gary Armstrong, *Principles of Marketing* (Pearson Prentice Hall, 2012), 189 (quoting former Best Buy CEO Anderson).

[124] See Tom Baker and Peter Siegelman, "Protecting Consumers from Add-On Insurance Products: New Lessons for Insurance Regulation from Behavioral Economics," *Connecticut Insurance Law Journal* 20 (2013): 13 (estimating that a "3-year in-home master protection agreement" priced at $349 on the Sears website has a 90 percent markup); Tao Chen, Aiay Kalra, and Baohong Sun, "Why Do Consumers Buy Extended Service Contracts?" *Journal of Consumer Research* 36 (2009): 611; Rafi Mohammed, *The Art of Pricing: How to Find the Hidden Profits to Grow Your Business* (Crown Business, 2005), 71: "These warranties are highly profitable add-ons to a company's core products. . . . Extended warranties offered by the Dixons Group (a leading European electronics retailer) and Comet . . . accounted for 47% and 80%, respectively, of their pre-tax profits."

[125] This lack of attention may partly be due to deliberate "shrouded pricing," that is, revealing prices only after consumers have decided to buy the primary product. On shrouded pricing, see Xavier Gabaix and David Laibson, "Shrouded Attributes, Consumer Myopia, and Information Suppression in Competitive Markets," *Quarterly Journal of Economics* 121 (2006): 505–40.

[126] See endnote 221 and accompanying text.

[127] Alexander Durst, "Greasing the Wheels of Justice? Deceptive Sales Practices by Jiffy Lube and Other Oil Change Companies" (unpublished student paper, Washington University School of Law, December 2011) (statements on neutral expert opinions based on interviews). See also http://www.edmunds.com/car-care/choosing-and-using-the-right-engine-oil.html ("Synthetic: Worth It? The short answer: Modern synthetic engine oil . . .

can extend oil-change intervals. However, unless you subject your vehicle to extreme conditions, synthetic may not be worth the extra cost") and http://www.edmunds.com/car-care/top-7-urban-legends-about-motor-oil.html ("Synthetic oil is better for your car's engine and it improves your fuel economy[?] Myth. Steve Mazor, manager of the American Automobile Association's Research Center, says his testing shows that synthetic oil is generally a superior lubricant, but adds, 'I'm not sure it is worth the extra cost").

[128] The 2010 Dodd-Frank Wall Street Reform and Consumer Protection Act amended the Truth in Lending Act (TILA), Regulation Z. The prohibition of yield spread premiums (12 CFR §1026.36 (d)) applies only to "certain home mortgage transactions." There is no similar compensation restraint on home equity loans, car loans, or student loans. The regulation regarding these loans is largely limited to disclosure requirements.

[129] Howell E. Jackson and Laurie Burlingame, "Kickbacks or Compensation: The Case of Yield Spread Premiums," *Stanford Journal of Law, Business and Finance* 12 (2007): 289– 361.

[130] See Christopher R. Leslie, "A Market-Based Approach to Coupon Settlements in Antitrust and Consumer Class Action Litigation," *UCLA Law Review* 49 (2002): 991– 1098.

[131] The Class Action Fairness Act of 2005 requires that, to the extent attorney fees are based on the value of coupons, the actually redeemed rather than the theoretically available number has to be taken into consideration. 28 U.S.C. §1712(a).

[132] Gerrit De Geest, "The Signing-Without-Reading Problem: An Analysis of the European Directive on Unfair Contract Terms," in *Konsequenzen wirtschaftsrechtlicher Normen*, ed. Hans-Bernd Schäfer and Hans-Jürgen Lwowski (Wiesbaden: Gabler Verlag, 2002), 213–35.

[133] Yannis Bakos, Florencia Marotta-Wurgler, and David R. Trossen, "Does Anyone Read the Fine Print? Testing a Law and Economics Approach to Standard Form Contracts," *Journal of Legal Studies* 43 (2014): 1–35.

[134] Joseph M. Perillo, *Calamari and Perillo on Contracts*, 6th ed. (West, 2009): 341–57. Courts are slowly carving out exceptions to this duty to read.

[135] See, for instance, Florencia Marotta-Wurgler, "What's in a Standard Form Contract? An Empirical Analysis of Software License Agreements," *Journal of Empirical Legal Studies* 4 (2007): 677–713 (nearly all software license contracts are pro-seller biased); Florencia Marotta-Wurgler and Robert Taylor, "Set in Stone: Change and Innovation in Consumer Standard-Form Contracts," *NYU Law Review* 88 (2013): 240–85 (standard terms have become longer and less buyer friendly over the past decade).

[136] UCC 2-316(2) requires that to exclude the implied warranty of merchantability or the implied warranty of fitness for a particular purpose, the writing must be "conspicuous." The Magnussen-Moss Act also contains legal limitations on skeleton warranties. On case law regarding unconscionability, see Perillo, *Calamari and Perillo on Contracts*, 9.40; Edward A. Farnsworth, *Farnsworth on Contracts*, 3rd ed. (Aspen, 2004), 4.28a.

[137] See James R. Maxeiner, "Standard-Terms Contracting in the Global Electronic Age: European Alternatives," *Yale Journal of International Law* 28 (2003): 109–82; Gerrit De Geest, "Signing without Reading," in *Encyclopedia of Law and Economics: Basic Areas of Law*, ed. Alain Marciano and Giovanni Battista Ramello (Springer, forthcoming).

[138] If cartridges are overpriced, why aren't other companies offering similar cartridges for a lower price? In some cases, patents prevent them from making compatible cartridges. In other cases, quality fog makes consumers reluctant to buy the cheaper cartridges.

[139] Alaska Packers' Ass'n v. Domenico et al., Circuit Court of Appeals, Ninth Circuit. 117 F. 99 (1902). Technically, the case was decided on the basis of the absence of consideration because of a preexisting duty. Recent commentators consider it a poster child of economic duress. See, for instance, John E. Murray, *Murray on Contracts* (Matthew Bender, 2011), 515–17.

[140] To be more precise, the two parties in *Alaska Packers Assn. v. Domenico* were in a bilateral monopoly position: in theory, the employer could also have played a hold-up game against the fishermen once they had arrived in Alaska. The bilateral character does not change the analysis in that there was still opportunistic behavior by the fishermen as the employer had no reasonable alternative.

[141] *Eastman Kodak Co. v. Image Technical Services* (1992) carves out exception, but it has been de facto overruled by lower courts. See David A.J. Goldfine and Kenneth M. Vorrasi, "The Fall of the Kodak Aftermarket Doctrine: Dying a Slow Death in the Lower Courts," *Antitrust Law Journal* 72 (2004): 209–31.

[142] See, for instance, Nagle, Hogan, and Zale, *The Strategy and Tactics of Pricing*, 246 ("Price competitors do well, therefore, to forget what they learned about competing from sports and other positive-sum games, and to try instead to draw lessons from less familiar competitions such as warfare or dueling. . . . For marketers, as for diplomats, warfare should be a last resort, and even then the potential benefits of using it must be weighed against the cost. . . . Competing on price alone is at best a short-term strategy until competitors find it threatening enough to react").

[143] See, generally, Akshay R. Rao, Mark E. Bergen, and Scott Davis, "How to Fight a Price War," *Harvard Business Review on Pricing* (2008, originally published 2000): 75–100. See also Nagle, Hogan, and Zale, *The Strategy and Tactics of Pricing*, 246 ("Precisely because they create profits, rather than dissipate them, building capabilities for positive-sum forms of competition is the basis of a sustainable strategy.")

[144] Ibid., 253.

[145] Ibid., 262.

[146] Rao, Bergen, and Davis, "How to Fight a Price War," 91 ("If simple retaliatory price cuts are the chosen means of defense in a price war, then implement them quickly and unambiguously so competitors know that their sales gains from a price cut will be short-lived and monetarily unattractive").

[147] Nagle, Hogan, and Zale, *The Strategy and Tactics of Pricing*, 261–62.

[148] Ibid., 262.

[149] Mohammed, *The 1% Windfall*, 148; Nagle, Hogan, and Zale, *The Strategy and Tactics of Pricing*, 253–61.

[150] Sometimes new entrants offer better products at a higher price; but entrants rarely offer identical products. Mohammed, *The 1% Windfall*, 159 ("It's rare for a new competitor to enter the market with an identical product, as this would virtually guarantee a price war").

[151] Mohammed, *The 1% Windfall*, 148 ("The benefits of fighter brands are threefold. . . . First, high-valuation customers continue to pay full price for regular versions. Next, price-sensitive customers purchase the cheaper version.

Finally, once the economy recovers, fighter brands can be withdrawn from the market and their customers transitioned back to paying full price for the flagship product"). Nagle, Hogan, and Zale, *The Strategy and Tactics of Pricing,* 260 ("There is an obvious benefit . . . the ability to kill this new competitor when consumers again feel able to pay for its more value- added brands").

[152] "Payer externalities" is a new term. The underlying idea is that buyers are less price sensitive when they don't pay the full bill; this is conventional wisdom in the marketing literature. See, for instance, Robert J. Dolan, "How Do You Know When the Price Is Right?" *Harvard Business Review on Pricing* (2008, originally published 1995), 13 ("Price sensitivity increases—and a company's latitude thus decreases—to the degree that: The end user bears the cost as opposed to a third party"). Nagle, Hogan, and Zale, *The Strategy and Tactics of Pricing,* 132–33 ("Price Sensitivity Drivers . . . Shared costs: Buyers are less price sensitive when some or all the purchase price is paid by others. Does the buyer pay the full cost of the product? If not, what portion of the cost does the buyer pay?").

[153] The true costs of electronic payments are low. Note that in the EU, interchange fees are capped at 0.2 percent for consumer debit cards, based on the reasoning that the costs cannot be higher than for cash payments. See "Regulation on Interchange Fees," European Commission Fact Sheet Antitrust, Brussels, June 9, 2016, http://europa.eu/rapid/press-release_MEMO-16-2162_en.htm.

[154] A recent settlement gives merchants in the US the right to add surcharges for the use of Visa and Mastercard credit cards. See https://usa.visa.com/ content/ dam/VCOM/download/merchants/surcharging-faq-by-merchants. pdf. However, several conditions need to be fulfilled. First, the credit card company must be notified thirty days beforehand. Second, the surcharge must be clearly disclosed at the entry of the store and the point-of-sale. Third (and here it becomes interesting!), the same surcharge must be applied to American Express, whose contracts with the merchants forbid surcharges! This means that businesses can only use surcharges if they no longer accept American Express. In addition, ten US states (including California, New York, and Texas) forbid or restrict surcharging on the mistaken belief that the current practice is good for consumers.

[155] In this comparison, I left airport taxes out of the equation. Note that such fees are no exception—they have become the rule. The practice started more than a decade ago. See Peter Greenberg, "European Skyway Robbery," *Today,* May 16, 2007, https://www.today.com/news/european-skyway-robbery-wbna18700377.

[156] In most published rescue cases, the rescue happened at sea and contracts were held legally unenforceable under the admiralty doctrine of "salvage."

[157] Peter Diamond, "A Model of Price Adjustment," *Journal of Economic Theory* 3 (1971): 156–68.

[158] The Diamond equilibrium may help explain why compensation of CEOs, CFOs, and other executives has spectacularly increased in the last couple of decades. Suppose that at a given point in time, the yearly income of all CEOs of large corporations was $1 million. Since this was the market price, economic logic dictates that any CEO could have been replaced by a similarly skilled CEO who would have commanded a similar wage. Replacing a CEO, however, requires search costs and switching costs (the new CEO would have to spend months to study the new firm, and there may be efficiency loss in the vacuum). Suppose

these costs are $400,000 per year (for instance, $2 million in total, and a CEO stays five years on average). In this case, if the CEO demanded a pay increase of $200,000 per year, it would be in the interest of the firm to pay it because the alternative would cost more (if search and switching costs are taken into account). But if all CEOs succeed in increasing their annual income to $1,200,000 this way, this amount becomes the new market price. In the next round, CEOs ask for another wage increase of $200,000 and get it, so that the market price becomes $1,400,000. After many rounds, which may take a few decades, the market price may have increased to, for instance, $5 million.

Of course, executive compensation is a complex issue, and other factors may have played a role. See also Lucian Bebchuk and Jesse Fried, *Pay without Performance: The Unfulfilled Promise of Executive Compensation* (Harvard University Press, 2004); John Bizjak, Michael Lemmon, and Thanh Nguyen, "Are All CEOs Above Average? An Empirical Analysis of Compensation Peer Groups and Pay Design," *Journal of Financial Economics* 100 (2011): 538–55 (the practice of benchmarking may ratchet up the level of executive compensation, as peer groups are chosen in a way that biases compensation upward).

[159] While hard data on the magnitude of lock-in effects and information rents are unavailable, anecdotal evidence seems to be plentiful. One of my research assistants reported that he once called Best Buy to get his TV fixed (purchased a few years earlier for $2,400). The visit cost $175. Upon arrival, the technician recommended replacing the motherboard on the TV, which would have cost an additional $750. The total cost ($175 + $750) came close to 40 percent of $2,400. My research assistant, a savvy MBA student, eventually found a local repairman who fixed the problem for $25 ($10 for the parts, $15 for the labor).

[160] The FTC Act forbids all deceptive acts and practices. Incorrect former price or retail price comparisons explicitly violate the FTC Guides Against Deceptive Pricing, 16 CFR Part 233. These rules are repeated by consumer protection law in most states.

[161] David Adam Friedman, "Reconsidering Fictitious Pricing," Minnesota Law Review 100 (2016): 921–22. Former FTC Commissioner Pitofsky feared that intervention would stifle competition. See Robert Pitofsky, "Beyond Nader: Consumer Protection and the Regulation of Advertising," *Harvard Law Review* 90 (1977): 661, 687–88.

[162] Bart J. Bronnenberg, Jean-Pierre Dubé, Matthew Gentzkow, and Jesse Shapiro, "Do Pharmacists Buy Bayer? Sophisticated Shoppers and the Brand Premium," *Quarterly Journal of Economics* 130 (2015): 1669–726.

[163] See https://www.fda.gov/Drugs/ResourcesForYou/ConsumersQuestionsAns wersucm100100.htm#q1 ("Do generic medicines work the same as brand-name medicines? Yes. Any generic medicine modeled after a brand-name medicine must perform the same in the body as the brand-name medicine. This standard applies to all generic medicines. A generic medicine is the same as a brand-name medicine in dosage, safety, effectiveness, strength, stability, and quality, as well as in the way it is taken and the way it should be used. Generic medicines use the same active ingredients as brand-name medicines and work the same way, so they have the same risks and benefits as the brand-name medicines. The FDA Generic Drugs Program conducts a rigorous review to make certain generic medicines meet these standards, in addition to conducting 3,500 inspections of manufacturing plants a year and monitoring drug safety after the generic medicine has been approved and brought to market").

164 Ivan L. Preston, *The Great American Blow-Up: Puffery in Advertising and Selling* (University of Wisconsin Press, 1996), 134.

165 "Genuine Bayer Aspirin provides pain relief from headaches, backaches, muscle pain, toothaches, menstrual pain and minor arthritis pain—and has for over 100 years. It's also recommended, under a doctor's supervision, to help reduce the risk of a recurrent heart attack or ischemic stroke. No other leading brand of pain reliever can do that." http://www.wonderdrug.com/products/genuine-bayer-aspirin/.

166 "Is aspirin safe? Aspirin is one of the most extensively studied pain relievers in history with a 100-year track record of safety and efficacy. Bayer Aspirin is safe and effective for pain relief when used according to label directions." http://www.wonderdrug.com/faqs/.

167 Restatement of Contracts (Second) § 161. ("When Non-Disclosure Is Equivalent to an Assertion. A person's non-disclosure of a fact known to him is equivalent to an assertion that the fact does not exist in the following cases only: (a) where he knows that disclosure of the fact is necessary to prevent some previous assertion from being a misrepresentation or from being fraudulent or material. (b) where he knows that disclosure of the fact would correct a mistake of the other party as to a basic assumption on which that party is making the contract and if non-disclosure of the fact amounts to a failure to act in good faith and in accordance with reasonable standards of fair dealing.")

168 Kronman, "Mistake, Disclosure, Information, and the Law of Contracts."

169 Bronnenberg, Dubé, Gentzkow, and Shapiro, "Do Pharmacists Buy Bayer?" The used methodology underestimates the potential savings because the benchmark is not perfect information but the information an average pharmacist possesses. The study found only a 1 percent potential saving on branded, food-related products, but here the reference group (professional cooks) may be far from perfectly informed.

170 Arthur A. Leff, *Swindling and Selling: The Story of Legal and Illegal Congames* (Free Press, 1976).

171 Ibid., 4, 19–29.

172 FTC Guides concerning the Use of Endorsements and Testimonials in Advertising, §255.1 (c) ("where the advertisement represents that the endorser uses the endorsed product, then the endorser must have been a bona fide user of it at the time the endorsement was given").

173 Jeff Berman, "Why Lawyers Need To Understand The Art of Price Conditioning," AttorneySync, July 27, 2010, https://www.attorneysync.com/law-practice-management/do-you-offer-a-higher-priced-legal-service-learn-the-art-of-price- conditioning/.

174 To be fair, there is also a rosy interpretation of price conditioning, and it goes like this. All sellers have to make sure that their true costs are covered by their prices. Sometimes, however, customers underestimate these true costs. Such customers may refuse to pay a perfectly fair bill. To prevent this, sellers need to timely inform their customers about the market prices. Suppose that most law firms in your city charge $200 per hour and that preparing a case takes them ten hours so that the market price for this service is $2,000. Suppose you can do the same in eight hours and charge only $1,600, but your client thinks that it takes only two hours and therefore expects a $400 bill. Thanks to your price conditioning effort, your client will accept the fair price, and even be grateful that you have worked below the market price. Yet the rosy version is less likely to happen than

the previous, more sinister version, for one simple reason. Price conditioning is unnecessary in a fully transparent market, in which customers know the market price. Price conditioning only makes sense in nontransparent markets, and these are exactly the markets in which sellers have most room for manipulation.

175 See Ian Ayres and Gregory Klass, Insincere Promises: *The Law of Misrepresented Intent* (Yale University Press, 2005).

176 Hellmann's did this with its Real Mayonnaise in 2006, Kraft followed in 2010. See http://www.mouseprint.org/2010/05/24/kraft-miracle-whip-and-mayonnaise-downsized/. See also Sullivan, *Stop Getting Ripped Off*, 41 ("inflation by degradation . . . When a quart of mayonaise is suddenly a thirty-ounce jar . . . a twenty-nine-ounce jar . . . a twenty-eight-ounce-jar—you see a new kind of inflation in action"); Poundstone, *Priceless*, 5 ("In summer 2008 Kellogg's phased in thinner boxes of Cocoa Krispies, Froot Loops, Corn Pops, Apple Jacks, and Honey Smacks cereals. No one noticed").

177 "Surprise" is one of the two central elements in the unconscionability doctrine (the other one is "oppression"). In practice, however, a term must be truly surprising before it falls under the term "surprise." On unconscionability more generally, see Perillo, *Calamari and Perillo on Contracts*, 9.37–9.40; Farnsworth, *Farnsworth on Contracts*, 4.28.

178 Margaret Jane Radin, "An Analytical Framework for Legal Evaluation of Boilerplate," in Philosophical Foundations of Contract Law, ed. Gregory Klass, George Letsas, and Prince Saprai (Oxford University Press, 2015, arguing that the notion of reasonable expectation should be avoided because it implies that the more often something is imposed on people, the more it is permissible).

179 See also Leff, *Swindling and Selling*, 167–69.

180 Herb Sorensen, "The Science of Shopping," *Marketing Research* 15, no. 3 (2003): 30–35.

181 Rashmi Adaval and Robert S. Wyer, "Conscious and Nonconscious Comparisons with Price Anchors: Effects on Willingness to Pay for Related and Unrelated Products," *Journal of Marketing Research* 48 (2011): 355–65. Joel Huber and Christopher Puto, "Market Boundaries and Product Choice: Illustrating Attraction and Substitution Effects," *Journal of Consumer Research* 10 (1983): 31–44. See also Poundstone, *Priceless*, 153.

182 Kotler and Armstrong, *Principles of Marketing*, 321.

183 K. Gupta Omprakash and Anna S. Rominger, "Blind Man's Bluff: The Ethics of Quantity Surcharges," *Journal of Business Ethics* 15 (1996): 1299–312. It is not hard to find anecdotal evidence on the internet in blogs and readers' comments. For instance, http://www.epinions.com/review/gatorade-fruit-punch-thirst-quencher-sports-drink-32-oz-pack-of-12/content_593265593988?sb=1 ("Although it is available in assorted sizes, I often buy the 32-ounce size because it is the least expensive per ounce, saving me money even over the larger 64-ounce jugs").

184 AAA calculated that Americans waste $2 billion a year on premium gas. See Peter Valdes-Dapena, "Americans waste $2 billion a year on pricey premium gas," *CNN Money*, September 20, 2016, http://money.cnn.com/2016/09/20/autos/aaa-premium-gasoline/index.html.

185 These gut feelings make sense in some situations: sometimes in life, the cheapest is the best; sometimes the middle is the best; and sometimes the most expensive is the cheapest in the long run. So, the irrationality is not sheer craziness but the misapplication of general wisdom.

[186] Premium gas sales have decreased over the last decades, though they started to slightly increase in 2013 and 2014. See "The Value of Premium," 2015 NACS Retail Fuel Report, http://www.convenience.org/yourbusiness/fuelsreports/2015/fuels/pages/the-value-of-premium.aspx.

[187] Steven Shavell, "A Note on Efficiency vs. Distributional Equity in Legal Rulemaking: Should Distributional Equity Matter Given Optimal Income Taxation?" *American Economic Review* 71 (1981): 414–18; Louis Kaplow and Steven Shavell, "Why the Legal System Is Less Efficient Than the Income Tax in Redistributing Income," *Journal of Legal Studies* 23 (1994): 667–81; Louis Kaplow and Steven Shavell, "Should Legal Rules Favor the Poor? Clarifying the Role of Legal Rules and the Income Tax in Redistributing Income," *Journal of Legal Studies* 29 (2000): 821–35. See also Aanund Hyllund and Richard Zeckhauser, "Distributional Objectives Should Affect Taxes but Not Program Choice or Design," *Scandinavian Journal of Economics* 81 (1979): 264–84 (making a similar point on the superiority of tax system over government projects). An extensive literature has followed Kaplow and Shavell's work. See, for instance, Chris W. Sanchirico, "Taxes versus Legal Rules as Instruments for Equity: A More Equitable View," *Journal of Legal Studies* 29 (2000): 797–820; Chris W. Sanchirico, "Deconstructing the New Efficiency Rationale," *Cornell Law Review* 86 (2001): 1003– 89 (tort law might be better at redistributing income if it could better observe some proxies for income-earning ability, such as "klutziness"; increased tort liability related to leisure activities may also reduce the attractiveness of leisure, offsetting the labor/leisure incentive distortion of the tax system somewhat); Kyle Logue and Ronen Avraham, "Redistributing Optimally: Of Tax Rules, Legal Rules, and Insurance," *Tax Law Review* 56 (2003): 157–257; Nicholas L. Georgakopoulos, "Exploring the Shavellian Boundary: Violations from Judgment-Proofing, Minority Rights, and Signaling," *Journal of Law, Economics, and Policy* 3 (2006): 47–62 (ex post legal rules may be better at redistributing nonmonetary goods such as self-respect); Tomer Blumkin and Yoram Margalioth, "On the Limits of Redistributive Taxation: Establishing a Case for Equity-Informed Legal Rules," *Virginia Tax Review* 25 (2005): 1–29 (legal rules may be better when monetary transfers themselves are considered distasteful); Christine Jolls, "Behavioral Economic Analysis of Redistributive Legal Rules," *Vanderbilt Law Review* 51 (1998): 1653–77 (ex post redistribution through the legal system may distort behavior less if it is less "salient" so that individuals underestimate its extent; potential injurers tend to underestimate the probability of accidents, so that wealthy injurers would also underestimate the effects of a redistributive tort law system); Alex Raskolnikov, "Accepting the Limits of Tax Law and Economics," *Cornell Law Review* 98 (2013): 523–90 (the tax system may be less redistributive than assumed in Kaplow and Shavell, for instance, because tax rules have many other goals, such as deterrence of undesirable behavior); Brian D. Galle, "Is Local Consumer Protection Law a Better Redistributive Mechanism Than the Tax System?" *New York University Annual Survey of American Law* 65 (2010): 525–43 (the outcome may depend on imperfections in the political system).

While these papers have raised theoretical qualifications to the result of Kaplow and Shavell, hardly any examples of legal rules that should be adjusted because of these qualifications have been identified so far. As a result, law and economics textbooks consider the result of Kaplow and Shavell the leading principle (Cooter and Ulen 2008, 9–11; Polinsky 2003, 152–56; Posner 2011, 715). See also David A. Weisbach, "Should Legal Rules Be Used to Redistribute Income?" *University of Chicago Law Review* 70 (2003): 403–53.

[188] The Deep Pocket Rule is not an official legal rule but one that may be implicitly (and sometimes unconsciously) applied by jury members or judges. Stella Liebeck v. McDonald's Restaurants, P.T.S., Inc. and McDonald's International, Inc., 1994 Extra LEXIS 23 (Bernalillo County, N.M. Dist. Ct. 1994), 1995 WL 360309 (Bernalillo County, N.M. Dist. Ct. 1994) is often cited as an illustration of the Deep Pocket Rule. In this case, Mrs. Liebeck was awarded a $2.7 million judgment after she spilled her own cup of McDonald's coffee and burned her legs.

[189] The second fundamental theorem of welfare economics states that any Pareto efficient outcome can be achieved through lump-sum transfers. The first fundamental theorem of welfare economics states, in essence, that free markets reach efficient outcomes. Yet there can exist an infinite number of efficient outcomes, depending on the starting position. For instance, if markets start from a situation in which most land is owned by a few individuals, the efficient outcome may be one in which a few individuals live in efficiently built castles, while most others live in efficiently built small houses. If markets start from a situation in which resources are owned equally, the efficient outcome may be one in which no one lives in a castle and most people live in medium-sized houses. So, if the outcome with the castles is considered undesirable, the second welfare theorem suggests that there is no need to tamper with market mechanisms through overregulation—just redistribute wealth through lump-sum payments and let markets do their job. Thus, the second welfare theorem implies that redistribution and efficiency should be split: redistribution should be accomplished through taxes and transfers, and for all other issues efficiency should be the only concern.

[190] Smith, *Wealth of Nations.*

[191] I am simplifying the math for expositional purposes. To be precise, the sales tax has to be $46.67 (not $40) to make the sales tax the equivalent of a 40 percent income tax (so that in the end, 40 percent of your income goes to taxes).

[192] In 2017, federal, state, and local governments together were "guesstimated" to collect about 36.4 percent of GDP. See http://www.usgovernmentrevenue. com/current_revenue. Note that the values are expressed in GDP, while the calculations of chapter 3 are based on national income. The GDP double-counts investments by not taking depreciation into account; therefore, it is possible that the figure is higher than 36.4 percent.

[193] Rents do not distort the rent receiver's incentive to work if they are a lump sum, unrelated to the number of hours worked (which may be the case for a landlord or the co-owner of a company run by others).

[194] In theory, there is a zone in which rents reduce the leisure/labor distortion. Indeed, if someone receives less rents than he pays taxes and rents to others, it is possible that the received rent has an overall positive effect by cancelling out the negative effect of taxes and rents paid.

[195] Anthony B. Atkinson and Joseph E. Stiglitz, "The Design of Tax Structure: Direct versus Indirect Taxation," *Journal of Public Economics* 6 (1976): 55–75.

[196] A general, uniform rate commodity tax system may be analytically identical to an income tax system with a uniform rate, if the income tax system excludes savings.

[197] The textbook case of the diamonds may be a simplification, because De Beers has quite some market power, so that not all rents are Ricardian.

[198] Ricardian rents cause consumption choice distortion (and labor/leisure distortion) when they are higher than optimal. This may be the case when zoning regulations are overly restrictive. If the price of building land would be $50,000 per acre if zoning restrictions were optimally set, but in practice it is $500,000 per acre because of overly restrictive zoning, the Ricardian rent does not reflect real scarcity but artificial scarcity, and therefore distorts in the same way as non-Ricardian rents do.

[199] The only case, in theory, in which taxes would correct price distortions is if tax rates would be 100 percent. This would remove the incentives to acquire the rent in the first place and therefore also remove the price distortion associated with the rent. But that is a theoretical exception, because a 100 percent tax rate would also eliminate all incentives to work and therefore destroy the entire economy. While income taxes don't make consumption choices worse, they don't improve them either. Suppose that a product costs $100 but is priced at $150 because of a market failure that generates a $50 rent. If the legal system removes 90 percent of the market failure (and the rent), the price becomes $105. If the tax system would tax away 90 percent of the rent (by increasing tax rates to 90 percent), the price would still be $150. In a sense, *high income taxes transform private sales taxes into sales taxes that go to the government*; consumers keep paying the artificially high price; the only difference is that now most of the profit goes to the government. While this reduces inequality, it keeps the distortive effects of sales taxes unaffected.

[200] The difficulties associated with observing rents seem to have led tax scholars to completely abandon the rent tax idea of Henry George. Illustratively, the term "rent" does not even appear in the subject index of a recent monograph of Louis Kaplow, *The Theory of Taxation and Public Economics* (Princeton University Press, 2008).

[201] See Ibid., 90 ("in the United States, public and private collection costs for the income tax are approximately 10 percent of revenues"). For an even higher estimate, see Jason J. Fichtner and Jacob M. Feldman, *The Hidden Cost of Federal Tax Policy* (Mercatus Center, 2015).

[202] From a different angle, one problem with the standard economic viewpoint is that it assumes that the law is efficient. To be fair, this is more a problem of interpreting the standard models (of Kaplow and Shavell, for instance) than a problem with the models themselves, because they formally assume the law is set at an efficient level. So, these models can be interpreted as saying: If there is too much inequality, start by making the law more efficient. If there is then still too much inequality, use taxes to reduce it. But in practice, politicians (and macroeconomists!) overlook this nuance and immediately jump to the next step: if there is too much inequality, increase taxes.

[203] The theoretical answer is that we should balance the net costs of more legal intervention with the net costs of higher taxes. The net costs of more legal intervention are the additional administrative costs minus the additional benefits of further reducing labor/leisure distortion and consumption choice distortion. (Keep in mind we are talking about the net cost of an instrument that has costs and benefits.) The net costs of higher taxes (again, to obtain the same redistributive benefit) are the additional administrative costs of the tax system plus the additional costs of labor/leisure distortion. To what extent

you should use the legal system or the tax system in this case is ultimately an empirical question; it all depends on the parameters. However, under standard assumptions of convexity (these are common, technical assumptions meaning that an instrument becomes more distortive the more it is used), both the legal system and the tax system will have to do a part of the extra work.

[204] For instance, removing every information rent obtained by employees would require information that even employers don't have. Employers have a natural incentive not to overpay employees; if they do overpay, it is because they can't get the necessary information. But if employers can't, how could the legal system?

[205] This is a simplification that is usually correct if the distribution of rent components is symmetrical around the mean and if distortive effects increase exponentially as prices deviate more from true costs. With different distributions, ideal corrective taxes may differ from average rents. Another implication is that, since shareholders tend to capture more rents than bondholders, capital gains of shareholders should be taxed at a higher rate than capital gains of bondholders.

[206] This view goes against a widely held theorem in tax economics—that only labor income should be taxed, not capital income. The reasoning behind the standard view is that a *capital gains tax causes a double distortion*. Labor income, in this view, should be taxed because a labor income tax causes a single distortion. The underlying idea is that before you may receive capital gains, you should acquire capital. See it as a game with two rounds. In the first round, you must decide how hard you will work; in the second round, you must decide whether you will consume your wage immediately or invest (or "save") it. Capital gains taxes distort the latter decision: they "punish" people who invest the money. Still, don't labor income taxes distort the incentives to work? That is true, but— and here comes the surprising part of the reasoning—so do capital gains taxes. Indeed, capital gains taxes make working less attractive if your goal is to later invest the money. Therefore, labor income taxes distort only once (the labor/ leisure decision), whereas capital income taxes distort twice (the labor/leisure decision and the consumption/investment decision). While the view that capital gains should not be taxed may sound odd, it is just another application of the double-distortion argument. The reason for not taxing capital gains (but only labor income) is essentially the same as the reason for not using sales taxes (but only income taxes) and for not using tort law (but only income taxes) to redistribute income.

The problem with this argument is that it assumes that rents don't exist. In an economy full of rents, you have two chances to receive rents: when you work, and when you invest. Now, analogize rents to subsidies. Just like subsidies, rents distort in a different direction than taxes: they give an incentive to work too hard (at least to those who receive more rents than they pay as consumers), and they give an incentive to invest too much. If you don't invest your wage, you have a single chance to receive a subsidy (when you work). If you invest your wage, you have a double chance (when you work and when you invest). A double subsidy distorts incentives more than a single subsidy. To correct this additional distortion, taxes should tax away the second subsidy. In other words, in an economy with rents, there is a *double-subsidy argument* in favor of taxing capital gains! The implication of this double-subsidy problem for tax policy is that taxes should correct this second distortion by taxing capital gains at a rate that reflects the likelihood that a specific type of tax gain consists of a rent. Still, it should be repeated that this capital gains tax argument is no more than a second best. The first-best policy is to make sure that the rents are not gained, through more aggressive legal rules that attack the underlying market failures. Yet, after the legal system has done all it could, capital gains taxes may be desirable to further reduce the consumption/investment distortion.

207 The problem with patents and copyrights, as we have seen, is that their duration is the same for all inventions, irrespective of their costs, so that they nearly automatically give rise to cherry-picking rents. This leads in turn to income inequality. There are two ways to reduce this income inequality. First, income from patents could be taxed (for instance, at a 50 percent tax rate, to give a simple example). Second, patent duration could be reduced (for instance, from twenty years to ten years). If we assume for simplicity that the patent income in all twenty years is the same, both measures have the same effect. For instance, if an inventor received $20 million income in the past, she now receives only $10 million. Since they have the same effect on net income, they also have the same effect on innovation effort. Because patents also distort consumption choices (as a result of monopoly pricing), reducing patent duration is less distortive than taxing patent income.

208 Empirically, it is not clear either that more college degrees reduce income inequality. The variance of years of schooling has declined since 1945, while the rate of return to a college degree (and income inequality more generally) has increased since 1975. See Edward N. Wolff, *Poverty and Income Distribution* (Wiley-Blackwell, 2009), 286–90.

209 See, e.g., Glyn, *Capitalism Unleashed*; Rosenfeld, *What Unions No Longer Do*.

210 Most economists, in contrast, hold negative views toward labor unions. For an overview of the economic literature, see Kenneth G. Dau-Schmidt and Arthur R. Traynor, "Regulating Unions and Collective Bargaining," in *Labor and Employment Law and Economics*, ed. Kenneth G. Dau-Schmidt, Seth D. Harris, and Orly Lobel (Edward Elgar, 2009), 96–128.

211 Artificially increasing wages in some sectors can also be analogized to levying sales taxes on labor (the proceeds of which go to the workers rather than the government). These (implicit) commodity taxes cause the same labor/leisure distortion as income taxes, but since they are nonneutral commodity taxes, they also distort consumption choices.

212 Gene A. Marsh, *Consumer Protection Law in a Nutshell* (West, 1999), 59–60 (explaining UDAP statutes that make estimates for auto repair jobs mandatory); Funeral Industry Practices, 16 C.F.R. §453.2 (2007) (creating a duty to reveal prices over the phone, or in the form of a printed price list, but not on the internet). For hotel room prices, see, e.g., California Civil Code Section 1863 ("(a) Every keeper of a hotel . . . shall post in a conspicuous place in the office or public room, and in every bedroom of said hotel. . . a statement of rate or range of rates by the day for lodging. (b) No charge or sum shall be collected or received for any greater sum than is specified in subdivision (a)").

213 Ben-Shahar and Schneider, *More Than You Wanted to Know,* arguing that most disclosure duties miss their effect, for instance, because they allow information to be buried inside hard-to-read documents, and therefore proposing that most

disclosure regulation be abolished. My own view is that disclosure should not be abolished but made in a different (standardized, electronic) form.

214 See also Poundstone, *Priceless*, 179, on batteries ("What you're buying is battery life: how many pictures you can take in a camera, how often you have to replace the smoke detector battery, how long a flashlight lasts in an outage. But battery life isn't disclosed anywhere on the label. . . . Some batteries pack a lot more juice than others, and consumers are left to guess which ones they are").

215 For example, Walton H. Hamilton, "The Ancient Maxim Caveat Emptor," *Yale Law Journal* 40 (1931): 1133–87.

216 Baker and Siegelman, "Protecting Consumers from Add-On Insurance Products."

217 A legal duty to publish all prices in a standardized form on the internet would make it easy for search engines to connect retail prices with wholesale prices. But if the goods were not bought but custom-ordered by the retailer, search engines would not be able to find the wholesale prices.

218 See Ian Ayres, "Fair Driving: Gender and Race Discrimination in Retail Car Negotiations," *Harvard Law Review* 104 (1991): 817–72.

219 See "The Great Rebate Runaround," *Bloomberg*, November 22, 2005, https://www.bloomberg.com/news/articles/2005-11-22/the-great-rebate-runaround. See also Mohammed, *The 1% Windfall*, 90.

220 The United States Adopted Names (USAN) Council chooses the nonproprietary names for pharmaceuticals marketed in the United States. The USAN Council officially tries to choose simple names, but because names are based on pharmacological and chemical relationships, nonprofessionals have a hard time remembering them.

221 See Perillo, *Calamari and Perillo on Contracts,* 305; Farnsworth, *Farnsworth on Contracts,* 474 ("The relation need not involve one who is a true fiduciary as a matter of law (such as a trustee, an agent, a guardian, or an executor or administrator) but may, for example, be one involving trust and confidence as a matter of fact (as between members of the same family, between physician and patient, or between members of the clergy and parishioner). The one in whom trust and confidence is reposed is expected to speak up").

222 James C. Cooper and Joshua D. Wright, "Alcohol, Antitrust, and the 21st Amendment: An Empirical Examination of Post and Hold Laws," *International Review of Law and Economics* 32 (2012): 379–92.

223 See, for instance, Philip Kotler and Kevin Lane Keller, *Marketing Management* (Pearson Prentice Hall, 2012): 142–43, 343, 384.

224 For an analysis of network externalities and their legal implications, see William H. Page and John E. Lopatka, "Network Externalities," in *Encyclopedia of Law and Economics,* vol. 1, 952–80 (defending antitrust law's current reluctance to intervene). Indirectly, network externalities may have legal implications to the extent that they lead to "dominant position," which is a first step in applying the rules against the abuse of dominant positions. There are also some antitrust authorities on this planet who are still concerned about "network neutrality." But network externalities in themselves are not grounds for intervention.

225 According to World Bank data, Norway's rents from natural resources, compared to its GDP, were 15.11 percent in the period 2005–2014. These data include mineral rents (0.044 percent in 2005–2014) and forest rents (0.1 percent in 2013). World Bank, World Development Indicators, http://data.worldbank.org/.

226 In Texas, as in most US states, the owner of the surface land automatically owns the mineral and oil rights underneath it. For oil under public (federal or state) land, oil companies pay a fixed royalty rate, which leads to cherry-picking rents. In addition, oil companies need to make a bonus bid to acquire the lease, but in practice these payments do not fully capture the oil rents, partly because competition for leases is organized at a stage in which there is significant uncertainty.

227 See the website of the US Department of the Interior, Bureau of Land Management, http://www.blm.gov. See also Nicole Gentile, *Federal Oil and Gas Royalty and Revenue Reform*, Center for American Progress, June 19, 2015.

228 In law and economics terminology, we apply "liability rule protection" on Mary's property rights, which is generally seen as the optimal solution to get out of a "bilateral monopoly" that exists when two individuals own complementary rights. The seminal paper on liability rule versus property rule protection is Guido Calabresi and A. Douglas Melamed, "Property Rules, Liability Rules and Inalienability: One View of the Cathedral," *Harvard Law Review* 85 (1972): 1089–1128.

229 Such a right of first refusal, however, may destroy the market: if all interested parties expect the government to exercise its right to buy the land, no one may even start bidding. A right of first refusal should therefore be accompanied by a right for the owner to demand compensation under eminent domain, based on market values for similar lots of land.

230 It does not matter here whether the $1 billion came from explicit tax money or from "virtual taxes" through more expensive, patented products; the excessive profit margins on the patented goods could have generated 1,000 times more innovation. A counterargument could be that if the 999 other inventions are worth being made, taxes could be increased to get them financed. In other words, if all innovators end up being 1,000 times overpaid, the innovation budget in society could be increased from $1 billion to $1 trillion. But additional taxes increase labor/leisure distortion. To put it differently, given the same tax burden, more innovation can be realized if innovators are not overpaid.

231 Here is another example. In 1975, Eric Carmen had a hit song, "All By Myself," partly based on Rachmaninoff's second piano concerto. The estate of Rachmaninoff threatened to sue Carmen and quickly received a share of the copyrights. But Rachmaninoff composed that concerto in 1901, when copyright protection lasted only forty-two years in the US (and fifty years in Russia). So, his rights should have been expired by 1943, no? Well, for starters, the 1909 Copyright Act retroactively extended the term to fifty-six years. In addition, the clock started running only when the work was published with notice (rather than when it was created), so that authors could de facto extend the fifty-six-year term by delaying publication, receiving perpetual common law protection in the meantime. Rachmaninoff's second piano concerto was first published in the United States in 1918, the year he moved to this country. The fifty-six-year term should have expired in 1974, but it was retroactively extended by Congress in 1974, and then again retroactively extended to seventy-five years by the Copyright Act of 1976, meaning that protection eventually ran until 1993. Good news for his estate. Rachmaninoff's second piano concerto (op. 18) was originally published in Russia in October 1901 by Gutheil. The first publication of op. 18 in the US I could trace down is the

four-hands piano version, published by Schirmer (vol. 1576) in 1918. Note that if the work would have been published earlier, but no earlier than September 19, 1906, its protection would eventually still have been retroactively extended to seventy-five years, given that the interim retroactive extensions of 1962–74 covered all works from 1906 on.

232 The Sonny Bono Copyright Term Extension Act, informally called the Mickey Mouse Protection Act, extended copyright protection to seventy years after the death of the author, and to ninety-five years after publication (or one hundred twenty years after production, whichever is shorter) in case the work was created by a corporation. Before 1998, Congress had increased copyright protection several times; when Disney directed *Steamboat Willy* in 1928, the maximum duration of copyright protection was fifty-six years. (Under this rule, Mickey Mouse would have been in the public domain since 1984.) The Disney Company handed contributions to most of the bill's sponsors in the Senate and the House. See Ben Depoorter, "The Several Lives of Mickey Mouse: Expanding the Boundaries of Intellectual Property Law," *Virginia Journal of Law and Technology* 9, no. 4, (2004): 1–68.

233 Evergreening (the practice of extending the effective life span of patent protection through a set of strategies) can be seen as an example of a retroactive extension as well.

234 The Agreement on Trade-Related Aspects of Intellectual Property Rights (TRIPS) is administered by the World Trade Organization (WTO).

235 See Wikipedia, s.v. "epinephrine autoinjector," last visited September 30, 2016, https://en.wikipedia.org/wiki/Epinephrine_autoinjector.

236 I'm simplifying the math by assuming away the part of the $19,000 that goes to the government in the form of taxes and social security contributions.

237 From a scientific viewpoint, this empirical answer is largely indeterminate—it is hard to put exact numbers on each of the costs. When empirical data are indeterminate, people tend to stick with their prior beliefs—and so the political discussion seems to be blocked forever. See also Gerrit De Geest, "N Problems Require N Instruments," *International Review of Law and Economics* 35 (2013): 42–57.

238 Ben-Shahar and Schneider, *More Than You Wanted to Know.*

239 Ronald H. Coase, "The Federal Communications Commission," *Journal of Law and Economics* 2 (1959): 1–40. Coase liked the transferability but argued that radio frequency licenses had to be auctioned (granting them to the highest bidder from the start). But see Thomas W. Hazlett, "The Rationality of U.S. Regulation of the Broadcast Spectrum," *Journal of Law and Economics* 33 (1990): 133–75 (arguing that preventing radio interferences was not the main motive for this regulation).

240 Ronald H. Coase, "The Problem of Social Cost," *Journal of Law and Economics* 3 (1960): 1–44.

241 Transaction costs may be half of the economy. The classic study is John J. Wallis and Douglass C. North, "Measuring the Transaction Sector in the American Economy, 1870–1970," in *Long-Term Factors in American Economic Growth*, ed. Stanley L. Engerman and Robert E. Gallman (University of Chicago Press, 1986, estimating the size of the transaction sector at 54.7 percent of the GDP in 1970).

INDEX

ABOUT THE AUTHOR

Gerrit De Geest is the Charles F. Nagel Professor of International and Comparative Law at Washington University School of Law, where he teaches contracts, antitrust law, law and economics, and seminars on consumer contracts, and served as the director of the Center on Law, Innovation & Economic Growth. Before moving to St. Louis with his family, he was a chaired professor at the Utrecht School of Economics and president of the European Association of Law and Economics. He is the co-editor of the Encyclopedia of Law and Economics (Edward Elgar, 2000, 5 volumes).

www.gerritdegeest.com
Follow on Facebook.com/gerrit.degeest.944
Follow on Twitter @gerritdegeest

CPSIA information can be obtained
at www.ICGtesting.com
Printed in the USA
LVHW04s0423060918
589323LV00001B/1/P